# BRINGING THE CAPED CRUSADER TO THE SCREEN

GARY COLLINSON

Robert Hale • London

© Gary Collinson 2012
First published in Great Britain 2012

ISBN 978-0-7090-9413-5

Robert Hale Limited
Clerkenwell House
Clerkenwell Green
London EC1R 0HT

www.halebooks.com

A catalogue record for this book is available from the British Library

10 9 8 7 6 5 4 3 2 1

Design by Eurodesign

Printed in China

# Contents

## PART I    LIVE-ACTION BATMAN

## PART 2   ANIMATED BATMAN

# PART 3   BATMAN OF THE FUTURE

# ACKNOWLEDGEMENTS

I would like to express my heartfelt thanks and gratitude to the following: Amie, Billy and my mother for their encouragement and support throughout the entire process; Bill Ramey of *Batman-on-Film.com*, Matt MacNabb of *LegionsofGotham.org* and James Harvey of *WorldsFinestOnline.com* for allowing me access to the wealth of information on their fabulous websites; *AintItCool.com*, *AVClub.com*, *The Critical Eye*, *DenofGeek.com*, *Empire* magazine and all other reference sources used within the text; Gill Jackson, Nikki Edwards and the rest of the staff at Robert Hale publishers; the contributors and readers of *FlickeringMyth.com*; and lastly, Bob Kane, Bill Finger and all of the writers, artists, filmmakers and creative talent involved in bringing the *Batman* universe to life.

# Batman

## WHO HE IS AND HOW HE CAME TO BE

Two shots ring out from an alleyway in the murky, crime-ridden cesspit of Gotham City, leaving a young Bruce Wayne orphaned by the swift and brutal act of a petty street thug. As he kneels over the fallen bodies of his parents, the boy swears an oath of vengeance, vowing to devote his life and family fortune to bring justice to the streets of Gotham. Travelling the world for an intense period of physical and mental preparation, Bruce adopts the mantle of a bat, transforming himself into a masked vigilante and relying on his skills, cunning and a vast array of gadgetry to strike terror into the hearts of the underworld as the legendary grim avenger of the night, Batman.

Behind his comic book origins, the birth of the Caped Crusader can be traced back to 18 April 1938 when National Allied Publications (later DC Comics) unleashed *Action Comics* #1 (cover date June 1938), introducing the world to the first American superhero – the Man of Steel, Superman. Created by Jerry Siegel and Joe Shuster, Superman was an instant success and sales of *Action Comics* soon approached a million copies a month as America went 'superhero' crazy. With the publisher keen to expand on the blistering popularity of this new character archetype, an aspiring young artist by the name of Bob Kane went on to conceive an idea for a costumed crime-fighter known as 'the Bat-Man'.

Influenced by a Leonardo da Vinci design for a manned ornithopter glider, the 18-year-old Kane merged elements from masked heroes such as Zorro and the Shadow, along with that of the villain in the 1930 mystery film *The Bat Whispers* (1930), before working with writer and collaborator Bill Finger to refine his creation. At Finger's suggestion, Kane updated his initial sketches, removing the ornithopter-inspired 'bat-wings' and domino mask in favour of a cape and cowl and replacing red sections of the costume with a dark grey. Kane took Batman to National Allied Publications co-owner Jack Liebowitz, who agreed to debut the character in its flagship anthology title *Detective Comics*.

With his first appearance in the six-page story 'The Case of the Chemical Syndicate' by Bill Finger, published in *Detective Comics* #27 (May 1939), readers were immediately gripped by the pulp-inspired exploits of the Dark Knight as Batman despatched a lethal brand of justice to the criminal element of Gotham City. He quickly became the cornerstone of the *Detective Comics* title, and by the end of the year many elements of the *Batman* mythos had already been introduced, including his iconic utility belt, Batarangs and origin story, which was first explored by Bill Finger in the two-page story 'The Legend of the Batman – Who He Is and How He Came To Be', published in *Detective Comics* #33 (November 1939).

After a successful first year, Batman's popularity increased even further in 1940 with the arrival of the teenage side-kick Dick Grayson, who made his first appearance in the comic book story 'Robin the Boy Wonder' by Bill Finger, published in *Detective Comics* #38 (April 1940). Coinciding with Robin's debut was a shift towards a lighter tone, which was accompanied by the introduction of a moral code prohibiting the vigilante from using lethal force against his enemies. The Dark Knight gained his own solo title with the release of *Batman* #1 (Spring 1940) and just three years later the Caped Crusader made his first appearance outside of the comic book medium as Columbia Pictures developed a fifteen-chapter movie serial centred upon the adventures of the Dynamic Duo.

In the decades following his debut, the Dark Knight went on to secure his status as a cultural icon, enthralling fans from generation to generation and positioning himself as one of the most recognizable comic book characters of all time. After his early silver screen exploits, Batman struggled to sustain his initial popularity amid waning interest in the comic book medium during the early post-war period, only to emerge from the dark days of the 1950s with a hit television show that adopted a light-hearted, camp approach and led to the first outbreak of a craze that came to be known as 'Batmania'.

The staggering success of the 1960s *Batman* series was replicated more than twenty years later as Warner Bros launched their hugely lucrative feature film franchise in the summer of 1989 with *Batman*. A box-office hit, this cinematic reinvention marked a new beginning for the Caped Crusader, who has since gone on to captivate audiences across a series of blockbuster theatrical features and acclaimed animated offerings, all of which are detailed in this book as we explore the complete screen history of the Dark Knight Detective …

PART 1

# LIVE-ACTION BATMAN

# Batman of the silver screen

## BATMAN (1943)

**Release date:** 16 July 1943 (US)
**Certificate:** Not rated
**Running time:** 260 minutes (15 episodes)

### CAST

Lewis Wilson (*Bruce Wayne/Batman*); Douglas Croft (*Dick Grayson/Robin*); J. Carrol Naish (*Dr Tito Daka*); Shirley Patterson (*Linda Page*); William Austin (*Alfred Pennyworth*); Charles C. Wilson (*Police Captain Arnold*); Knox Manning (*Narrator*).

### KEY CREW

Lambert Hillyer (*Director*); Rudolph C. Flothow (*Producer*); Victor McLeod, Leslie Swabacker, Harry Fraser (*Screenplay*); Bob Kane (*Characters*); Lee Zahler (*Music*); James S. Brown Jr (*Cinematography*); Dwight Caldwell, Earl Turner (*Editing*).

### CHAPTER TITLES

(1) The Electrical Brain; (2) The Bat's Cave; (3) The Mark of the Zombies; (4) Slaves of the Rising Sun; (5) The Living Corpse; (6) Poison Peril; (7) The Phoney Doctor; (8) Lured by Radium; (9) The Sign of the Sphinx; (10) Flying Spies; (11) A Nipponese Trap; (12) Embers of Evil; (13) Eight Steps Down; (14) The Executioner Strikes; (15) The Doom of the Rising Sun.

### STORY

Millionaire playboy Bruce Wayne and his youthful ward Dick Grayson take to the streets of Gotham City as the costumed crime-fighters Batman and Robin, working for the United States government to battle criminals, spies and saboteurs during the height of World War II. Meanwhile, in the city's deserted Little Tokyo district, the Japanese scientist Dr Tito Daka has developed a sinister weapon that turns its victims into mindless zombies under the control of the Third Reich. With the tide of the war set to turn, the Dynamic Duo race to dismantle Daka's espionage ring, the League of the New Order, and protect democracy by thwarting preparations for a Japanese invasion. After tracking Daka to his base of operations, the Cave of Horrors, Batman and Robin successfully reverse the effects of the mind-control device and apprehend the spymaster, only for the villain to fall through a trap door into an alligator pit as he attempts to flee.

## BRINGING BATMAN TO THE SCREEN

Given the stunning early success of Superman and Batman, publishers immediately sought to capitalize on the blistering popularity of the comic book medium, with National Comics (later DC Comics) debuting a host of new characters including the Flash, Green Lantern and Wonder Woman, while rivals Timely Comics (later Marvel Comics) introduced the likes of Captain America, the Human Torch and the Sub-Mariner. As fans clamoured for tales of superhuman heroics and costumed crime-fighters, Hollywood soon turned its attention to the burgeoning superhero genre, which seemed a perfect match for the 'cliffhanger' approach of the weekly movie serial.

In 1940, Republic Pictures developed a serial entitled *Mysterious Doctor Satan*, which was originally intended to feature the screen debut of the Man of Steel. However, due to licensing issues between National Comics and Fleischer Studios – who had earlier secured the rights to the character for a series of animated theatrical shorts – Republic were forced to remove all traces of the *Superman* universe from their script. Instead, the studio gave Fawcett Comics' Captain Marvel the distinction of becoming the first screen superhero with the release of the twelve-part serial *Adventures of Captain Marvel* (1941). While Republic followed this up with another Fawcett Comics tale, *Spy Smasher* (1942), it was another year before a National Comics character finally reached the silver screen courtesy of Columbia Pictures, with Superman stepping aside for a fifteen-chapter serial based upon the Caped Crusader.

Entitled *Batman*, the first theatrical adventure of the Dark Knight Detective was based on a screenplay by Victor McLeod (*Gang Busters*, 1942), Leslie Swabacker (*Secret Agent X-9*, 1937) and Harry Fraser (*Randy Rides Alone*, 1934), with Lambert Hillyer (*Dracula's Daughter*, 1936) handling directing duties. Unsurprisingly, *Batman* was a product of its time, drawing upon the anti-Japanese sentiment post Pearl Harbor to deliver a patriotic tale peppered with racial slurs. Furthermore, censors at the Motion Picture Production Code expressed concerns about heroes taking the law into their own hands, resulting in a change that saw the Dynamic Duo forego their vigilante status to become government agents tasked with thwarting the diabolical schemes of Dr Tito Daka, a Japanese villain created specifically for the serial.

Making history as the first actor to don the cape and cowl of the Dark Knight was Lewis Wilson, a newcomer whose prior screen credits extended to an uncredited role in the propaganda piece *Good Luck, Mr Yates* (1943) and a supporting turn in the comedy *Redhead from Manhattan* (1943). Joining Wilson as the Boy Wonder was 16-year-old Douglas Croft, a child star with appearances in notable features such as *King's Row* (1942), *Yankee Doodle Dandy* (1942) and *The Pride of the Yankees* (1942), while veteran British actor William Austin (*Duck Soup*, 1927) was hired to portray Bruce Wayne's faithful butler Alfred Pennyworth, a character developed specifically for the serial who had recently made his debut in panel form with the comic book story 'Here Comes Alfred' by Don Cameron, published in *Batman* #16 (April–May 1943).

Although *Batman* enjoyed an increased budget next to other Columbia serials, financial constraints meant that much of the Caped Crusader's fledgling comic book mythos was overlooked, with notable absences including the Bat-Signal and the Batmobile (instead, the heroes used a black 1939 Cadillac Series 75 Convertible, which also doubled as transport for Bruce Wayne and Dick Grayson). Aside from Batman and Robin, the remaining characters were all original creations, with J. Carrol Naish (*Beau Geste*, 1939) starring as the villainous Dr Daka and other additions to the cast including Shirley Patterson (*Next in Line*, 1942) as love interest Linda Page and Charles C. Wilson (*It Happened One Night*, 1934) as Gotham's Chief of Police, Captain Arnold. *Batman* creator Bob Kane also made a cameo appearance as a newsboy in the first chapter, 'The Electrical Brain', while radio announcer and prolific voice actor Knox Manning (*Meet John Doe*, 1941) provided uncredited narration for the serial.

## RECEPTION

Just four years after the Dark Knight's first print appearance, Columbia Pictures launched their fifteen-part *Batman* 'Super Serial' on 16 July 1943, releasing subsequent chapters on a weekly basis. Despite low production values, loose-fitting costumes, unconvincing acting and repetitive storytelling, audiences were drawn to the theatrical adventures of the Caped Crusader and *Batman* was a hit with fans and critics alike. The serial went on to influence the comic book series, introducing the concept of the 'Bat's Cave' (renamed the Batcave) and its hidden entrance behind a grandfather clock situated in Wayne Manor, while Alfred's appearance was also adjusted to match that of actor William Austin. However, it would have an even greater impact on the *Batman* universe in 1965. Edited together and re-released as *An Evening with Batman and Robin*, the serial became popular among college students for its 'camp' entertainment value, ultimately paving the way for the Caped Crusader's hugely successful television debut (SEE 'SAME BAT-TIME, SAME BAT-CHANNEL').

Over the years, *Batman* received a number of home video releases, with a silent and abridged cut arriving on the Super 8 home video format in the late 1960s soon followed by a complete sound edition. *Batman* was revived once again in 1989, receiving numerous television broadcasts to coincide with the launch of Warner Bros' theatrical feature film series (SEE 'THE TIM BURTON/JOEL SCHUMACHER ERA'). The following year Goodtimes Home Video issued the serial across two VHS volumes in a heavily edited format that removed all offensive anti-Japanese content, while the uncut version was eventually made available in 2005 with a two-disc DVD set from Sony Pictures Home Entertainment entitled *Batman – The Complete 1943 Movie Serial Collection*.

# BATMAN AND ROBIN (1949)

**Release date:** 26 May 1949 (US)
**Certificate:** Not rated
**Running time:** 263 minutes (15 episodes)

## CAST

Robert Lowery (*Bruce Wayne/Batman*); John Duncan (*Dick Grayson/Robin*); Jane Adams (*Vicki Vale*); Lyle Talbot (*Commissioner Jim Gordon*); Eric Wilton (*Alfred Pennyworth*); Ralph Graves (*Winslow Harrison*); William Fawcett (*Professor Hammil*); Don C. Harvey (*Nolan*); Rick Vallin (*Barry Brown*); Leonard Penn (*Carter/The Wizard*); Knox Manning (*Narrator*).

## KEY CREW

Spencer Gordon Bennet (*Director*); Sam Katzman (*Producer*); George H. Plympton, Joseph F. Poland, Royal K. Cole (*Screenplay*); Bob Kane (*Characters*); Mischa Bakaleinikoff (*Music*); Ira H. Morgan (*Cinematography*); Dwight Caldwell, Earl Turner (*Editing*).

## CHAPTER TITLES

(1) Batman Takes Over; (2) Tunnel of Terror; (3) Robin's Wild Ride; (4) Batman Trapped; (5) Robin Rescues Batman; (6) Target – Robin!; (7) The Fatal Blast; (8) Robin Meets the Wizard; (9) The Wizard Strikes Back; (10) Batman's Last Chance;

(11) Robin's Ruse; (12) Robin Rides the Wind; (13) The Wizard's Challenge; (14) Batman vs Wizard; (15) Batman Victorious.

## STORY

After their heroic war efforts, Batman and Robin turn their attention to cleaning up the streets of Gotham City, encountering a new enemy in the form of a mysterious hooded villain known as the Wizard. After stealing Professor Hammil's latest invention – the so-called 'Remote Control Device' that can operate any machine within a fifty-mile radius – the Wizard and his gang hold the city to ransom, with Commissioner Gordon calling upon the Dynamic Duo for assistance. As Batman and Robin track down the gang, the Wizard takes photojournalist Vicki Vale hostage, leading to a climactic showdown within the criminal mastermind's cave hideout. The Wizard is eventually unmasked as Professor Hammil's assistant, Carter, before being subdued by the costumed crime-fighters and handed over to the Gotham City Police Department to face justice for his crimes.

## BRINGING BATMAN TO THE SCREEN

Although the movie serial market was beginning to dwindle towards the end of the 1940s, producer Sam Katzman (*The Case of the Missing Brides*, 1942) revitalized the format in 1948 with the release of *Superman*. Spurred on by the box-office success of the Man of Steel's live-action debut,

Columbia Pictures tasked Katzman with turning his hand to the Caped Crusader for a new fifteen-part adventure entitled *Batman and Robin*. Joining Katzman on the project were several members of the creative team behind *Superman*, including 'King of the Serial Directors' Spencer Gordon Bennet (*Son of Zorro*, 1947) and experienced scriptwriters George H. Plympton (*Flash Gordon*, 1936), Joseph F. Poland (*Captain America*, 1944) and Royal K. Cole (*The Masked Marvel*, 1943).

In the years following the release of *Batman*, both members of the original Dynamic Duo – Lewis Wilson and Douglas Croft – had enjoyed but a handful of credits, opening the door for Robert Lowery (*The Mark of Zorro*, 1940) and John Duncan (*Clancy Street Boys*, 1943) to step in and become the second actors to portray Batman and Robin respectively. As with its predecessor, the antagonist of *Batman and Robin* was an original creation, with Leonard Penn (*Marie Antoinette*, 1938) cast as the Wizard and his alter ego Carter; meanwhile, veteran actor Eric Wilton (*A Christmas Carol*, 1938) took over from William Austin for an uncredited turn as Alfred Pennyworth, and Lyle Talbot (*A Shriek in the Night*, 1933) portrayed Police Commissioner James Gordon, giving a screen debut to a character that originated in the Caped Crusader's very first comic book adventure in *Detective Comics* #27 in May 1939. The only actor to return from the original was Knox Manning, who once again served as narrator, albeit uncredited.

Although the *Superman* movie serial had been financially successful, producer Sam Katzman was determined to produce *Batman and Robin* on a shoe-string budget, which necessitated a host of cost-cutting measures. Not only did this impact the quality of the sets, props and costumes – including an ill-fitting Batsuit tailored to *Superman* star Kirk Alyn (*The Three Musketeers*, 1948) as opposed to Robert Lowery – but it also meant that the Batmobile was noticeably absent once more, with the Dynamic Duo this time employing a 1949 Lincoln Convertible. Despite suffering from shoddy production values, the serial would, however, mark the first screen appearance of the Bat-Signal in addition to the character of Vicki Vale, with Jane Adams (*House of Dracula*, 1945) starring as the roving reporter and love interest who first appeared in the comic book story 'The Scoop of the Century' by Bill Finger, published in *Batman* #49 (October 1948).

## RECEPTION

*Batman and Robin* began its theatrical run on 26 May 1949 and was moderately successful, although it failed to generate anywhere near the same level of excitement as the previous year's *Superman* serial, or that of the original *Batman*. Having received a number of theatrical re-releases in the 1950s and 1960s, *Batman and Robin* finally made its way to home video in 1997 as Sony Pictures Home Entertainment collected the fifteen chapters together on VHS. As with its predeces-

sor, Sony also released the serial to DVD, with a two-disc set in 2005 entitled *Batman and Robin – The Complete 1949 Movie Serial Collection*.

By the time that Batman's movie serial adventures drew to a close, the comic book industry was in a state of flux; following the end of World War II, sales of popular superhero titles began to fall and this continued for much of the next decade as comic books made way for other forms of cheap entertainment. It was also during this period of Batman's history that the German-American psychiatrist Frederic Wertham began his crusade against the medium, publishing a book entitled *Seduction of the Innocent* (1954) which criticized comic books for their corrupting influence on children. Along with concerns over violence, Wertham accused Superman of being 'un-American' and suggested that Batman and Robin were homosexual lovers. As a moral panic brewed, comic books were blamed for a rise in crime statistics, leading the United States Senate to establish a Subcommittee on Juvenile Delinquency. To counter these concerns, comic book publishers created the Comics Code Authority – a regulatory body designed to promote 'wholesome' entertainment by restricting excessive violence, sexualized imagery and the glamorization of criminal activities.

As a result of dwindling sales and the newly imposed limitations of the Comics Code Authority, the Batman character underwent a number of changes during the 1950s, shifting from his noir-soaked roots towards a much more colourful and light-hearted approach. Along with a greater emphasis on sci-fi orientated tales, several new characters were introduced to the *Batman* canon, including the canine crime-fighter Ace the Bat-Hound and the dimension-hopping Imp Bat-Mite, yet still sales continued to fall. Although DC Comics ushered in the dawn of the 'Silver Age of Comic Books' with the debut of the Flash in *Showcase* #4 (October 1956), by the close of the decade it seemed that the Golden Age of the superhero had truly come to an end. The next few years saw the Caped Crusader at serious risk of cancellation, but his popularity would soon be revived with a new live-action television series that pushed the franchise into new levels of 'camp' and led to a pop-culture phenomenon known as 'Batmania'.

# Same Bat-time, same Bat-channel

## BATMAN (1966–8)

**Premiere:** 12 January 1966 (US);
21 May 1966 (UK)
**Episode count:** 120

### CAST

Adam West (*Bruce Wayne/Batman*); Burt Ward (*Dick Grayson/Robin*); Alan Napier (*Alfred Penny-worth*); Neil Hamilton (*Police Commissioner James Gordon*); Stafford Repp (*Chief O'Hara*); Madge Blake (*Aunt Harriet Cooper*); William Dozier (*Narrator*); Yvonne Craig (*Barbara Gordon/Batgirl*) (Season Three only).

### KEY CREW

William Dozier (*Executive Producer*); Howie Horwitz (*Producer*); William P. D'Angelo (*Associate Producer*); Bob Kane (*Characters*); Nelson Riddle (*Music*); Neal Hefti (*Batman Theme*).

### STORY

For a full breakdown of the *Batman* television series, along with a synopsis of the 1966 theatrical *Batman* movie, see the episode guide that follows later in this chapter.

### BRINGING BATMAN TO THE SCREEN

Although *Batman* had been one of only three DC Comics superhero titles to have survived the dark days of the 1950s unscathed (the others being *Superman* and *Wonder Woman*), it was the success of rival publisher Marvel Comics in the early 1960s that ultimately paved the way for the Caped Crusader's revival. Headed up by the prolific creative genius of Stan Lee and artists such as Jack Kirby and Steve Ditko, Marvel ushered in a new wave of 'flawed' superheroes with the publication of *Fantastic Four* #1 in November 1961. While Marvel continued to grip the public's imagination with popular titles such as *The Amazing Spider-Man* and *The Avengers*, over at DC Comics – who were, at the time, still going by the official name of National Periodical Publications – *Batman* creator Bob Kane feared for the survival of his Dark Knight Detective.

In the early 1960s sales of *Batman* reached an all-time low and, faced with the blistering popularity of Marvel's line of superheroes, it was clear that the character was in desperate need of an overhaul. This task fell to DC editor Julius

Schwartz, who had previously overseen reimaginings of Golden Age heroes such as the Flash, Green Lantern and Hawkman, and he was given just six months to save the title. Working in collaboration with his regular artist Carmine Infantino, Schwartz debuted his 'New Look' Batman in *Detective Comics* #327 (May 1964). Gone were the fantastical sci-fi elements of the 1950s as *Batman* was given a much greater basis in reality, alongside aesthetic changes such as a redesigned crest that added a yellow oval behind the black Bat-Insignia. Fortunately this revamp helped to revive flagging sales, although the Caped Crusader was about to achieve an unprecedented level of popularity thanks to the arrival of a big-budget, prime-time television series that would ultimately go on to define the character for a generation.

Having enjoyed strong ratings for their broadcasts of the syndicated television series *Adventures of Superman* (1952–8), ABC executives Harve Bennett and Edgar J. Scherick believed the time was right to introduce a new comic book character into their prime-time schedule. ABC were enjoying success with programmes such as *The Addams Family* (1964–6) and *Bewitched* (1964–72), and felt they could make up further ground on higher-rated rivals NBC and CBS by tapping into the comic book boom to capture viewers in the all-important 7.30 timeslot. Undertaking market research to discover which comic book properties would prove popular with audiences,

ABC compiled a wish list that was headed up by *Superman*, along with *Dick Tracy*, Chester Gould's incorruptible police detective who had first appeared in the *Detroit Mirror* in October 1941.

Unable to secure the rights to either of their top two choices, the network turned to a recommendation from Yale Udoff, then Director of Late-Night Programming at ABC. A *Batman* fan during his childhood, Udoff had recently attended a screening of *An Evening with Batman and Robin* – the re-released 1943 *Batman* movie serial – at Chicago's Playboy Club, where he was amazed by the positive reception from the hip young clientele. Sensing the potential for a new and vibrant take on the Dynamic Duo that would cater to both adults and children alike, Udoff took his idea to Douglas Cramer, ABC's Vice President in Charge of New Program Development. Cramer was immediately sold on the concept, and once he convinced Scherick to get behind the idea the network made contact with DC Comics to express their interest in bringing the Caped Crusader to the small screen.

Prior to the introduction of their 'New Look' Caped Crusader, DC Comics had entered negotiations with Ed Graham Productions, who planned to develop *Batman* as a children's adventure series for CBS. The proposal had reached the casting stage, with former Pittsburgh Steelers and Los Angeles Rams linebacker Mike Henry set to don the cape and cowl, even going as far as to pose for publicity photographs in character.

However, when negotiations stalled with Ed Graham Productions, DC seized the opportunity to reacquire the rights and quickly made a deal with Bennett and Scherick in early 1965. ABC then approached Twentieth Century Fox to handle production duties and the search began to find a creative talent capable of realizing their vision.

William Dozier had started his career as a literary agent before shifting to the film industry as an associate producer on the World War II drama *The Hour Before the Dawn* (1944). In 1948 he produced *Letter from an Unknown Woman* and *You Gotta Stay Happy*, both starring his second wife, Joan Fontaine (*Suspicion*, 1941), and after their divorce in 1951 he gravitated to the small screen where he was employed by CBS as Executive Producer of Dramatic Programs. Rising through the ranks to Vice President of Hollywood Programming, Dozier's credits included the weekly sci-fi series *Rod Brown of the Rocket Rangers* (1953–4) and dramatic anthology shows such as *Suspense* (1949–54), *Climax!* (1954–8) and *Playhouse 90* (1956–60). Following a brief stint as Vice President of Columbia Pictures' Screen Gems, Dozier went on to form Greenway Productions and helped to develop *The Loner* (1965–6), a short-lived Western created by Rod Serling (*The Twilight Zone*, 1959–64) and starring Lloyd Bridges (*Sea Hunt*, 1958–61).

Along with his extensive television experience, Dozier was also familiar to ABC, where he had recently pitched a drama based on Charlie Chan's son entitled *Number One Son*, only for the network to pull out at the last minute amid concerns over the ethnicity of its lead character (an aspiring actor by the name of Bruce Lee was set to star in the title role, having come to Dozier's attention during a martial arts exhibition in Long Beach, California). Nevertheless, they felt that Dozier could be a perfect fit for *Batman* and he was invited by Douglas Cramer to attend a meeting in New York for a preliminary discussion about the project. Dozier left the meeting intrigued by the potential for a show based on the character, despite the fact that he knew absolutely nothing of the Caped Crusader, nor did he have the slightest of interest in comic books. 'ABC had bought the concept without any idea what to do with it,' Dozier told *TV Guide* in 1966. 'I bought a dozen comic books and felt like a fool doing it. I read them – if that is the word – and asked myself, "what do I do with *this*?" Then I hit on the idea of camping it.'

Dozier attended another meeting the following week to pitch his concept to a room full of ABC executives. Inspired by the work of pop artists such as Andy Warhol and Roy Lichtenstein, his plan was to take full advantage of the boom in colour TV to recreate a dynamic visual style unlike anything else on television, with bright, garish designs and on-screen graphics depicting sound effects such as 'POW!' and 'ZAP!' The show itself would be presented as 'high camp', playing it overly straight while pushing the outrageous elements of the comic books to the verge of absurdity, thus appealing to both adults and children alike. Furthermore, the characters would be introduced via a feature-length theatrical movie, laying the foundations for the television launch of *Batman* in September 1966. Impressed with Dozier's vision, executives immediately struck a deal for Greenway Productions to develop a pilot.

In order to turn his ideas into a workable script, Dozier turned to Lorenzo Semple Jr, a writer who had broken into the business in the 1950s penning the Broadway plays *Tonight in Samarkand* (1955) and *The Golden Fleecing* (1959) before collaborating with Dozier on a number of television pitches, included the aborted *Number One Son*. To give him inspiration for the pilot, Dozier sent Semple four issues of the comic book, including *Batman* #171 (May 1965); this particular issue featured a Gardner Fox story entitled 'Remarkable Ruse of the Riddler', which would serve as the basis for Semple's script. It was also decided that rather than taking the form of one hour-long episode, each story would be split into two parts and broadcast over consecutive nights, enabling the series to retain the 'cliff-hanger' approach of the 1940s movie serials.

As Semple completed the script, Dozier turned his attention to the task of casting the Dynamic Duo. Initially, the executive producer had earmarked Ty Hardin, star of the popular Western series *Bronco* (1958–62), as his number one choice for the role of Batman. When Hardin proved unavailable his agent recommended another of his clients, a rising star by the name of Adam West. After meeting with the up-and-coming actor, Dozier felt that West's understanding of the approach towards the material made him perfect for the role, although he knew from experience that ABC would expect to be given a choice over their leading man. As a result, Dozier invited West and Lyle Waggoner – a then-unknown actor who would later gain attention for his work on *The Carol Burnett Show* (1967–78) and *Wonder Woman* (1975–9) – to screen test for the role of Batman, alongside their preferred candidates from auditions held to find the Boy Wonder.

After starting his career in the entertainment business with a run on the local Hawaiian children's programme *The Kino Popo Show*, in 1959 Adam West made the shift to Hollywood where he landed a supporting role alongside Paul Newman in Warner Bros' *The Young Philadelphians*. This opened up the door to television and West quickly amassed a number of credits, with guest roles in popular series such as *Maverick* (1957–62), *Bonanza* (1959–73), *Perry Mason* (1957–66), *The Outer Limits* (1963–5) and *Bewitched*. However, it was his dead-pan turn as Captain Q in a commercial for Nestlé that convinced Dozier of his suitability for the role. 'They actually signed me the first day I talked to them, because they had seen a series of Nestlé Quik commercials in which I spoofed James Bond,' recalled West in an interview with Matt Mac Nabb of *LegionsofGotham.org* in 2004. 'Twentieth Century Fox and Greenway Productions tested Lyle [Waggoner] and others to appease the suits at ABC, but they had already decided on me. Kind of a little casting trick.'

'When I tried out for the part, I didn't even know what show I was trying out for,' Burt Ward told *SliceofSciFi.com* in 2011. 'It was one of those quick things, "Get over to Twentieth Century Fox right away and go see this person."' At just 20 years of age, Ward – then known as Burton Gervis – was studying acting at UCLA when he attended his first audition, becoming one of more than a thousand aspiring actors to try out for the part of Robin. Dressed in a prototype Robin suit, Ward impressed with his martial arts abilities and was invited to film a screen test alongside Adam West, with the duo competing against Lyle Waggoner and former child actor Peter Deyell (*Shirley Temple's Storybook*, 1958–61) for the highly coveted roles. The footage – which consisted of scenes from the pilot and, in Ward's case, a demonstration of his martial arts skills – was then screened for ABC executives who found themselves in agreement with Dozier; deals were signed and Adam West and Burt Ward were announced as the latest actors to have the distinction of bringing the Caped Crusader and the Boy Wonder to the screen.

Preceding the casting of Batman and Robin was the appointment of veteran English actor Alan Napier as Alfred, the faithful butler of Bruce Wayne and Dick Grayson, who had recently met his demise in the comic book story 'Gotham Gang Line-Up!' by Bill Finger, published in *Detective Comics* #328 (June 1964). The cousin of former British prime minister Neville Chamberlain, Napier had extensive experience on both sides of the Atlantic, with his Hollywood credits including appearances in the likes of *Macbeth* (1948), *Julius Caesar* (1953), *My Fair Lady* (1964) and *Marnie* (1964). Napier was joined in Wayne Manor by Madge Blake, a character actress whose CV included roles in the MGM musicals *An American in Paris* (1951) and *Singin' in the Rain* (1952), along with small-screen appearances in television shows such as *Leave It to Beaver* (1957–63) and *The Real McCoys* (1957–63) in addition to the pilot episode of *The Addams Family*. Blake was cast as Aunt Harriet Cooper, the maternal aunt of Dick Grayson who had also made her first appearance in 'Gotham Gang Line-Up!'; as with her introduction to the comic book series, Aunt Harriet's presence in the *Batman* television show was designed primarily to counter rumours of homosexuality within Wayne Manor.

To portray the face of the Gotham City Police Department, Dozier secured another two veteran character actors with extensive television experience. For Police Commissioner Gordon, Dozier turned to Neil Hamilton (*Tarzan the Ape Man*,

1932), a leading man of the silent and early-sound eras who had been rescued from a career slump in the 1940s by the advent of television. TV regular Stafford Repp (*The New Phil Silvers Show*, 1963–4) was hired as Gordon's right-hand man, Gotham City Chief of Police O'Hara, a newly created character who would eventually debut in panel form in the comic book story 'Bruce Wayne … Bait in a Bat-Trap' by Bob Rozakis and Michael Uslan, published in *Detective Comics* #461 (July 1976). Finally, after failing to find a suitable candidate to supply voiceover work as the narrator, Dozier was encouraged by his assistant Charles FitzSimons to take on the role himself, adopting a style that parodied Knox Manning's narration on the earlier *Batman* serials along with Walter Winchell's work on *The Untouchables* (1959–63).

Hoping to have a hit on their hands, ABC devoted considerable financial resources to the *Batman* pilot. On top of a production budget of around $500,000, the network spent $800,000 on the creation of the Batcave set, which was at the time an astronomical figure for a television production. Another key design consideration was that of the Batmobile, an iconic aspect of the *Batman* mythos that had been sorely overlooked in the Caped Crusader's earlier screen appearances. Hollywood car customizer Dean Jeffries was initially tasked with the design, although he left the project amid concerns over his ability to meet the strict three-week deadline. Dozier then turned to another notable customizer, George Barris, who had previously created vehicles for shows such as *The Beverly Hillbillies* (1962–71) and *The Munsters* (1964–6). Barris was the owner of the Lincoln Futura, a one-off concept car built in 1955 at a cost of $250,000; the distinctive Futura had played a prominent role in the romantic comedy *It Started with a Kiss* (1959) and underwent $30,000 of modifications in order to convert it to the Batmobile in time for filming.

'As a kid, I'd read the comic books,' Adam West told *LegionsofGotham.org*. 'Consequently, when I first pulled on the cape and cowl, I'd had flash-backs to running through the house in my blue bath-towel cape. So, it was really déjà vu time when we began to film.'

Joining West, Ward and company in the pilot was Frank Gorshin, an actor, impressionist and comedian best known for guest spots on the likes of *The Tonight Show* and *The Ed Sullivan Show*, including an appearance on the famous 9 February 1964 broadcast which had introduced The Beatles to American audiences. Gorshin would star as the very first 'Special Guest Villain', the Riddler, then a minor *Batman* antagonist with just three comic book appearances to his name, including his debut in 'The Riddler!' by Bill Finger, published in *Detective Comics* #140 (October 1948). Meanwhile the pilot would be helmed by Robert Butler, an experienced television director with past credits on the likes of *Bonanza*, *The Detectives Starring Robert Taylor* (1961), *The Untouchables* and *The Twilight Zone*.

Along with the sets constructed at Twentieth Century Fox Studios and Desilu Studios, filming for the pilot would also take place on location at Bronson Caves in Bronson Canyon, Los Angeles, which doubled as the entrance to the Batcave, while 380 South San Rafael Avenue, Pasadena, was used as the exterior to Wayne Manor. 'With each script and new situation, I saw something funny in it. But I could never let the audience think that I thought it was funny,' reflected Adam West on his approach to the character in an interview with Martin Anderson of *DenofGeek.com* in 2008. 'It was a conscious effort that I always felt. I was at war with the producers at the beginning because of that. They wanted it to be stiff and at one level I wouldn't do it. So the letters and memos flew back and forth, but after a week or so, a wonderful thing happened – they trusted me. They said, "Let him go, let him do what he's doing".'

Midway through the production of the *Batman* pilot, dailies were screened to ABC executives who were greatly impressed by what they saw. Confident that *Batman* would prove a ratings success, the network made the unusual decision to green-light the show there and then, ordering a further sixteen two-part stories and using the pilot episode as the season opener. Dozier enlisted Lorenzo Semple Jr as executive story editor, granting him input into all of the scripts for the first season, while he was also charged with adapting a further three comic books; these stories would introduce two of Batman's major nemeses, the Joker and the Penguin, along with Mr Freeze. Together with the pilot, these would form the first eight episodes of the *Batman* television series. Meanwhile Semple was also contracted to write the screenplay for the *Batman* theatrical feature, although Twentieth Century Fox – who were solely responsible for the financing of the movie – decided to hold off on production until they had a chance to see how viewers would respond to the series.

By the time that filming had come to an end on the *Batman* pilot, ABC found themselves struggling against rivals CBS and NBC in terms of prime-time ratings. Their schedule for the fall of 1965 had failed to take off and the network knew they needed to take drastic action to make up ground on their competitors. Hoping to boost ratings, ABC announced what they referred to as the 'Second Season', an influx of new programming that would air as midseason replacements for their failing shows, with *Batman* topping their list of priorities. However, despite their earlier confidence in the project, ABC executives were left dumbfounded when test scores from a preview screening of the pilot came back ten points lower than what was considered a passing grade. In an effort to salvage something from their investment, the network requested two further test screenings, one featuring a laugh-track and the other with additional narration. Still this failed to impress.

Having devoted considerable financial resources to the pilot – not to mention the purchase of an entire season at an approximate cost of $75,000 per episode – the network were left with little choice but to push on with their plans to debut the series in January 1966, a full nine months earlier than Dozier had originally anticipated. The executive producer was forced to employ two units to work concurrently in the hope of ensuring that the series would be ready on time. Using his Hollywood contacts, Dozier managed to lure a number of star names to feature as Special Guest Villains, including Golden Globe nominee Cesar Romero (*If a Man Answers*, 1962) as the Joker and Burgess Meredith (*The Twilight Zone*) as the Penguin. Julie Newmar (*Seven Brides for Seven Brothers*, 1954) was chosen to portray Catwoman, a popular character last seen prior to the introduction of the Comics Code, while other notable first-season guest stars included Roddy McDowall (*Cleopatra*, 1963), Victor Buono (*Whatever Happened to Baby Jane?*, 1962) and Academy Award-winner Anne Baxter (*The Razor's Edge*, 1946).

If the feedback from the *Batman* test screenings was to be believed, ABC and Twentieth Century Fox were about to suffer the biggest disaster in television's fledgling history. With the January premiere fast approaching, the network embarked on a multi-million-dollar publicity campaign to promote the series. Amid countless television promos, magazine and billboard advertisements, ABC even hired a skywriter to spell out the phrase 'Batman is coming' during the 52nd

Rose Bowl game held on 1 January 1966. Now all they could do was sit back and hope that the general viewing public were ready to embrace Dozier's 'camp' take on the Caped Crusader…

## RECEPTION

After generating a huge amount of hype in the days leading up to its premiere, *Batman* received its first airing in the United States on Wednesday 12 January 1966 in ABC's prime-time lead-in slot of 7.30 p.m. Eastern Time/6.30 p.m. Central Time and became, quite literally, an overnight success. Nielsen ratings for the first episode came in at 27.3/49, meaning that 49 per cent of American households equipped with a TV set (estimated at 93 per cent in 1966) had tuned in to catch the television debut of Adam West and Burt Ward's Dynamic Duo. Despite a mixed reaction from critics, the second episode (arriving 'Same Bat-time, same Bat-channel' the following day) drew an even bigger audience, pulling in a rating of 29.6/59. It was official: 'Batmania' had begun.

Over the coming weeks and months *Batman* continued to maintain astonishing ratings as America went Caped Crusader crazy and the series became a true pop-culture phenomenon. There was an immediate spike in sales of the *Batman* comic book, with the latest issue shifting just under a million copies. By the time of Adam West's appearance on the cover of *Life* magazine on 11 March 1966 over a thousand official products had been licensed, including books, bicycles, bubblegum cards, die-cast vehicles, fancy-dress costumes, food products, lunchboxes, model kits, play-sets, posters and even toiletries. The fervour seemed to reach its peak on 17 March 1966, when the Gemini 8 spacecraft suffered an in-flight system failure and ABC were inundated with complaints after interrupting Julie Newmar's Catwoman debut in 'The Purr-fect Crime' in order to report on the emergency. Meanwhile Batmania soon spread across the Atlantic, with *Batman* arriving in the UK on 21 May 1966, where it enjoyed a similar level of success to that of its domestic market.

Along with the general public, celebrities were also finding themselves swept up in the Batmania craze. Neal Defti's 'Batman Theme' was covered by a number of groups including The Marketts, The Ventures and British rockers The Who, while a guest spot on the show quickly became one of the most sought-after credits in Tinseltown. A host of famous names signed on to appear as villains and villainesses, with the likes of Tallulah Bankhead (*Lifeboat*, 1944), Art Carney (*The Honeymooners*, 1955–6), Joan Collins (*Island in the Sun*, 1957), Otto Preminger (*Stalag 17*, 1953), Vincent Price (*House on Haunted Hill*, 1959), George Sanders (*All About Eve*, 1950), Eli Wallach (*The Good, the Bad and the Ugly*, 1966) and Shelley Winters (*The Diary of Anne Frank*, 1959) each paid a flat fee of $2,500 for their work; it was also rumoured that Clint Eastwood (*A Fistful of Dollars*, 1964) was in negotiations to appear as

Two-Face, a character whose grotesque appearance concerned network executives, but the series would draw to an end before this could materialize.

To cope with the demand for celebrity appearances the 'Bat-Climb' cameo was created, whereby a famous face would pop out of a window as the Dynamic Duo scaled the side of a building. Stars who managed to secure Bat-Climb cameos included Sammy Davis Jr (*Ocean's Eleven*, 1960), Jerry Lewis (*The Nutty Professor*, 1963) and Edward G. Robinson (*Double Indemnity*, 1944). Carolyn Jones, John Astin and Ted Cassidy of fellow ABC show *The Addams Family* would also feature during the series, while the second season played host to crossovers between *Batman* and Dozier's latest costumed crime-fighting show, *The Green Hornet* (1966–7). Launched on 9 September 1966, *The Green Hornet* ran for a single season, with stars Van Williams (*Bourbon Street Beat*, 1959–60) and Bruce Lee (*The Kid*, 1950) appearing in character for a Bat-Climb cameo and a two-part episode that saw them credited as 'Visiting Hero' and 'Assistant Visiting Hero', respectively.

As the first season of *Batman* drew to a close in April 1966, production got underway on the feature film, which Twentieth Century Fox intended to use as a promotional tool to sell the series in foreign markets where Batmania was yet to take hold. Evidence of *Batman's* success was further confirmed as it became the first television show to feature twice in Neilsen's 'Top Twenty-five' of the season (a feat that would not be matched until the 1999/2000 season of *Who Wants to Be a Millionaire?*), with the Wednesday episode featuring at number 10 and the Thursday episode coming in at number 5. *Batman* also received industry recognition with three nominations at the 18th Primetime Emmy Awards, where it competed for Outstanding Comedy Series, Individual Achievements in Sound Editing (Ralph Hickey, Dick Le Grand, Ross Taylor and Harold E. Wooley) and Outstanding Performance by an Actor in a Supporting Role in a Comedy (Frank Gorshin, for the episode 'Hi Diddle Riddle').

With Batmania reaching such dizzying heights during the series' first season (including over $150m in sales of official merchandise), it was inevitable that *Batman* would struggle to sustain such an intense level of popularity. In July 1966, *Batman: The Movie* was released to only moderate box-office success, and in the face of declining merchandise sales ABC – who had naturally ordered a second season of the hit show – made the decision to trim the budget for the next run of episodes. Along with recycled footage from both the first season and the theatrical movie, the second season also saw a change to the superimposed overlays used during fight scenes, which were replaced by intercut title cards in order to save on production costs.

The second season of *Batman* launched in September 1966 and the show initially managed

to retain strong ratings, although these were considerably lower than the phenomenal figures it enjoyed in the early part of the year. However, as the mammoth season of sixty episodes progressed, the show began to stagnate and slipped into an overly predictable formula. Typically, episodes followed a regular pattern that began with the Special Guest Villain committing a crime, leading Commissioner Gordon to call upon Batman and Robin for assistance. The resulting investigation would see the Dynamic Duo captured by the crooks and placed into an elaborate death-trap, ending on a cliff-hanger as the narrator questioned how the heroes could possibly survive. This was quickly resolved in the opening scenes of the concluding part, with Batman and Robin making their escape and tracking down the villain for a climactic 'Bat Fight' from which the heroes would emerge victorious, having saved the day once again.

While younger viewers still tuned in regularly to catch the latest adventures of the Dynamic Duo, by the end of *Batman's* second season the adult audience had severely dwindled, leaving ABC undecided about whether to renew the series for a third outing. In an attempt to freshen up proceedings Dozier planned to introduce a new female crime-fighter, Batgirl, based on the Barbara Gordon incarnation of the character who had recently debuted in the comic book story 'The Million Dollar Debut of Batgirl' by Gardner Fox, published in *Detective Comics* #359 (January

1967). Dozier's first choice for Batgirl was former Miss America and Golden Globe-winner Mary Ann Mobley (*Harum Scarum*, 1965), and when Mobley proved unavailable he turned to Yvonne Craig, a trained ballet dancer whose previous acting experience included the likes of *High Time* (1960), *It Happened at the World's Fair* (1963) and *Kissin' Cousins* (1964). Producing a seven-and-a-half minute promotional short entitled *Batgirl* (1967), Dozier managed to convince the network to renew the series, albeit with a dramatically reduced budget and a solitary weekly airing on a Thursday night.

Despite the introduction of Yvonne Craig's Batgirl, ratings continued to fall throughout the third season, and ABC soon announced their intention to scale things back even further by dropping Robin and Chief O'Hara from the line-up of the proposed fourth season. However, before this could happen the network made the decision in January 1968 to call time on the series; two weeks later NBC made an offer to Greenway Productions to finance a fourth season but pulled out of negotiations after learning that the sets had already been destroyed, and *Batman* came to an end on 14 March 1968 with the broadcast of its 120th and final episode, 'Minerva, Mayhem and Millionaires'. The show remained popular as it entered syndication and to this day it receives regular airings around the world. Owing to complex rights issues between Fox and Warner Bros, the television series is yet to receive any kind of home entertainment release, although the 1966 theatrical movie has been made available on VHS, DVD and Blu-ray.

Had it not been for the *Batman* television series, there is every chance that the 1960s would have seen the end of the Dark Knight's war on the criminal element of Gotham City. *Batman* had introduced a new generation to Bob Kane's most famous creation, and in the two years since its premiere the Caped Crusader had grown to become America's number one comic book character. Nevertheless, this success would prove to be a double-edged sword, both for its cast and for the characters they portrayed on screen. Stars Adam West, Burt Ward and Yvonne Craig found it increasingly difficult to distance themselves from the show (for details on additional *Batman* appearances and reunions, SEE 'THE EARLY ADVENTURES OF THE ANIMATED BATMAN' AND 'MISCELLANEOUS SPIN-OFFS'), while the camp tone of the series left a lasting impression on the public and quickly came to define the character. Although DC Comics embarked on a push towards a darker interpretation of the Caped Crusader in the 1970s, it would be more than twenty years before audiences were ready to embrace a new incarnation, courtesy of an inexperienced director and an unpopular casting choice for the Dark Knight.

# BATMAN (1966—8) EPISODE GUIDE
# BATMAN: SEASON ONE (1966)

**Episode 1.1 'Hi Diddle Riddle'**
Original US air date: 12 January 1966

**Episode 1.2 – 'Smack in the Middle'**
Original US air date: 13 January 1966

Key crew: Robert Butler (*Director*); Lorenzo Semple Jr (*Teleplay*)
Special Guest Villain: Frank Gorshin (*The Riddler*)
Notable Guest Star: Jill St John (*Molly*)

## STORY

After tricking Batman into making a false arrest, the Riddler launches legal action against the Caped Crusader as a smoke-screen for his latest plan – the theft of an ancient mammoth stuffed with priceless Moldavian postage stamps.

## BAT-FACTS

Based on the comic book story 'Remarkable Ruse of the Riddler' by Gardner Fox, published in *Batman* #171 (May 1965). Frank Gorshin became *Batman's* first Special Guest Villain and received an Emmy Award nomination for Outstanding Performance by an Actor in a Supporting Role in a Comedy for 'Hi Diddle Riddle', while an uncredited William Dozier also supplied the voice of a maitre d' in the same episode. 'Smack in the Middle' was one of three episodes in the series to feature the death of a character (the Riddler's henchwoman, Molly, who falls to her death after infiltrating the Batcave), and one of only three to end with the Special Guest Villain evading justice.

**Episode 1.3 – 'Fine Feathered Finks'**
Original US air date: 19 January 1966

**Episode 1.4 – 'The Penguin's a Jinx'**
Original US air date: 20 January 1966

Key crew: Robert Butler (*Director*); Lorenzo Semple Jr (*Teleplay*)
Special Guest Villain: Burgess Meredith (*The Penguin*)
Notable Guest Star: Leslie Parish (*Dawn Robbins*)

## STORY

Upon his release from prison, the Penguin hopes to trick Batman and Robin into plotting his next crime by listening in on the Dynamic Duo as they investigate a series of random umbrella incidents, leading to a kidnap attempt on movie star Dawn Robbins.

## BAT-FACTS

Based on the comic book story 'Partners in Plunder!' by France Eddie Herron, published in *Batman* #169 (February 1965). Burgess Meredith debuted in the role of the Penguin, with David Lewis (*The Apartment*, 1960) also making his first appearance in 'Fine Feathered Finks' as recurring character Warden Crichton. Former child star Mickey Rooney (*Babes in Arms*, 1939) was among the actors considered for the Penguin, along with twice Academy Award-winner Spencer Tracy (*Captains Courageous*, 1937 and *Boys Town*, 1938), who said that he would only accept the role on the condition that he killed Batman.

Episode 1.5 – 'The Joker is Wild'
Original US air date: 26 January 1966

Episode 1.6 – 'Batman is Riled'
Original US air date: 27 January 1966

Key crew: Don Weis (*Director*); Robert Dozier (*Teleplay*)
Special Guest Villain: Cesar Romero (*The Joker*)
Notable Guest Star: Nancy Kovack (*Queenie*)

## STORY

When his latest crime spree is foiled by the Dynamic Duo, the Joker creates his own utility belt in an effort to even the playing field. Capturing Batman and Robin, the Clown Prince of Crime sets out to unmask them live on television with his twisted game show, *What's My Crime?*

## BAT-FACTS

Based on the comic book story 'The Joker's Utility

Belt!' by David Reed, published in *Batman* #73 (October 1952). The episodes were written by Robert Dozier, son of executive producer William Dozier, in his only contribution to the series. Cesar Romero made his first appearance as the Joker, with the make-up department forced to cover his moustache after he refused to shave for the role. Other actors considered for the Joker included Academy Award-winner José Ferrer (*Cyrano de Bergerac*, 1950) and later Oscar recipient Gig Young (*They Shoot Horses, Don't They?*, 1969).

Episode 1.7 – 'Instant Freeze'
Original US air date: 2 February 1966

Episode 1.8 – 'Rats Like Cheese'
Original US air date: 3 February 1966

Key crew: Robert Butler (*Director*); Max Hodge (*Teleplay*)
Special Guest Villain: George Sanders (*Mr Freeze*)

## STORY

Blaming Batman for an accident that left him dependent on a cryogenic suit for survival, Mr Freeze returns to Gotham City to exact his revenge and kidnaps a star baseball player, offering to release his hostage in exchange for the Caped Crusader.

## BAT-FACTS

Based on the comic book story 'The Ice Crimes of Mr Zero!' by Dave Wood, published in *Batman*

#121 (February 1959). This issue introduced the villainous Mr Zero, who was renamed Mr Freeze by the producers of *Batman* in a move that soon crossed over into the comics. 'Instant Freeze' was the second episode to feature the death of a character (a butler, who is frozen and knocked over by Mr Freeze, smashing to pieces off-screen).

**Episode 1.9 – 'Zelda the Great'**
Original US air date: 9 February 1966

**Episode 1.10 – 'A Death Worse than Fate'**
Original US air date: 10 February 1966

**Key crew:** Norman Foster (*Director*); Lorenzo Semple Jr (*Teleplay*)
**Special Guest Villainess:** Anne Baxter (*Zelda the Great*)
**Notable Guest Star:** Jack Kruschen (*Eivol Ekdal*)

## STORY

Hoping to uncover the thief behind a bank robbery, Batman plants a newspaper story suggesting the stolen money is counterfeit. The trail soon leads to Zelda the Great, an escape artist who needs to raise funds to pay designer Eivol Ekdal for his latest creation, the Inescapable Doom-Trap.

## BAT-FACTS

Based on the comic book story 'Batman's Inescapable Doom-Trap!' by John Broome, published in *Detective Comics* #346 (December 1965).

'A Death Worse than Fate' was the third and final episode to feature death (two of Eivol Ekdal's henchmen shoot each other when Batman and Robin duck their gunfire), and one of only two episodes not to include a 'Bat Fight'.

**Episode 1.11 – 'A Riddle a Day Keeps the Riddler Away'**
Original US air date: 16 February 1966

**Episode 1.12 – 'When the Rat's Away, the Mice Will Play'**
Original US air date: 17 February 1966

**Key crew:** Tom Gries (*Director*); Fred De Gorter (*Teleplay*)
**Special Guest Villain:** Frank Gorshin (*The Riddler*)

## STORY

King Boris arrives in Gotham City to present the Museum of Fame with a replica statue from his home country. However, the King is soon kidnapped by the Riddler, who plants a bomb inside the statue and demands a ransom of $1m in order to deactivate it.

## BAT-FACTS

The actor who played King Boris, Reginald Denny (*Cat Ballou*, 1965), would make his final screen appearance as Commodore Schmidlapp in the *Batman* theatrical movie.

Episode 1.13 – 'The Thirteenth Hat'
Original US air date: 23 February 1966

Episode 1.14 – 'Batman Stands Pat'
Original US air date: 24 February 1966

Key crew: Norman Foster (*Director*); Charles
Hoffman (*Teleplay*)
Special Guest Villain: David Wayne (*The Mad
Hatter*)

## STORY

As a spate of hat-related disappearances grips
Gotham, the Dynamic Duo unearth a plot by the
Mad Hatter to gain revenge against the jurors
responsible for his previous conviction, with key
prosecution witness Batman his number one target.

## BAT-FACTS

Based on the comic book story 'The New Crimes
of the Mad Hatter' by Dave Wood, published in
*Batman* #161 (February 1964).

Episode 1.15 – 'The Joker Goes to School'
Original US air date: 2 March 1966

Episode 1.16 – 'He Meets His Match, the
Grisly Ghoul'
Original US air date: 3 March 1966

Key crew: Murray Golden (*Director*); Lorenzo
Semple Jr (*Teleplay*)

Special Guest Villain: Cesar Romero (*The Joker*)

## STORY

With the Joker undermining student morale in
order to recruit high school drop-outs into his new
gang, the Bad Pennies, Dick Grayson embarks on
a dangerous undercover assignment to bring the
dastardly criminal to justice.

## BAT-FACTS

The Joker's One-Armed Bandit Novelty Company originated from an idea by Semple to create
a new villain called the One-Armed Bandit,
whose speciality would have been using gimmick
vending machines to commit his crimes.

Episode 1.17 – 'True or False Face'
Original US air date: 9 March 1966

Episode 1.18 – 'Holy Rat Race'
Original US air date: 10 March 1966

Key crew: William A. Graham (*Director*);
Stephen Kandel (*Teleplay*)
Special Guest Villain: Malachi Throne (*False Face*)

## STORY

Investigating the theft of the priceless Mergenberg
Crown, the Dynamic Duo soon find themselves
on the trail of False Face, a master of disguise who
plans to rob a bank and replace the money in the
vault with counterfeit notes.

## BAT-FACTS

To tie in with the mystery surrounding False Face, Malachi Throne (*The Young Lovers*, 1964) was credited as '?' until the end title sequence of 'Holy Rat Race'. Throne would later voice characters on both *The New Batman Adventures* (as the Judge in the episode 'Judgement Day') and *Batman Beyond* (as Fingers in the episode 'Speak No Evil'), while Gary Owens (who voices a TV newscaster in 'Holy Rat Race') went on to lend his vocal talents to the 1950s Batman in an episode of *The New Batman Adventures* entitled 'Legends of the Dark Knight' (SEE 'THE DARK KNIGHT IN THE DC ANIMATED UNIVERSE').

Episode 1.19 – 'The Purr-fect Crime'
Original US air date: 16 March 1966

Episode 1.20 – 'Better Luck Next Time'
Original US air date: 17 March 1966

Key crew: James Sheldon (*Director*); Stanley Ralph Ross, Lee Orgel (*Teleplay*)
Special Guest Villainess: Julie Newmar (*Catwoman*)

## STORY

Following the theft of one half of a matching pair of golden cat statuettes, the Caped Crusader and Boy Wonder find themselves protecting the other figurine from Catwoman, who hopes to combine the artefacts to reveal a map leading to the buried treasure of Captain Manx.

## BAT-FACTS

Julie Newmar made her first appearance of the series – winning the role against competition from Suzanne Pleshette (*The Birds*, 1963) – and would go on to become the most prolific Special Guest Villainess. Meanwhile, Catwoman became only the second antagonist to avoid apprehension by the Dynamic Duo.

Episode 1.21 – 'The Penguin Goes Straight'
Original US air date: 23 March 1966

Episode 1.22 – 'Not Yet, He Ain't'
Original US air date: 24 March 1966

Key crew: Leslie H. Martinson (*Director*); Lorenzo Semple Jr, John Cardwell (*Teleplay*)
Special Guest Villain: Burgess Meredith (*The Penguin*)

## STORY

Fresh from his latest spell in jail, the Penguin announces that he's shifting from crime to crime-fighting with the establishment of the Penguin Protective Agency. Batman and Robin soon find themselves framed for robbery and must fake their own deaths in order to expose the true culprit to the citizens of Gotham.

## BAT-FACTS

The episode 'Not Yet, He Ain't' featured the debut of the Batcycle, although the design would be updated for the theatrical movie and its subsequent appearances within the series.

Episode 1.23 – 'The Ring of Wax'
Original US air date: 30 March 1966

Episode 1.24 – 'Give 'Em the Axe'
Original US air date: 31 March 1966

Key crew: James B. Clark (*Director*); Jack Paritz, Bob Rodgers (*Teleplay*)
Special Guest Villain: Frank Gorshin (*The Riddler*)

## STORY

When a waxwork statue of Batman is replaced by that of the Riddler, the Caped Crusader and Boy Wonder follow a trail of clues that sees them uncover a plot by the Riddler to steal the lost treasure of the Incas, which is hidden inside an ancient sarcophagus at the Gotham City Museum.

## BAT-FACTS

Based on the comic book story 'A Hairpin, a Hoe, a Hacksaw, a Hole in the Ground!' by Bill Finger, published in *Batman* #53 (June 1949).

Episode 1.25 – 'The Joker Trumps an Ace'
Original US air date: 6 April 1966

Episode 1.26 – 'Batman Sets the Pace'
Original US air date: 7 April 1966

Key crew: Richard C. Sarafian (*Director*); Francis M. Cockrell, Marian B. Cockrell (*Teleplay*)
Special Guest Villain: Cesar Romero (*The Joker*)

## STORY

For his latest criminal caper the Joker targets the solid gold golf clubs of the Maharajah of Nimpah, only to kidnap the visiting monarch and demand a hefty ransom for his release. With time running out, Batman and Robin strive to avoid an international incident.

## BAT-FACTS

Byron Keith (*The Stranger*, 1946) made his first appearance of the series in 'The Joker Trumps an Ace', portraying the recurring character Mayor Linseed.

Episode 1.27 – 'The Curse of Tut'
Original US air date: 13 April 1966

Episode 1.28 – 'The Pharaoh's in a Rut'
Original US air date: 14 April 1966

Key crew: Charles R. Rondeau (*Director*); Earl Barret, Robert C. Dennis (*Teleplay*)
Special Guest Villain: Victor Buono (*King Tut*)

## STORY

After sustaining a head injury during a student riot, a former Yale scholar of Egyptology believes himself to be the King of the Nile; erecting a giant sphinx in Gotham Central Park, Tut plans to turn the city into a modern day Thebes with himself as ruler and Batman as his slave.

## BAT-FACTS

King Tut was the first Special Guest Villain to have been specifically created for the television series (he would finally make his comic debut in *Batman Confidential* #26 in April 2009). Olan Soule (*Dragnet*, 1951–9), who supplied voice work as a newscaster in the episode 'The Pharaoh's in a Rut', went on to voice Batman in the 1968 Filmation cartoon *The Batman/Superman Hour* (1968–9), in addition to two episodes of *The New Scooby-Doo Movies* (1972) and the various incarnations of Hanna-Barbera's *Super Friends* produced between 1973 and 1982 (SEE 'THE EARLY ADVENTURES OF THE ANIMATED BATMAN').

Episode 1.29 – 'The Bookworm Turns'
Original US air date: 20 April 1966

Episode 1.30 – 'While Gotham City Burns'
Original US air date: 21 April 1966

**Key crew:** Larry Peerce (*Director*); Hendrik Vollaerts (*Teleplay*)

**Special Guest Villain:** Roddy McDowall (*The Bookworm*)
**Celebrity Bat-Climb cameo:** Jerry Lewis (*Himself*)

## STORY

The Bookworm stages a false assassination of Commissioner Gordon to lure Batman and Robin to police headquarters; leaving a trail of clues that lead the Dynamic Duo into a deadly trap inside a giant cookbook, the Bookworm heads to Gotham Library with plans to pilfer its collection of rare books.

## BAT-FACTS

Jerry Lewis' appearance in 'The Bookworm Turns' marked the first inclusion of the celebrity Bat-Climb cameo, while Roddy McDowall later returned to Gotham City as the voice of the Mad Hatter in *Batman: The Animated Series* and *The New Batman Adventures*.

Episode 1.31 – 'Death in Slow Motion'
Original US air date: 27 April 1966

Episode 1.32 – 'The Riddler's False Notion'
Original US air date: 28 April 1966

**Key crew:** Charles R. Rondeau (*Director*); Richard Carr (*Teleplay*)
**Special Guest Villain:** Frank Gorshin (*The Riddler*)

## STORY

Posing as Charlie Chaplin and the Keystone Cops, the Riddler and his gang raid a film festival of its box-office receipts before embarking on a celluloid crime spree. Capturing the Riddler's moll, Pauline (Sherry Jackson), Batman invites Commissioner Gordon to the Batcave where their interrogation unearths a plan to steal a priceless silent film collection.

## BAT-FACTS

Based on the comic book story 'The Joker's Comedy Capers!' by John Broome, published in *Detective Comics* #341 (July 1965). After he had been the most prolific villain of the first season, a pay dispute meant that Frank Gorshin declined the opportunity to return for the second season, although he would enjoy a prominent role in the theatrical movie and made one final appearance as the Riddler in Season Three.

Episode 1.33 – 'Fine Finny Fiends'
Original US air date: 4 May 1966

Episode 1.34 – 'Batman Makes the Scenes'
Original US air date: 5 May 1966

Key crew: Tom Gries (*Director*); Sheldon Stark (*Teleplay*)
Special Guest Villain: Burgess Meredith (*The Penguin*)

## STORY

During preparations for the Multimillionaires Annual Awards Dinner, Alfred is kidnapped by the Penguin and brainwashed into revealing the event's secret location. Hoping to rob the wealthy guests, the Penguin infiltrates the dinner only to discover that Batman and Robin are in attendance on behalf of Bruce Wayne and Dick Grayson.

## BAT-FACTS

A selection of mug shots seen in the episode 'Fine Finny Fiends' includes photographs of producer Howie Horwitz and executive producer William Dozier.

## BATMAN (A.K.A. BATMAN: THE MOVIE) (1966)

**Release date:** 30 July 1966 (US); 16 December 1966 (UK)
**Certificate:** PG (US); U (UK)
**Running time:** 105 minutes
**Budget:** $1,377,800

### CAST

Adam West (*Bruce Wayne/Batman*); Burt Ward (*Dick Grayson/Robin*); Lee Meriwether (*Miss Kitka/Catwoman*); Cesar Romero (*The Joker*); Burgess Meredith (*The Penguin*); Frank Gorshin (*The Riddler*); Alan Napier (*Alfred Pennyworth*); Neil Hamilton (*Commissioner James Gordon*); Stafford Repp (*Chief O'Hara*); Madge Blake (*Aunt Harriet Cooper*); Reginald Denny (*Commodore Schmidlapp*); Milton Frome (*Vice Admiral Fangschliester*); Gil Perkins (*Bluebeard*); Dick Crockett (*Morgan*); George Sawaya (*Quetch*); William Dozier (*Narrator*).

### KEY CREW

Leslie H. Martinson (*Director*); William Dozier (*Producer*); Charles B. Fitzsimons (*Associate Producer*); Lorenzo Semple Jr (*Written by*); Bob Kane (*Characters*); Nelson Riddle (*Music*); Howard Schwartz (*Cinematography*); Harry W. Gerstad (*Editing*).

### STORY

Bruce Wayne and Dick Grayson are enjoying a peaceful afternoon drive when they find themselves summoned back to Wayne Manor after receiving an anonymous tip concerning the safety of Commodore Schmidlapp and his revolutionary 'Total Dehydrator' invention. Switching to their crime-fighting alter egos, Batman and Robin embark on a search and rescue mission in the Batcopter to locate Commodore Schmidlapp's yacht but fall into a trap when they discover the vessel to be a holographic decoy. Attacked by an exploding shark, the Caped Crusader only narrowly manages to escape his doom with the aid of Shark Repellent Bat Spray.

In light of the mysterious happenings a press conference is held at Gotham City police headquarters where Catwoman – posing as Miss Kitka Karenska of the *Moscow Bugle* – attempts to unmask the Dynamic Duo for a photo opportunity. After deflecting questions about Commodore Schmidlapp and his machine, Batman, Robin, Commissioner Gordon and Chief O'Hara discuss the incident in private. Suspecting that the real yacht must have been hijacked at another location, the foursome highlight four potential culprits – the Joker, the Riddler, the Penguin and Catwoman – and deduce that, should the supervillains be working together, they could have but one goal – world domination.

As Batman and Robin head to the Batcave to investigate a clue, Miss Kitka returns to her hideout, Ye Olde Benbow Taverne, where the heroes' worst fears are realized – the arch-criminals have come together as the United Underworld and taken Commodore Schmidlapp prisoner. Realizing that Batman and Robin will soon be on their trail, the crooks prepare to take to sea in a pre-atomic submarine that the Penguin has purchased from the military. Meanwhile the Dynamic Duo trace the holographic decoy to an illegal marker buoy and set out in the Batboat to investigate; ambushed by torpedoes from the Penguin's submarine, the crime-fighters are saved from certain death by the brave sacrifice of a passing porpoise.

Hatching a new plan to lure Batman into a trap, Catwoman visits Wayne Manor as Miss Kitka and passes Bruce a pair of riddles written on stationery from the Wayne Foundation. Fearing that her life is in danger, Bruce agrees to spend the evening with Miss Kitka but finds himself attacked in her apartment by the terrible trio of the Joker, the Riddler and the Penguin. Awaking in the villains' sea-front hideout, Bruce demands to see Miss Kitka and is led into a side room where Catwoman awaits in disguise. Knowing that his captors will be listening, Bruce tricks them into thinking he has a transmitter up his sleeve. When they untie him to remove it, Bruce manages to fight the dastardly crooks off long enough to make his escape.

While Bruce Wayne races back to Wayne Manor, the Penguin launches the next stage of his plan. Using the Total Dehydrator to drain all of the moisture from five of his men and turn them into small piles of dust, the Penguin intends to sneak the goons into the Batcave where he will rehydrate them to overpower the Dynamic Duo. Batman and Robin arrive at the hideout to rescue Miss Kitka but instead find a giant bomb, which Batman eventually succeeds in disposing of safely. The Penguin approaches dressed as Commodore Schmidlapp, and while the crime-fighters immediately see through his disguise they agree to take him to the Batcave. Unfortunately for the Penguin, the Batcave's heavy-water system leaves his men highly unstable, with the thugs reverting to anti-matter and disappearing upon the slightest of impacts.

The Penguin manages to escape by hijacking the Batmobile and sets off to join his fellow fiends at the United World headquarters; Batman and Robin use the Batcycle to race to the airport and set off in pursuit using the Batcopter, which is then shot down by a missile from the Riddler. They make their way to the United World building on foot but arrive too late to prevent the supervillains from carrying out their master plan – the dehydration of the United World Security Council. Realizing that their foes have escaped by submarine, the crime-fighters locate the submarine and force it to surface using Bat Charges. Boarding the submarine, the Caped Crusader and Boy Wonder manage to subdue the villains after a large Bat Fight that culminates with Batman making the startling discovery of Miss Kitka's true identity.

Burying his emotions in order to preserve his secret identity, Batman contacts the coastguard and prepares to retrieve the rack of vials containing the dehydrated members of the Security Council. However, disaster strikes when Commodore Schmidlapp enters and trips over, smashing the vials and mixing all the representatives together. With the world holding its breath, the Dynamic Duo are successful in separating the mingled dust particles using the Batcave's Super Molecular Dust Separator. Back at the United World building the Security Council are rehydrated, only for the members to start speaking in foreign languages. Realizing their work is now complete, Batman and Robin contemplate the impact of this 'mixing of the minds' on humanity before making an inconspicuous exit through the window.

## BAT-FACTS

Although William Dozier initially planned to launch the series with a feature, production would not get underway on the theatrical *Batman* movie until filming wrapped on the first season of the television show in April 1966. Working on an increased budget, *Batman* enabled the producers to introduce three new vehicles – the Batcopter (a fully functional helicopter leased to Fox by the National Helicopter Service at a cost of $750 per day), the Batcycle and the Batboat, all of which were beyond the financial limitations of the series. The flying umbrellas used by the villains were taken from the comic book story 'Partners in Plunder!' by France Eddie Herron, published in *Batman* #169 (February 1965), which had earlier been adapted into the episodes 'Fine Feathered Finks' and 'The Penguin's a Jinx'.

With regular Catwoman actress Julie Newmar unavailable due to a back injury, former Miss America Lee Meriwether (*Dr Kildare*, 1961–5) won the role; she would later return to the series as Bruce Wayne's love interest Lisa Carson in the Season Two episodes 'King Tut's Coup' and 'Batman's Waterloo'. Van Williams also made an uncredited appearance in the movie as the US president and would debut as Britt Reid in William Dozier's *The Green Hornet* series that September. Finally, whereas only three characters were ever killed in the entire run of the series, six of the Penguin's henchmen meet their demise in the theatrical *Batman* feature – one via an exploding octopus and the other five as a result of the Total Dehydrator – while Bruce Wayne uncharacteristically threatens to break his vow not to kill when the United Underworld 'kidnap' Miss Kitka.

# BATMAN: SEASON TWO (1966-7)

**Episode 2.1 – 'Shoot a Crooked Arrow'**
Original US air date: 7 September 1966

**Episode 2.2 – 'Walk the Straight and Narrow'**
Original US air date: 8 September 1966

**Key crew:** Sherman Marks (*Director*); Stanley Ralph Ross (*Teleplay*)
**Special Guest Villain:** Art Carney (*The Archer*)
**Celebrity Bat-Climb cameo:** Dick Clark (*Himself*)

## STORY

A medieval-style crook known as the Archer loots the safe of Wayne Manor with the aid of his band of merry mercenaries, winning favour with the public by handing the cash over to the poor. However, their intentions prove wholly dishonourable when Batman and Robin uncover a ploy to steal $10m of charitable donations from the Wayne Foundation and escape to Switzerland.

## BAT-FACTS

Although a villain known as the Archer had debuted in *Superman* #13 (November–December 1941), the character portrayed by Art Carney was a wholly original creation of Stanley Ralph Ross.

**Episode 2.3 – 'Hot Off the Griddle'**
Original US air date: 14 September 1966

**Episode 2.4 – 'The Cat and the Fiddle'**
Original US air date: 15 September 1966

**Key crew:** Don Weis (*Director*); Stanley Ralph Ross (*Teleplay*)
**Special Guest Villainess:** Julie Newmar (*Catwoman*)
**Notable Guest Star:** James Brolin (*Ralph Staphylococcus*)

## STORY

Suspecting that Catwoman has returned to Gotham City, Batman plants a fake news story concerning the arrival of a rare canary to the National History Museum. After escaping the trap, Catwoman poses as a rich recluse to go after her number one target – a pair of rare Stradivarius violins.

## BAT-FACTS

A then-unknown actor and room-mate of *Batman* casting director Michael McLean, James Brolin made the first of four appearances on the series, portraying a driver named Ralph Staphylococcus.

**Episode 2.5 – 'The Minstrel's Shakedown'**
Original US air date: 21 September 1966

**Episode 2.6 – 'Barbecued Batman?'**
Original US air date: 22 September 1966

**Key crew:** Murray Golden (*Director*); Francis M. Cockrell, Marian B. Cockrell (*Teleplay*)
**Special Guest Villain:** Van Johnson (*The Minstrel*)

## STORY

A lute-playing electronics genius known as the Minstrel holds the Gotham City Stock Exchange to ransom, tampering with the quotations and demanding $1,000 a week from each Exchange member to avoid a market crash. With the Dynamic Duo hot on his trail, the Minstrel threatens to destroy the Exchange building unless his demands are met within the hour.

## BAT-FACTS

'The Minstrel's Shakedown' and 'Barbecued Batman?' marked the first occasion where non-rhyming titles were used within the series.

**Episode 2.7 – 'The Spell of Tut'**
**Original US air date:** 28 September 1966

**Episode 2.8 – 'Tut's Case is Shut'**
**Original US air date:** 29 September 1966

**Key crew:** Larry Peerce (*Director*); Earl Barret, Robert C. Dennis (*Teleplay*)
**Special Guest Villain:** Victor Buono (*King Tut*)
**Celebrity Bat-Climb cameos:** Van Williams (*The Green Hornet*); Bruce Lee (*Kato*)

## STORY

King Tut returns to Gotham City to carry out his latest scheme, creating a mind-control potion known as 'abu raubu simbu tu' from the essence of ancient scarab beetles. With the Gotham Police under Tut's spell, Batman and Robin race to prevent him from contaminating the water supply and taking control of the entire population of the city.

## BAT-FACTS

Van Williams and Bruce Lee appeared in character as the Green Hornet and side-kick Kato for the series' third Bat-Climb cameo; inspired by the early success of *Batman*, executive producer William Dozier had launched *The Green Hornet* series on ABC earlier that month.

**Episode 2.9 – 'The Greatest Mother of Them All'**
**Original US air date:** 5 October 1966

**Episode 2.10 – 'Ma Parker'**
**Original US air date:** 6 October 1966

**Key crew:** Oscar Rudolph (*Director*); Harry Slesar (*Teleplay*)
**Special Guest Villainess:** Shelley Winters (*Ma Parker*)
**Notable Guest Stars:** Julie Newmar (*Catwoman*); Milton Berle (*Lefty*)

## STORY

When Ma Parker and her brood rob the audience at a ceremony for the Ladies Auxiliary's Mother of the Year Awards, the Dynamic Duo waste no time in rounding up the gang and putting them behind bars. However, little do they know it's all part of Ma's cunning plan to take control of Gotham State Penitentiary.

## BAT-FACTS

Oscar Rudolph made his directorial debut on *Batman* with 'The Greatest Mother of Them All'; he would go on to become the most prolific director of the series, helming a total of thirty-six episodes. Meanwhile Julie Newmar's Catwoman also featured in a brief cameo and Milton Berle (*Texaco Star Theater*, 1948–55) made an uncredited appearance in 'Ma Parker' as Lefty, before going on to portray Special Guest Villain Louie the Lilac in the third season.

Episode 2.11 – 'The Clock King's Crazy Crimes'
**Original US air date:** 12 October 1966

Episode 2.12 – 'The Clock King Gets Crowned'
**Original US air date:** 13 October 1966

**Key crew:** James Neilson (*Director*); Charles Sinclair, Bill Finger (*Teleplay*)
**Special Guest Villain:** Walter Slezak (*The Clock King*)

**Celebrity Bat-Climb cameo:** Sammy Davis Jr (*Himself*)

## STORY

After using a trick timepiece to rob a jewellery store, the Clock King and his gang of Second Hands continue their chronographic crime-wave, breaking into Wayne Manor to steal Bruce's collection of antique pocket watches and retrieve a mistakenly rigged clock that holds the key to his master plan.

## BAT-FACTS

Bill Finger served as co-writer, marking the only occasion that the *Batman* co-creator would pen a screen adventure for the Caped Crusader.

Episode 2.13 – 'An Egg Grows in Gotham'
**Original US air date:** 19 October 1966

Episode 2.14 – 'The Yegg Foes in Gotham'
**Original US air date:** 20 October 1966

**Key crew:** George Waggner (*Director*); Ed Self (*Story*); Stanley Ralph Ross (*Teleplay*)
**Special Guest Villain:** Vincent Price (*Egghead*)
**Notable Guest Star:** Edward Everett Horton (*Chief Screaming Chicken*)
**Celebrity Bat-Climb cameo:** Bill Dana (*Jose Jimenez*)

## STORY

Egghead uncovers a clause in the City Charter that would see ownership of the city revert to Chief Screaming Chicken of the Mohican Indians without a tribute from Gotham's richest families. Kidnapping Bruce Wayne, the self-proclaimed 'world's smartest criminal' intends to forge his own agreement with the Chief and test his theory on the identity of Batman by extracting information directly from Bruce's mind.

## BAT-FACTS

Egghead's henchman Foo Yung was portrayed by Ben Weldon, a veteran character actor who had made eight appearances in the television series *The Adventures of Superman*, starring George Reeves as the Man of Steel.

Episode 2.15 – 'The Devil's Fingers'
Original US air date: 26 October 1966

Episode 2.16 – 'The Dead Ringers'
Original US air date: 27 October 1966

Key crew: Larry Peerce (*Director*); Lorenzo Semple Jr (*Teleplay*)
Special Guest Villain: Liberace (*Chandell/Harry*)

## STORY

Renowned concert pianist Chandell finds himself the victim of blackmail at the hands of his evil twin Harry. Needing to raise $5m, Chandell concocts a plan to woo Aunt Harriet before disposing of Bruce and Dick in order to get his fingers on the Wayne fortune.

## BAT-FACTS

*Batman* received the highest ratings of its run with the inclusion of flamboyant musician and entertainer Liberace, who made his only appearance of the series in the dual role of pianist Chandell and his conniving brother Harry.

Episode 2.17 – 'Hizzoner the Penguin'
Original US air date: 2 November 1966

Episode 2.18 – 'Dizzoner the Penguin'
Original US air date: 3 November 1966

Key crew: Oscar Rudolph (*Director*); Stanford Sherman (*Teleplay*)
Special Guest Villain: Burgess Meredith (*The Penguin*)

## STORY

After a staging a series of heroic deeds to endear himself to the public, the Penguin rides a wave of popularity to take a firm lead in the race for mayor. However, the façade is exposed when Batman embarks on his own campaign, causing the Penguin to kidnap the members of the election board in an attempt to rig the outcome.

## BAT-FACTS

Popular American rockers Paul Revere and the Raiders enjoyed an extended cameo in 'Hizzoner the Penguin' as a local band, performing two songs at a fundraiser organized by the Penguin. The concept of the Penguin running for mayor would also be utilized by Tim Burton in his 1992 theatrical sequel *Batman Returns* (SEE 'THE TIM BURTON/JOEL SCHUMACHER ERA').

**Episode 2.19 – 'Green Ice'**
Original US air date: 9 November 1966

**Episode 2.20 – 'Deep Freeze'**
Original US air date: 10 November 1966

**Key crew:** George Waggner (*Director*); Max Hodge (*Teleplay*)
**Special Guest Villain:** Otto Preminger (*Mr Freeze*)

## STORY

Breaking out of jail, the nefarious Mr Freeze sets out to find a bride by kidnapping the Miss Iceland entrant from the Miss Galaxy Beauty Pageant. He soon enacts a plan to discredit the Dynamic Duo before threatening to freeze the city unless he receives a ransom of $1bn.

## BAT-FACTS

Although Lee Meriwether had appeared as Catwoman in the *Batman* feature film, Otto Preminger became the first actor to take over as a Special Guest Villain within the television series, replacing George Sanders as Mr Freeze.

**Episode 2.21 – 'The Impractical Joker'**
Original US air date: 16 November 1966

**Episode 2.22 – 'The Joker's Provokers'**
Original US air date: 17 November 1966

**Key crew:** James B. Clark (*Director*); Charles Hoffman, Jay Thompson (*Teleplay*)
**Special Guest Villain:** Cesar Romero (*The Joker*)
**Celebrity Bat-Climb cameo:** Howard Duff (*Detective Sam Stone*)

## STORY

The Ace of Knaves returns to Gotham with a series of key-related acts of vandalism, using his latest invention – a magic box with the ability to tamper with time – to steal the Jewelled Key of Kaincordins. When Batman discovers a plan to contaminate the city's water supply, Alfred must go undercover as his identical cousin Egbert, night-watchman of the Gotham Reservoir, in an attempt to foil the Joker.

## BAT-FACTS

Actress Kathy Kersh (*The Beverly Hillbillies*), who would become Burt Ward's second wife in 1967, made an appearance as the Joker's moll Cornelia, while 'The Impractical Joker' sees the Clown

Prince of Crime interrupting a television broadcast of ABC's other costumed crime-fighting show, *The Green Hornet*.

**Episode 2.23 – 'Marsha, Queen of Diamonds'**
**Original US air date:** 23 November 1966

**Episode 2.24 – 'Marsha's Scheme of Diamonds'**
**Original US air date:** 24 November 1966

**Key crew:** James B. Clark (*Director*); Stanford Sherman (*Teleplay*)
**Special Guest Villainess:** Carolyn Jones (*Marsha, Queen of Diamonds*)
**Notable Guest Star:** Estelle Winwood (*Aunt Hilda*)

## STORY

Entrancing Commissioner Gordon and Chief O'Hara with Aunt Hilda's potent love-potion, Marsha, Queen of Diamonds, casts her spell on Robin, offering to release the Boy Wonder in exchange for the priceless Bat-Diamond. When Batman counters that no stranger can enter the Batcave, Marsha then demands the Caped Crusader's hand in marriage.

## BAT-FACTS

With her turn as the Special Guest Villainess Marsha, Queen of Diamonds, Carolyn Jones became the first of three cast members of *The Addams Family* to appear in *Batman*.

**Episode 2.25 – 'Come Back, Shame'**
**Original US air date:** 30 November 1966

**Episode 2.26 – 'It's How You Play the Game'**
**Original US air date:** 1 December 1966

**Key crew:** Oscar Rudolph (*Director*); Stanley Ralph Ross (*Teleplay*)
**Special Guest Villain:** Cliff Robertson (*Shame*)
**Celebrity Bat-Climb cameo:** Werner Klemperer (*Colonel Klink*)

## STORY

The cowboy criminal Shame and his gang of outlaws steal a racing car as part of a scheme to construct a vehicle capable of outperforming the Batmobile. After tracking Shame to his hideout, the Dynamic Duo discover that Shame's ultimate goal is the theft of four prize rodeo bulls, leading to a showdown at the KO Corral.

## BAT-FACTS

Having undergone a redesign for the *Batman* theatrical feature, the new look Batcycle made its first appearance in the television series in the episode 'Come Back, Shame'. Special Guest Villain Cliff Robertson had enjoyed an early lead role in the CBS series *Rod Brown of the Rocket Rangers*, executive produced by William Dozier.

**Episode 2.27 – 'The Penguin's Nest'**
**Original US air date:** 7 December 1966

Episode 2.28 – 'The Bird's Last Jest'
Original US air date: 8 December 1966

Key crew: Murray Golden (*Director*); Lorenzo Semple Jr (*Teleplay*)
Special Guest Villain: Burgess Meredith (*The Penguin*)
Celebrity Bat-Climb cameo: Ted Cassidy (*Lurch*)

## STORY

The Penguin opens an exclusive new restaurant called the Penguin's Nest in order to acquire writing samples from all of the city's elite, which he plans to pass on to a forger upon his inevitable return to prison. Hoping to thwart his plan, Batman has Alfred go undercover as legendary forger Quill-Pen Quertch, but the plan backfires when the Penguin recognizes Alfred and demands a million-dollar ransom from Bruce Wayne.

## BAT-FACTS

Based on the comic book story 'The Penguin's Nest' by Alvin Schwartz, published in *Batman* #36 (August 1946). With his Bat-Climb cameo in character as Lurch in 'The Penguin's Nest', Ted Cassidy became the second cast member of *The Addams Family* to appear in *Batman*, while series writer Stanley Ralph Ross also made uncredited appearances in both episodes as forger Ballpoint Baxter.

Episode 2.29 – 'The Cat's Meow'
Original US air date: 14 December 1966

Episode 2.30 – 'The Bat's Kow Tow'
Original US air date: 15 December 1966

Key crew: James B. Clark (*Director*); Stanley Ralph Ross (*Teleplay*)
Special Guest Villainess: Julie Newmar (*Catwoman*)
Celebrity Bat-Climb cameo: Don Ho (*Himself*)

## STORY

Catwoman tests her latest invention, the Voice-Eraser, on a television presenter as a test run for her latest fiendish plot – stealing the voices of Chad and Jeremy, visiting British musicians who happen to be staying as guests of Bruce Wayne at Wayne Manor.

## BAT-FACTS

English folk duo Chad Stuart and Jeremy Clyde portrayed themselves in both episodes, while Judy Strangis – sister of *Batman* production manager and later episode director Sam Strangis – also featured in 'The Cat's Meow' as a concertgoer.

Episode 2.31 – 'The Puzzles are Coming'
Original US air date: 21 December 1966

Episode 2.32 – 'The Duo is Slumming'
Original US air date: 22 December 1966

**Key crew:** Jeffrey Hayden (*Director*); Fred De Gorter (*Teleplay*)
**Special Guest Villain:** Maurice Evans (*The Puzzler*)
**Celebrity Bat-Climb cameo:** Andy Devine (*Santa*)

## STORY

When a toy plane delivers a cryptic clue through the window of Commissioner Gordon's office, the Caped Crusader uncovers a scheme by the Puzzler to hijack the Retsoor, a supersonic plane belonging to multi-billionaire Artemus Knab.

## BAT-FACTS

This two-part story was originally conceived for the Riddler under the episode titles 'A Penny for Your Riddles' and 'They're Worth a Lot More'; however, with Frank Gorshin opting against a return to his signature role for the second season, writer Maurice Evans decided to change the villain to the Puzzler, a comic book enemy of Superman who had debuted in *Action Comics* #49 (June 1942).

Episode 2.33 – 'The Sandman Cometh'
Original US air date: 28 December 1966

Episode 2.34 – 'The Catwoman Goeth'
Original US air date: 29 December 1966

**Key crew:** George Waggner (*Director*); Ellis St Joseph (*Story*); Ellis St Joseph, Charles Hoffman (*Teleplay*)
**Special Guest Villain:** Michael Rennie (*The Sandman*)
**Extra Special Guest Villainess:** Julie Newmar (*Catwoman*)
**Notable Guest Stars:** James Brolin (*Young Policeman, Reggie*); Gypsy Rose Lee (*TV Newscaster*)

## STORY

Teaming up to steal the fortune of the wealthy insomniac J. Pauline Spaghetti, the Sandman and Catwoman devise a plot that sees the Sandman posing as sleep therapist Dr Somnambula. While the Dynamic Duo strive to expose the masquerade, the Sandman double-crosses Catwoman and elopes with Spaghetti to her own private island.

## BAT-FACTS

James Brolin made his second and third appearances of the series, portraying a young policeman in 'The Sandman Cometh' and Reggie in 'The Catwoman Goeth', while former burlesque dancer and striptease artist Gypsy Rose Lee (*Screaming Mimi*, 1958) featured in a short cameo role in 'The Catwoman Goeth'. This second part is also known by its original title, 'A Stitch in Time', having been renamed once Julie Newmar was confirmed to appear as the Extra Special Guest Villainess.

Episode 2.35 – 'The Contaminated Cowl'
Original US air date: 4 January 1967

Episode 2.36 – 'The Mad Hatter Runs Afoul'
Original US air date: 5 January 1967

Key crew: Oscar Rudolph (*Director*); Charles Hoffman (*Teleplay*)
Special Guest Villain: David Wayne (*Mad Hatter*)

## STORY

Breaking out of prison during a game of baseball, the Mad Hatter plans to steal a priceless ruby from the head of the Golden Buddha of Bergama at the Gotham Art Center, but first he has one final hat to add to his collection – the cowl of the Batman.

## BAT-FACTS

Based on the comic book story 'The Mad Hatter of Gotham City' by Bill Finger, published in *Detective Comics* #230 (April 1956).

Episode 2.37 – 'The Zodiac Crimes'
Original US air date: 11 January 1967

Episode 2.38 – 'The Joker's Hard Times'
Original US air date: 12 January 1967

Episode 2.39 – 'The Penguin Declines'
Original US air Date: 18 January 1967

Key crew: Oscar Rudolph (*Director*); Stephen Kandel (*Story*); Stanford Sherman (*Teleplay*)
Special Guest Villain: Cesar Romero (*The Joker*)
Extra Special Guest Villain: Burgess Meredith (*The Penguin*)
Notable Guest Star: Rob Reiner (*Delivery Boy*)

## STORY

Aided by the evil temptress Venus, the Joker and the Penguin hatch a plan to commit a series of crimes relating to the twelve signs of the Zodiac. After Venus switches sides to help the Dynamic Duo, the Penguin pleads with her to remove his criminal record from the Batcomputer, but it is merely a ruse to help the villains gain access to the Batcave.

## BAT-FACTS

The first three-part *Batman* story, produced to celebrate the show's one-year anniversary. Rob Reiner, who briefly appeared as a pizza delivery boy in the episode 'The Penguin Declines', would go on to develop a successful career as a filmmaker, directing the likes of *Stand By Me* (1986) and *When Harry Met Sally …* (1989).

Episode 2.40 – 'That Darn Catwoman'
Original US air date: 19 January 1967

Episode 2.41 – 'Scat! Darn Catwoman'
Original US air date: 25 January 1967

Key crew: Oscar Rudolph (*Director*); Stanley Ralph Ross (*Teleplay*)
Special Guest Villainess: Julie Newmar (*Catwoman*)
Notable Guest Star: Lesley Gore (*Pussycat*)

## STORY

Concocting a 'Cataphrenic' potion, Catwoman orders her protégé Pussycat to administer the drug to Robin via a cat-scratch, turning the Boy Wonder into the feline fatale's newest recruit. Catwoman and her gang then rob Wayne Manor, leading to a showdown between the Caped Crusader and the Boy Wonder.

## BAT-FACTS

Pop singer Lesley Gore (niece of series producer Howie Horowitz) starred in both episodes as Catwoman's side-kick Pussycat. 'Scat! Darn Catwoman' was also the final episode where Batman and Robin failed to capture their adversary, leaving Catwoman as the only member of the Rogues Gallery to evade the Dynamic Duo on more than one occasion.

Episode 2.42 – 'Penguin is a Girl's Best Friend'
Original US air date: 26 January 1967

Episode 2.43 – 'Penguin Sets a Trend'
Original US air date: 1 February 1967

Episode 2.44 – 'Penguin's Disastrous End'
Original US air date: 2 February 1967

Key crew: James B. Clark (*Director*); Stanford Sherman (*Teleplay*)
Special Guest Villain: Burgess Meredith (*The Penguin*)
Extra Special Guest Villainess: Carolyn Jones (*Marsha, Queen of Diamonds*)
Notable Guest Star: Estelle Winwood (*Aunt Hilda*)

## STORY

Batman and Robin find themselves tricked into taking part in a movie after mistakenly interrupting the filming of a hold-up scene featuring the Penguin and Marsha, Queen of Diamonds. As the shoot continues it becomes clear that the Penguin is up to his usual tricks, stealing top secret military plans from the Hexagon in an effort to construct a tank made from solid gold bullion.

## BAT-FACTS

Bob Hastings (*McHale's Navy*, 1962–6), who appeared as Major Beasley in 'Penguin Sets a Trend', also supplied the voice of Superboy in Filmation's *The New Adventures of Superman* (1966–70) and would later lend his vocal talents to Commissioner Gordon in the DC Animated Universe.

Episode 2.45 – 'Batman's Anniversary'
Original US air date: 8 February 1967

Episode 2.46 – 'A Riddling Controversy'
Original US air date: 9 February 1967

Key crew: James B. Clark (*Director*); William P. D'Angelo (*Teleplay*)
Special Guest Villain: John Astin (*The Riddler*)

## STORY

The Gotham City Police Department throw a surprise party for Batman and Robin, celebrating the anniversary of their crime-fighting partnership with the Dynamic Duo. Unfortunately proceedings are interrupted by the Riddler, who steals a golden calf filled with $200,000 in charitable donations in order to purchase a destructive weapon called the De-Molecularizer.

## BAT-FACTS

Based on the comic book story 'The Riddler' by Bill Finger, published in *Detective Comics* #140 (October 1948). John Astin became the third member of *The Addams Family* cast to appear in the series, replacing Frank Gorshin for his only appearance as the Prince of Puzzlers.

Episode 2.47 – 'The Joker's Last Laugh'
Original US air date: 15 February 1967

Episode 2.48 – 'The Joker's Epitaph'
Original US air date: 16 February 1967

Key crew: Oscar Rudolph (*Director*); Peter Rabe (*Story*); Lorenzo Semple Jr (*Teleplay*)
Special Guest Villain: Cesar Romero (*The Joker*)

## STORY

Hoping to uncover evidence that the Joker has been flooding counterfeit money into the city, Batman approaches his nemesis as Bruce Wayne. Citing financial difficulties, Bruce asks the Joker to print him money but his plan backfires when he becomes the victim of blackmail and Commissioner Gordon calls in a psychiatrist who then declares him insane.

## BAT-FACTS

'The Joker's Last Laugh' and 'The Joker's Epitaph' were the last episodes of the series to be penned by *Batman*'s executive story editor Lorenzo Semple Jr, while 'The Joker's Last Laugh' is also notable for featuring the first appearance of the Clown Prince of Crime's 'Jokemobile'.

Episode 2.49 – 'Catwoman Goes to College'
Original US air date: 22 February 1967

Episode 2.50 – 'Batman Displays His Knowledge'
Original US air date: 23 February 1967

Key crew: Robert Sparr (*Director*); Stanley Ralph Ross (*Teleplay*)
Special Guest Villainess: Julie Newmar (*Catwoman*)

Notable Guest Star: Jacques Bergerac (*Freddy the Fence*)
Celebrity Bat-Climb cameo: Art Linkletter (*Himself*)

## STORY

Released from her latest prison sentence early after Bruce Wayne endorses her parole, Catwoman finds herself a guest at Wayne Manor and enrols in a criminology course at Gotham University. Of course, it's only a matter of time before she plots her latest caper – the theft of a fortune in Batagonian Cat's Eye Opals.

## BAT-FACTS

Julie Newmar made her final appearance as the feline fatale Catwoman in the episode 'Batman Displays His Knowledge', while French actor Jacques Bergerac (*Les Girls*, 1957) portrayed Freddy the Fence, a role he would reprise in the series finale, 'Minerva, Mayhem and Millionaires'.

Episode 2.51 – 'A Piece of the Action'
Original US air date: 1 March 1967

Episode 2.52 – 'Batman's Satisfaction'
Original US air date: 2 March 1967

Key crew: Oscar Rudolph (*Director*); Charles Hoffman (*Teleplay*)
Visiting Hero: Van Williams (*The Green Hornet*)
Assistant Visiting Hero: Bruce Lee (*Kato*)

Notable Guest Star: Roger C. Carmel (*Colonel Gumm*)
Celebrity Bat-Climb cameo: Edward G. Robinson (*Himself*)

## STORY

The Green Hornet and Kato arrive in Gotham City on the trail of stamp counterfeiter Colonel Gumm but are mistaken for criminals by Commissioner Gordon, who calls upon the Dynamic Duo to investigate. As the four costumed crimefighters prepare to square off against each other, Colonel Gumm sets his sights on raiding the International Stamps Exhibition of its most valuable collection.

## BAT-FACTS

Van Williams and Bruce Lee appeared as their characters from *The Green Hornet* for the second time after a Bat-Climb cameo in 'Batman's Satisfaction'. Diane McBain featured as damsel in distress Pinky Pinkston, having portrayed the Mad Hatter's moll Lisa in the first season episodes 'Batman Stands Pat' and 'The Thirteenth Hat', while Roger C. Carmel's (*Gambit*, 1966) Colonel Gumm became the first and only antagonist not to receive the 'Special Guest Villain' billing.

Episode 2.53 – 'King Tut's Coup'
Original US air date: 8 March 1967

Episode 2.54 – 'Batman's Waterloo'
Original US air date: 9 March 1967

Key crew: James B. Clark (*Director*); Leo Townsend, Pauline Townsend (*Story*), Stanley Ralph Ross (*Teleplay*)
Special Guest Villain: Victor Buono (*King Tut*)
Notable Guest Stars: Lee Meriwether (*Lisa Carson*); Grace Lee Whitney (*Neila, Goddess of the Nile*)
Celebrity Bat-Climb cameo: Suzie Knickerbocker (*Herself*)

## STORY

Relapsing into his old ways after another blow to the head, King Tut mistakes Lisa Carson – a millionaire's daughter and friend of Bruce Wayne – for the beautiful Egyptian Queen Cleopatra. Sneaking into a ball at Wayne Manor, Tut kidnaps Lisa and holds her to ransom, demanding that Batman act as courier.

## BAT-FACTS

Having stood in for Julie Newmar in the *Batman* feature film, Lee Meriwether returned to Gotham City as Lisa Carson, love interest to Bruce Wayne. 'Batman's Waterloo' was also notable for delivering the first mention of Commissioner Gordon's daughter Barbara, laying the foundations for the introduction of Batgirl in the third season.

Episode 2.55 – 'Black Widow Strikes Again'
Original US air date: 15 March 1967

Episode 2.56 – 'Caught in the Spider's Den'
Original US air date: 16 March 1967

Key crew: Oscar Rudolph (*Director*); Robert Mintz (*Teleplay*)
Special Guest Villainess: Tallulah Bankhead (*The Black Widow*)

## STORY

The Black Widow robs a string of banks using her paralysing Cerebrium Short-Circuiter device, which she soon turns on the Dynamic Duo when they locate her hideout. Receiving word that Batman has held up the Heritage First National Bank, Commissioner Gordon issues a warrant for his arrest while the Black Widow prepares to make off with the loot.

## BAT-FACTS

Tallulah Bankhead's turn as the Special Guest Villainess Black Widow proved to be the final screen role for the veteran actress.

Episode 2.57 – 'Pop Goes the Joker'
Original US air date: 22 March 1967

Episode 2.58 – 'Flop Goes the Joker'
Original US air date: 23 March 1967

**Key crew:** George Waggner (*Director*); Stanford Sherman (*Teleplay*)
**Special Guest Villain:** Cesar Romero (*The Joker*)

## STORY

Fancying himself as an artist, the Joker defaces the paintings at an exhibition only for his handiwork to be praised as 'art'. After further success in a prestigious competition he opens his own exclusive art school. Suspicious of his motives, Bruce and Dick enrol only to uncover a scheme to pilfer priceless Renaissance art from the Gotham City Museum.

## BAT-FACTS

'Pop Goes The Joker' would not be the last time the Clown Prince of Crime explored his creative side, 'broadening his mind' by disfiguring the masterpieces of the Flugelheim Museum in Tim Burton's 1989 feature, *Batman*.

Episode 2.59 – 'Ice Spy'
Original US air date: 29 March 1967

Episode 2.60 – 'The Duo Defy'
Original US air date: 30 March 1967

**Key crew:** Oscar Rudolph (*Director*); Charles Hoffman (*Teleplay*)
**Special Guest Villain:** Eli Wallach (*Mr Freeze*)
**Celebrity Bat-Climb cameo:** Cyril Lord (*Carpet King*)

## STORY

In his latest quest to bring Gotham to its knees, Mr Freeze kidnaps the notable Icelandic scientist Isaac Isaacson and forces him into constructing a devastating Ice-Ray beam. As the villainous scientist threatens to turn the country into a frozen wasteland, Batman and Robin race to bring their frosty foe to justice.

## BAT-FACTS

Mr Freeze became the first villain to be portrayed by three different actors as Eli Wallach followed in the footsteps of George Sanders and Otto Preminger, whom he replaced in the role. The Bat-Climb cameo was included for the final time in the episode 'Ice Spy' and featured British textiles magnate Cyril Lord, a.k.a. the Carpet King.

# BATMAN: SEASON THREE (1967-8)

Episode 3.0 – 'Batgirl'
Original US air date: Never aired

Key crew: Howie Horwitz (*Producer*)
Special Guest Villain: Tim Herbert (*Killer Moth*)

## STORY

Killer Moth and his henchmen descend on Gotham City Library, locking librarian Barbara Gordon in a closet as Batman and Robin arrive to confront the gang. Subdued by Killer Moth's spray-gun, the heroes are held captive until Batgirl makes her entrance, freeing the Dynamic Duo and helping to defeat Killer Moth before disappearing into the night on her Batgirlcycle.

## BAT-FACTS

*Batgirl* was a seven-and-a-half minute promotional film created in order to showcase the female crime-fighter to network executives. It was never broadcast, although bootleg copies of the film have since emerged. While Killer Moth had also appeared as the villain in Batgirl's first comic book appearance, the presentation film took the form of a wholly original story that bore no further resemblance to 'The Million Dollar Debut of Batgirl'.

Episode 3.1 – 'Enter Batgirl, Exit Penguin'
Original US air date: 14 September 1967

Key crew: Oscar Rudolph (*Director*); Stanford Sherman (*Teleplay*)
Special Guest Villain: Burgess Meredith (*The Penguin*)

## STORY

Attending the opera with Bruce, Dick, Chief O'Hara and her father the Commissioner, Barbara Gordon is snatched by the Penguin. However, he hadn't reckoned on her double life as the costumed crime-fighter Batgirl, who must come to the aid of Batman and Robin after a failed rescue attempt.

## BAT-FACTS

Following a number of allusions to the character during the second season, Barbara Gordon/Batgirl made her *Batman* television debut in the first episode of the series to present a single, self-contained story.

Episode 3.2 – 'Ring Around the Riddler'
Original US air date: 21 September 1967

Key crew: Sam Strangis (*Director*); Charles Hoffman (*Teleplay*)
Special Guest Villain: Frank Gorshin (*The Riddler*)
Notable Guest Stars: Joan Collins (*The Siren*); James Brolin (*Kid Gulliver*)

## STORY

The King of Conundrums hopes to control

Gotham's prize-fighting circuit by kidnapping boxing champion Kid Glover and brainwashing him into throwing his next bout, before issuing a challenge himself to the Caped Crusader to step into the ring at the Garden.

## BAT-FACTS

For his final outing of the series, Frank Gorshin reprised his role as the Riddler after declining the opportunity during the second season. Gorshin would later return to Gotham City to voice Professor Hugo Strange in three episodes of the animated series *The Batman* (SEE 'THE FURTHER ANIMATED ADVENTURES OF THE CAPED CRUSADER'), while 'Ring Around the Riddler' marked the final *Batman* episode to feature James Brolin.

Episode 3.3 – 'The Wail of the Siren'
**Original US air date:** 28 September 1967

**Key crew:** George Waggner (*Director*); Stanley Ralph Ross (*Teleplay*)
**Special Guest Villainess:** Joan Collins (*The Siren*)

## STORY

The seductive siren Loreli Circe casts her spell on Commissioner Gordon, hoping to discover the location of the Batcave by having him stow away in the trunk of the Batmobile. Meanwhile the Siren sets her sights on Bruce Wayne in a ploy to get her hands on the vast Wayne fortune.

## BAT-FACTS

In his autobiography, Adam West suggested that Special Guest Villainess Joan Collins was given a rough ride by director George Waggner during the production of 'The Wail of the Siren' because of her reputation of being difficult to work with. The episode also marked the first use of the 'Batgirl Theme', composed by country musician Billy May.

Episode 3.4 – 'The Sport of Penguins'
**Original US air date:** 5 October 1967

Episode 3.5 – 'A Horse of Another Color'
**Original US air date:** 12 October 1967

**Key crew:** Sam Strangis (*Director*); Charles Hoffman (*Teleplay*)
**Special Guest Villain:** Burgess Meredith (*The Penguin*)
**Extra Special Guest Villainess:** Ethel Merman (*Lola Lasagne*)

## STORY

Teaming up with down-on-her-luck racehorse owner Lola Lasagne, the Penguin hopes to rig the prestigious Wayne Handicap by swapping Lasagne's prize thoroughbred for a tired old nag, before stealing a priceless collection of parasols in order to raise his betting stake.

Episode 3.6 – 'The Unkindest Tut of All'
**Original US air date:** 19 October 1967

Key crew: Sam Strangis (*Director*); Stanley Ralph Ross (*Teleplay*)
Special Guest Villain: Victor Buono (*King Tut*)

## STORY

Tricking the police into thinking he's gone straight by tipping them off to a series of robberies, King Tut hopes to send them on a wild goose chase while he orchestrates his own master plan, which involves uncovering the identity of the Caped Crusader by tracking the Batmobile to Wayne Manor.

Episode 3.7 – 'Louie, the Lilac'
Original US air date: 26 October 1967

Key crew: George Waggner (*Director*); Dwight Taylor (*Teleplay*)
Special Guest Villain: Milton Berle (*Louie the Lilac*)

## STORY

Cornering the city's floral industry, Louie the Lilac hatches a plan to control Gotham's flower children by brainwashing the leader of their group, Princess Primrose, with his aromatic mind-control spray. When the Princess' followers protest over the abduction, it is left to Batman, Robin and Batgirl to try and avert a riot.

Episode 3.8 – 'The Ogg and I'
Original US air date: 2 November 1967

Episode 3.9 – 'How to Hatch a Dinosaur'
Original US air date: 9 November 1967

Key crew: Oscar Rudolph (*Director*); Stanford Sherman (*Teleplay*)
Special Guest Villain: Vincent Price (*Egghead*)
Extra Special Guest Villainess: Anne Baxter (*Olga, Queen of the Cossacks*)

## STORY

With help from Olga, Queen of the Cossacks, the self-proclaimed 'world's smartest criminal' captures Commissioner Gordon and demands a tax of ten cents on every egg consumed by the citizens of Gotham, before embarking on a scheme to hatch an ancient dinosaur egg and feed the Terrific Trio to the carnivorous baby Neosaurus.

## BAT-FACTS

Anne Baxter returned to the series after appearing as magician Zelda the Great in the first season episodes 'Zelda the Great' and 'A Death Worse than Fate', becoming the only credited guest star to have appeared as two different villains (or villainesses, as it were).

Episode 3.10 – 'Surf's Up! Joker's Under!'
Original US air date: 16 November 1967

Key crew: Oscar Rudolph (*Director*); Charles Hoffman (*Teleplay*)
Special Guest Villain: Cesar Romero (*The Joker*)

## STORY

For his latest mad-cap caper the Joker kidnaps champion surfer Skip Parker and absorbs his skills using the Surfing Experience and Ability Transferometer and Vigor Reverser. As the Clown Prince of Crime descends on a surfing tournament, only the Caped Crusader can prevent him from achieving a decisive victory.

## BAT-FACTS

Having debuted in the second season episode 'The Joker's Last Laugh', the infamous Jokemobile made its second and final appearance.

Episode 3.11 – 'The Londinium Larcenies'
Original US air date: 23 November 1967

Episode 3.12 – 'The Foggiest Notion'
Original US air date: 30 November 1967

Episode 3.13 – 'The Bloody Tower'
Original US air date: 7 December 1967

Key crew: Oscar Rudolph (*Director*); Elkan Allan (*Story*); Elkan Allan, Charles Hoffman (*Teleplay*)
Special Guest Villain: Rudy Vallee (*Lord Marmaduke Ffogg*)
Extra Special Guest Villainess: Glynis Johns (*Lady Penelope Peasoup*)

## STORY

When the devious siblings Lord Marmaduke Ffogg and Lady Penelope Peasoup steal the Queen's collection of snuffboxes from a Londinium museum, Ireland Yard call upon the Caped Crusader to investigate the crime and protect the Crown Jewels in the Tower of Londinium.

## BAT-FACTS

Madge Blake delivered her final screen performance in the episode 'The Bloody Tower', which also proved to be the last three-part story of the series.

Episode 3.14 – 'Catwoman's Dressed to Kill'
Original US air date: 14 December 1967

Key crew: Sam Strangis (*Director*); Stanley Ralph Ross (*Teleplay*)
Special Guest Villainess: Eartha Kitt (*Catwoman*)

## STORY

The fashion-conscious feline felon Catwoman interrupts a luncheon to honour Gotham's best-dressed women, frazzling their hair and stealing an exclusive collection of dresses. Catwoman then kidnaps Batgirl, hoping to distract the Dynamic Duo while she steals the solid-gold dress of the visiting Queen of Belgravia.

## BAT-FACTS

With Julie Newmar busy filming *Mackenna's Gold* (1969), Catwoman became only the second of Batman's adversaries to have been portrayed by three different people with the casting of Eartha Kitt (*Anna Lucasta*, 1959). This was the first time that an African-American actress had taken on the role of the feline felon, a move that would be repeated with the casting of Halle Berry in the 2004 feature *Catwoman* (SEE 'MISCELLANEOUS SPIN-OFFS').

Episode 3.15 – 'The Ogg Couple'
Original US air date: 21 December 1967

Key crew: Oscar Rudolph (*Director*); Stanford Sherman (*Teleplay*)
Special Guest Villain: Vincent Price (*Egghead*)
Extra Special Guest Villainess: Anne Baxter (*Olga, Queen of the Cossacks*)

## STORY

Egghead and Olga, Queen of the Cossacks, unite once more to rob the Gotham City Museum of the silver Sword of Bulbul and the golden Egg of Ogg. Batgirl investigates only to find herself held captive by the terrible twosome, who aim to dispose of the Dominoed Daredoll until Batman and Robin arrive to save the day.

## BAT-FACTS

'The Ogg Couple' was originally planned as the third of a three-part story and filmed alongside the 'The Ogg and I' and 'How to Hatch a Dinosaur' before the producers decided to adapt it into a stand-alone episode.

Episode 3.16 – 'The Funny Feline Felonies'
Original US air date: 28 December 1967

Episode 3.17 – 'The Joke's on Catwoman'
Original US air date: 4 January 1968

Key crew: Oscar Rudolph (*Director*); Stanley Ralph Ross (*Teleplay*)
Special Guest Villain: Cesar Romero (*The Joker*)
Extra Special Guest Villainess: Eartha Kitt (*Catwoman*)

## STORY

The Joker wastes no time in resuming his illegal activities upon his release from prison as he teams up with Catwoman to locate a stash of hidden gunpowder. Hoping to prevent the crooks from getting their hands on the explosives, Batman, Robin and Batgirl track the dastardly duo to a lighthouse on Phoney Island where they engage in a climactic confrontation.

## BAT-FACTS

Having taken over from Julie Newmar for the third season, 'The Joke's on Catwoman' marked Eartha Kitt's final appearance in the series.

Episode 3.18 – 'Louie's Lethal Lilac Time'
Original US air date: 11 January 1968

Key crew: Sam Strangis (*Director*); Charles Hoffman (*Teleplay*)

**Special Guest Villain:** Milton Berle (*Louie the Lilac*)

## STORY

When Barbara Gordon witnesses the kidnapping of Bruce Wayne and Dick Grayson by Louie the Lilac's henchmen, she calls her father and asks him to contact Batman. When the Commissioner's request goes unanswered Batgirl investigates only to fall captive herself, forcing Bruce to turn to his latest invention, the Instant Unfolding Batcostumes with Utility Belts.

Episode 3.19 – 'Nora Clavicle and the Ladies' Crime Club'
Original US air date: 18 January 1968

**Key crew:** Oscar Rudolph (*Director*); Stanford Sherman (*Teleplay*)
**Special Guest Villain:** Barbara Rush (*Nora Clavicle*)

## STORY

Acting on the encouragement of his wife, Mayor Linseed replaces Commissioner Gordon with women's rights advocate Nora Clavicle, who immediately fires all of the male policemen. By replacing them with women, Nora hopes the police force will be too concerned with their make-up to prevent her from robbing a series of banks.

## BAT-FACTS

'Nora Clavicle and the Ladies Crime Club' was only the second episode in the series not to feature a climactic 'Bat Fight'.

Episode 3.20 – 'Penguin's Clean Swoop'
Original US air date: 25 January 1968

**Key crew:** Oscar Rudolph (*Director*); Stanford Sherman (*Teleplay*)
**Special Guest Villain:** Burgess Meredith (*The Penguin*)

## STORY

Breaking into the National Mint, the Penguin contaminates the money supply with germs of the dreaded Lygerian Sleeping Sickness, only for Batman to warn the public of the threat, rendering him bankrupt. As a last resort, the Penguin threatens to unleash the sickness on Gotham by releasing five hundred Lygerian fruit flies.

## BAT-FACTS

This episode marked the final outing for Burgess Meredith, whose Penguin proved to be Batman's most regular adversary, receiving twenty credits as Special Guest Villain in addition to a starring role in the theatrical movie and an uncredited cameo in 'The Wail of the Siren'.

Episode 3.21 – 'The Great Escape'
Original US air date: 1 February 1968

Episode 3.22 – 'The Great Train Robbery'
Original US air date: 8 February 1968

Key crew: Oscar Rudolph (*Director*); Stanley Ralph Ross (*Teleplay*)
Special Guest Villain: Cliff Robertson (*Shame*)
Extra Special Guest Villainess: Dina Merrill (*Calamity Jan*)
Notable Guest Star: Hermione Baddeley (*Frontier Fanny*)

## STORY

The outlaw Shame escapes from prison with help from his cowgirl side-kick Calamity Jan and her mother, Frontier Fanny. Discovering his goal of re-creating the Great Train Robbery by stealing a shipment of old money heading to the Treasury Department, Batman hopes to foil Shame's plan by challenging him to a showdown.

## BAT-FACTS

Cliff Robertson reprised his second-season role as Shame, with his then-wife Dina Merrill (*Operation Petticoat*, 1959) starring as partner-in-crime Calamity Jan.

Episode 3.23 – 'I'll Be a Mummy's Uncle'
Original US air date: 22 February 1968

Key crew: Oscar Rudolph (*Director*); Stanley Ralph Ross (*Teleplay*)
Special Guest Villain: King Tut (*Victor Buono*)

## STORY

King Tut discovers a deposit of nilanium, the world's strongest metal, directly beneath Wayne Manor. When Tut buys an adjacent property and begins tunnelling, Batman and Robin race to protect their secret identities but are too late to prevent him from drilling directly into the Batcave.

Episode 3.24 – 'The Joker's Flying Saucer'
Original US air date: 29 February 1968

Key crew: Sam Strangis (*Director*); Charles Hoffman (*Teleplay*)
Special Guest Villain: Cesar Romero (*The Joker*)

## STORY

Using plans devised by a mad scientist, the Joker aims to construct a flying saucer that he hopes will pave the way for world domination. In order to do so, the Ace of Knaves sends his goons to obtain a rare lightweight metal from the Wayne Foundation, while planting a bomb on the Batmobile that detonates inside the Batcave.

## BAT-FACTS

'The Joker's Flying Saucer' marked Byron Keith's final turn as Mayor Linseed. He had made a total of ten appearances throughout the series. It was the last episode to feature Cesar Romero; although his Clown Prince of Crime tied with Burgess Meredith's Penguin for total appearances this included two uncredited cameos by Romero as opposed to Meredith's one.

Episode 3.25 – 'The Entrancing Dr Cassandra'
Original US air date: 7 March 1968

**Key crew:** Sam Strangis (*Director*); Stanley Ralph Ross (*Teleplay*)
**Special Guest Villainess:** Ida Lupino (*Dr Cassandra Spellcraft*)
**Extra Special Guest Villain:** Howard Duff (*Cabala*)

## STORY

Rendered invisible by camouflage pills, Dr Cassandra and her husband Cabala embark on a concealed crime wave until they clash with Batman, Robin and Batgirl, turning the Terrific Trio into two-dimensional figures using a ray gun. While Alfred struggles to restore the heroes' dimensions, the crooked couple break into Gotham State Penitentiary to release a sextet of super criminals.

## BAT-FACTS

Although this penultimate episode briefly included the Joker, Catwoman, the Riddler, the Penguin, King Tut and Egghead, the characters were performed by stand-ins as opposed to the recurring cast members. David Lewis made the last of eight appearances as Warden Crichton, while the episode was also the only instance in the series where the Special Guest Villainess received top billing over her male counterpart.

Episode 3.26 – 'Minerva, Mayhem and Millionaires'
Original US air date: 14 March 1968

**Key crew:** Oscar Rudolph (*Director*); Charles Hoffman (*Teleplay*)
**Special Guest Villainess:** Zsa Zsa Gabor (*Minerva*)
**Notable Guest Star:** Jacques Bergerac (*Freddy the Fence*)

## STORY

The proprietress of a luxurious spa catering to Gotham's elite, Minerva places her Deepest Secret Extractor within a modified hair-dryer, which she uses to learn the location of her clients' valuables. Discovering the combination to the Wayne Foundation vault, Minerva steals a collection of diamonds as Alfred goes undercover to investigate.

## BAT-FACTS

Hungarian actress Zsa Zsa Gabor (*Moulin Rouge*, 1952) had been linked to a role in *Batman* since the first season when the *New York Daily News* reported that she would portray Marsha, Queen of Diamonds. Gabor finally arrived in Gotham City as Minerva, a character originally intended for silver-screen icon Mae West (*She Done Him Wrong*, 1933), while series producer Howie Horwitz and executive producer William Dozier made cameo appearances as two of Minerva's customers.

# The Tim Burton/Joel Schumacher era

## BATMAN (1989)

**Release date:** 23 June 1989 (US); 11 August 1989 (UK)
**Certificate:** PG-13 (US); 12 (cinema), 15 (home video) (UK)
**Running time:** 126 minutes
**Budget:** $40m
**Global box office:** $411,348,924

### CAST

Jack Nicholson (*Jack Napier/The Joker*); Michael Keaton (*Batman/Bruce Wayne*); Kim Basinger (*Vicki Vale*); Robert Wuhl (*Alexander Knox*); Pat Hingle (*Commissioner James Gordon*); Billy Dee Williams (*Harvey Dent*); Michael Gough (*Alfred Pennyworth*); Jack Palance (*Carl Grissom*); Jerry Hall (*Alicia Hunt*); Tracey Walter (*Bob the Goon*); William Hootkins (*Lieutenant Eckhardt*); Lee Wallace (*Mayor William Borg*).

### KEY CREW

Tim Burton (*Director*); Peter Guber, Jon Peters (*Producers*); Michael E. Uslan, Benjamin Melniker (*Executive Producers*); Sam Hamm (*Story*); Sam Hamm, Warren Skaaren (*Screenplay*); Bob Kane (*Characters*); Danny Elfman (*Music*); Roger Pratt (*Cinematography*); Ray Lovejoy (*Editing*); Anton Furst (*Production Design*); Bob Ringwood (*Costume Design*); Marion Dougherty (*Casting*).

### STORY

As night falls on Gotham, a couple and their young son become the latest victims of the crime wave gripping the city, with a pair of street punks robbing the family before retreating to the city's towering rooftops in search of sanctuary. Unfortunately for the thieves, a winged assailant emerges from the shadows – the masked vigilante known throughout the underworld as the Bat, who is there to deliver his own brand of justice, along with a potent message designed to strike fear into the hearts of his enemies:

'I want you to tell all your friends about me … I'm Batman.'

Day breaks, and with it comes renewed hope for the law-abiding population of Gotham as the city's Mayor and new District Attorney Harvey Dent vow to root out corruption and end the reign of mob boss Carl Grissom. However, the crime lord has problems closer to home – his right-hand man Jack Napier is sleeping with his moll, Alicia

Hunt, and also harbours ambitions of succeeding Grissom as the head of the syndicate. Concerned that the DA could tie him into illegal dealings at the Axis Chemical Factory, Grissom arranges for Napier to stage a break-in at the plant and destroy any incriminating evidence — a task he can only entrust to his number one guy.

With rumours circulating the city of a giant bat striking out at Gotham's criminal element, investigative reporter Alexander Knox joins forces with photojournalist Vicki Vale in order to uncover the truth about the 'Bat-Man'. Hoping to catch an official comment from Police Commissioner James Gordon, Knox and Vale attend a benefit fundraiser thrown by the mysterious billionaire Bruce Wayne. While the Commissioner, District Attorney and Mayor all refuse to be drawn into discussion, the journalists do enjoy a brief conversation with Bruce, only for their host to cut things short after being informed by his butler, Alfred, that Commissioner Gordon has made an unexpected departure. Watching on security footage, Bruce learns that the police have received an anonymous tip that Jack Napier is leading a raid on Axis Chemicals.

Breaking into the office to find it empty, Napier realizes that he has been set up by Grissom in retaliation for his transgressions. As the gang attempt to make their escape, they find themselves in a stand-off with the police, who have specific orders from Gordon to take Napier alive. Batman arrives on the scene and despatches Napier's goons before confronting the gangster on a platform high above a boiling vat of chemicals. Napier takes a shot at Batman only to have the bullet deflected back, catching him in the cheek and sending the mobster toppling over the railings into the toxic waste below. Batman makes his exit through the roof as the police close in; outside a pale white hand emerges from the Gotham River, accompanied by a disfigured Joker playing card.

In a shabby back-street doctor's, a plastic surgeon trembles in fear as he exposes the results of his botched attempt at plastic surgery to a hysterical Jack Napier, who then staggers out into the night for his revenge on Grissom. In Grissom's penthouse, Napier reveals his shocking new visage of bone-white skin, luminous green hair and hideous maniacal grin to his former boss, introducing himself as the Joker before gunning down the crime lord and taking control of his empire. After assuming control of all the criminal activities in Gotham, the Joker enacts a plan to poison all of its citizens by tampering with their supply of hygiene products, creating lethal combinations and leaving Batman as the city's only hope for survival.

Having embarked on a relationship with Bruce Wayne, Vicki Vale finds herself intrigued by the mystery surrounding Gotham's wealthiest citizen. Searching for clues into his past, Vicki follows Bruce to an alley where she watches as he lays roses on the ground. Moving on to the Gotham courthouse, Bruce comes face to face with the Joker and realizes that Napier has somehow managed to survive their earlier encounter. Later, Vicki Vale is invited to dinner at the Flugelheim Museum, where she is soon joined by the Joker, who intends on wooing the reporter and making her his latest moll. Crashing through the museum's glass ceiling, Batman rescues Vicki and takes her to the Batcave where he hands over details of the deadly product combinations, foiling the Joker's diabolical plot and saving the people of Gotham.

As the Joker vows to kill Batman for disrupting his plans, Bruce arrives at Vicki's apartment hoping to tell her the truth behind his nocturnal activities. They are interrupted by the Joker, who recites a familiar catchphrase to the billionaire before shooting him in the chest. The Joker departs and Vicki rushes to Bruce's aid, only to find a dented silver platter in place of his body. She later learns from Knox that, as a child, Bruce witnessed the brutal murder of his parents at the hands of a street thug. Heading to Wayne Manor, Vicki is led into the Batcave at the very moment that Bruce remembers a young Jack Napier as the gunman responsible for the birth of Batman; shocked by these startling reservations, Bruce and Vicki agree to put their feelings aside until the Joker's reign of terror has been brought to an end once and for all.

After Batman destroys the Axis Chemical Factory, the Joker challenges the Dark Knight to confront him at Gotham's 200th anniversary celebrations, during which time he plans to unleash his poisonous gas from the parade balloons. The scheme is foiled when Batman arrives in the Batwing, cutting the balloons free before his aircraft is shot down by the Joker. Climbing from the burning wreckage of the Batwing, the masked vigilante watches as the Clown Prince of Crime takes Vicki hostage and begins to ascend the steps of the towering Gotham Cathedral. Batman pursues the Joker to the summit of the Cathedral roof for a final showdown where the two archenemies come to realize that they are directly responsible for the creation of one another. In the ensuing confrontation, the Joker pulls Batman and Vicki over the ledge of the roof and attempts to make his escape via helicopter. Batman fires his grappling hook around the Joker's leg and attaches the wire to a gargoyle, sending his nemesis plummeting to his death on the streets far below.

With the public free from the grasp of the Joker, District Attorney Harvey Dent and Police Commissioner Gordon hold a press conference, announcing Batman as the city's protector and unveiling a new signal that pierces the night sky with hope for the citizens of Gotham City.

## BRINGING BATMAN TO THE SCREEN

It was Superman's debut in *Action Comics* #1 (June 1938) that had led to the creation of the Batman character in May 1939, and four decades later the box-office success of Richard Donner's *Superman: The Movie* (1978) would also prove the catalyst for bringing the Dark Knight back to the big screen. Acquiring the *Batman* film rights in April 1979, former comic book writer Michael E. Uslan (who had himself written for the *Batman* line during the mid-1970s) and producing partner Benjamin Melniker (*Shoot*, 1976) intended to reboot the character for a new generation, differentiating from the campy approach of the 1960s television series by taking the Caped Crusader back to the dark roots of his early comic book appearances. 'I wanted to make the definitive, dark, serious version of Batman – the way Bob Kane and Bill Finger had envisioned him in 1939,' Uslan told Bill Ramey of *Batman-on-Film.com* in 2005. 'A creature of the night; stalking criminals in the shadows.'

To develop his vision of the Dark Knight, Uslan approached screenwriter Richard Maibaum and director Guy Hamilton, who had previously collaborated on the Bond films *Goldfinger* (1964), *Diamonds Are Forever* (1971) and *The Man with the Golden Gun* (1974), and when they passed on his offer he then turned his attention to another regular Bond scribe, Tom Mankiewicz. Mankiewicz had written Roger Moore's first 007 outing *Live and Let Die* (1973) and shared screenwriting credits with Maibaum on *Diamonds Are Forever* and *The Man with the Golden Gun*, while – perhaps most importantly – his CV also included uncredited writing duties on both *Superman* and *Superman II* (1980).

With Mankiewicz busy developing the screenplay it seemed as though the Dark Knight was on the verge of his return. However, Uslan hit a stumbling block with his efforts to convince Hollywood executives that the idea was viable. Although the comic book line had seen a deliberate shift away from the camp approach of the 1960s television series – largely thanks to the efforts of writer Denny O'Neil and artist Neal Adams – public perception of *Batman* remained synonymous with Adam West's portrayal and the project was rejected by many of the top studios, including Columbia Pictures and United Artists. Uslan and Melniker then approached fledgling production company Casablanca, headed up by the young and ambitious producing team of Peter Guber (*The Deep*, 1977) and Jon Peters (*A Star is Born*, 1976), and a contract was signed between the two partnerships in November 1979 that effectively handed control of the project to Guber–Peters. Eventually *Batman* was brought to the attention of Warner Bros Pictures, where the producers were successful in negotiating a deal, albeit one that relegated Uslan and Melniker to nominal executive producer credits and entitled them to a reduced cut of 13 per cent net from their original terms of 40 per cent gross. Nevertheless, *Batman* was officially given the go-ahead in 1981 with a predicted budget of $15m, but it would be a further two years before Mankiewicz delivered his first draft of the script.

Entitled *The Batman*, Mankiewicz's screenplay was essentially an origin tale with a narrative structure closely resembling the template laid down by *Superman*. Inspired by the *Batman: Strange Apparitions* story arc that had proven popular with fans during its run in *Detective Comics* #469–76 from 1977 to 1978, *The Batman* opened in the 1960s with a young Bruce Wayne witnessing the murder of his parents at the hands of hitman Joe Chill, an associate of the Joker whom we discover to be acting on behalf of Thomas Wayne's political rival, Rupert Thorne. Transforming himself into the masked vigilante Batman, the Dark Knight combats street thugs and rogues such as the Joker and the Penguin, while his playboy alter ego embarks on a romantic relationship with Thorne's intern, Silver St Cloud, a character who had debuted in the comic book story 'The Master Plan of Doctor Phosphorus!' by Steve Englehart, published in *Detective Comics* #470 (June 1977).

Following the introduction of Robin the Boy Wonder (the young Dick Grayson having been orphaned by the Joker during a circus performance of the Flying Graysons), the Dynamic Duo face off against Thorne and the Clown Prince of Crime in an over-the-top climax befitting of the 1960s television show. Thorne meets his demise by falling into a gigantic pencil-sharpener, while Batman's victory is marred by his failure to prevent the death of Silver St Cloud, with the script ending as he vows to continue his struggle to bring justice to the streets of Gotham City.

In 1983 *The Batman* was announced with a tentative release date set for 1985 and, with its budget having inflated to $20m, the search began for a director to helm the project. Over the next two years a number of filmmakers were either attached or under consideration, including Ivan Reitman (*Ghostbusters*, 1984), Joe Dante (*Gremlins*, 1984), Robert Zemeckis (*Back to the Future*, 1985) and Joel and Ethan Coen (*Blood Simple*, 1984), while the script underwent rewrites at the hands of nine different writers. For a time it seemed as if *The Batman* was teetering on the verge of development hell until Warner Bros turned their attention to up-and-coming director Tim Burton, who had just delivered a hit for the studio with his feature debut *Pee-Wee's Big Adventure* (1985).

Graduating from the California Institute of the Arts in 1979, Burton had begun his career at Disney working as an animator and concept artist. Having contributed to titles such as *The Fox and the Hound* (1981) and *The Black Cauldron* (1985), Burton cut his directing teeth with the short films *Vincent* (1982) and *Frankenweenie* (1984), along with an adaptation of *Hansel and Gretel* that received a solitary airing on the Disney Channel in October 1983. Although he was enjoying a growing reputation, the filmmaker's dark artistic sensibilities put him at odds with Disney's clean, family-friendly ethos; following Burton's departure from the studio, *Frankenweenie* came to the attention of Paul Reubens, a.k.a. Pee-Wee Herman, who enlisted the young director to oversee the big-screen adaptation of the popular children's TV show *Pee-Wee's Playhouse* for Warner Bros. During its theatrical run the resulting film grossed over $40m from an investment of just $7m, which was enough to convince the studio to approach Burton with a view to taking on the challenge of *Batman*.

Examining Makiewicz's draft, Burton felt that there were inherent problems in both the structure and the approach of the screenplay. Not only was it a retread of *Superman*, but the script also failed to acknowledge and explore the psychological aspect of the character, while remaining too similar in tone to the camp take of the television series. In an attempt to rectify his concerns, Burton collaborated with *Frankenweenie* producer and then-girlfriend Julie Hickson to develop a treatment of their own. Dated 21 October 1985, the 43-page outline roughly followed the plot structure established by Mankiewicz, taking Bruce through his tragic childhood – the murder of his parents occurring after a costume party in which Thomas Wayne is dressed in a bat suit, paying homage to 'The First Batman' by Bill Finger, published in *Detective Comics* #235 (September 1965) – and exploring the rise of the Batman as Gotham's protector.

Despite Burton's misgivings over the original script, the new treatment also retained many of the key story elements and characters. Along with the Joker, Rupert Thorne, Silver St Cloud and Robin, Hickson's outline also featured cameos by the Penguin, the Riddler and Catwoman, with the three villains cropping up to assist the Joker in the murder of the Flying Graysons. It does differ considerably in its climax, with Batman saving the people of Gotham from the Joker's diabolical plan to unleash his Grimacing Gas during a Christmas parade, while Silver – whose role is considerably reduced here – also lives to see another day. By early 1986 *Batman* had received a further two treatments by Steve Englehart, a veteran comic book writer who had worked extensively for both Marvel and DC during the 1970s on popular titles such as *The Avengers*, *Justice League of America* and *Detective Comics*, in addition to penning the acclaimed *Strange Apparitions* run which had served to influence Makiewicz's first draft. However, it wasn't until Burton met Sam Hamm, a young writer and Bat-fan who had just secured a two-year contract with Warner Bros on the back of a hot spec-script entitled *Pulitzer Prize*, that he found a screenwriter who shared his artistic vision.

In the relatively untried pairing of Burton and Hamm, producers Jon Peters and Peter Guber had found the ideal combination to develop Michael Uslan's initial vision for a 'definitive, dark and serious' *Batman* movie. The studio, however, remained apprehensive about straying too far towards this new direction, until they were buoyed by the popularity of Frank Miller's seminal limited series *Batman: The Dark Knight Returns* (February–June 1986). This classic tale, which saw a weary, middle-aged Bruce Wayne coming out of retirement to fight crime and corruption, not only reinvigorated the character but also laid the foundations for storylines such as Miller's *Batman: Year One* (published in *Batman* #404–7, February–May 1987) and Alan Moore's *Batman: The Killing Joke* (1988), while simultaneously convincing the studio of the potential behind Burton's vision.

On 20 October 1986 Sam Hamm delivered his first draft of *Batman*, foregoing the earlier focus on an origin tale in favour of presenting the character as a fait accompli, with his journey from innocent victim to Dark Knight gradually revealed through flashbacks as the main story unfolds. Rupert Thorne was replaced by an original creation, mob boss Carl Grissom, while the bulk of the narrative dealt with the emergence of the Joker and his eventual confrontation with the Caped Crusader. Hamm also relegated Dick Grayson to a cameo (which would be abandoned prior to filming for pacing purposes) and dropped Silver St Cloud as the love interest, replacing her with reporter Vicki Vale, a prominent supporting player of the Silver Age who had not been seen on screen since Jane Adams' depiction in Columbia Pictures' 1949 *Batman and Robin* serial.

Although Sam Hamm's script was well received by the studio – and endorsed by Bob Kane himself – Warner executives were still reluctant to give production the official green light and Burton moved on to develop his second feature, the black comedy *Beetlejuice* (1988), while Hamm worked on further revisions to the

screenplay. Produced for $15m, *Beetlejuice* was released on 1 April 1988 by Warner Bros in the US, where the film enjoyed an $8m opening weekend, going on to eclipse the success of *Pee-Wee's Big Adventure* with a worldwide gross of $73.7m and confirming to the studio that in Burton they had found their man.

Almost a decade after Uslan and Melniker had first acquired the rights to produce a new movie – during which time they had released a live-action adaptation of another DC property, *Swamp Thing* (1982) – *Batman* was finally a go. Working on an increased budget of $35m (along with an additional $5m in interest charges), *Batman* commenced pre-production in April 1988 and one of the first moves was to secure a legendary Hollywood star to portray Jack Napier, the unhinged mobster who would go on to become the Joker. Created by Bob Kane, Bill Finger and Jerry Robinson, the Joker had made his debut in the comic book story 'The Joker', published in *Batman* #1 (Spring 1940), and had since gone on to become a mainstay of the Rogues Gallery and the Dark Knight's greatest adversary.

While Burton and screenwriter Sam Hamm had discussed the likes of Willem Dafoe (*Platoon*, 1986), James Woods (*Once Upon a Time in America*, 1984) and David Bowie (*Labyrinth*, 1986) in relation to the role – and, despite the best efforts of Robin Williams (*Good Morning Vietnam*, 1987), who lobbied hard for the part – the studio had but one name on their shortlist, that of Jack Nicholson. Having firmly established himself as one of Hollywood's leading men with memorable roles in classics such as *Easy Rider* (1969), *Five Easy Pieces* (1970) and *Chinatown* (1974), the then twice Academy Award-winner (Best Actor *One Flew Over the Cuckoo's Nest*, 1975, and Best Supporting Actor – *Terms of Endearment*, 1983) had delivered one of the greatest screen psychopaths in cinema history with his turn as Jack Torrance, the antagonist of Stanley Kubrick's acclaimed horror, *The Shining* (1980). It seemed a match made in heaven.

First approached by producer Jon Peters in 1986 while filming *The Witches of Eastwick* (1987), Nicholson had been a favourite of both Michael Uslan and Bob Kane as far back as 1980, during which time the *Batman* creator sent Warner Bros a doctored image of *The Shining*'s Jack Torrance, presenting the actor with the iconic green hair and chalk-white skin of the Joker. To secure Nicholson's participation the studio granted him one of the most lucrative contracts in Hollywood history; in addition to an 'off-the-clock' agreement specifying a set number of hours' leave from the set each day to compensate for the gruelling two-and-a-half hour make-up sessions that were required to convert him into the maniacal Clown Prince of Crime, Nicholson received a $6m up-front salary and a percentage of the total box-office gross and merchandizing sales, a deal which is rumoured to have netted the star between $50m and $75m in total.

Initially the filmmakers presumed that an unknown actor would take on the crucial role of the Caped Crusader, as had been the case with the casting of Christopher Reeve (*Gray Lady Down*, 1978) in *Superman: The Movie*. However, the arrival of Nicholson quickly led to a change in thinking. With the hunt underway to find a Dark Knight capable of holding his own alongside Nicholson, a host of actors were rumoured by the Hollywood press to be under consideration, including Pierce Brosnan (*The Fourth Protocol*, 1987), Daniel Day-Lewis (*The Unbearable Lightness of Being*, 1988), Mel Gibson (*Lethal Weapon*, 1987), Charlie Sheen (*Wall Street*, 1987) and even comedian Bill Murray (*Ghostbusters*). Executive producer Michael Uslan listed Kevin Costner (*The Untouchables*, 1987), Harrison Ford (*Raiders of the Lost Ark*, 1981) and Dennis Quaid (*Innerspace*, 1987) as his preferred three choices and even Adam West threw his name into the hat, although perhaps unsurprisingly the producers chose to ignore the pleas of the then 60-year-old former Caped Crusader.

Acting on the recommendation of producers Peters and Guber – and resisting studio pressure to secure a big-name star – Burton turned to his *Beetlejuice* leading man, Michael Keaton, in a move that immediately sparked unprecedented levels of controversy. Known for his comic performances, Keaton had been plucked from TV obscurity by Ron Howard, who cast him in a co-starring role in the 1982 comedy *Night Shift* alongside Henry

Winkler of *Happy Days* (1974–84) fame. Going on to appear in a further six comedies, Keaton gained critical acclaim and a National Society of Film Critics Award for Best Actor with his first dramatic role in *Clean and Sober* (1988), but this was far from enough to quell the backlash.

Angry fans, already anxious over the appointment of an unproven director and fearing that Keaton's casting pointed towards a continuation of the 'jokey' tone established by the television series, soon established a petition against the production and bombarded Warner Bros with over 50,000 letters of complaint. The likes of Bob Kane, Michael Uslan and Adam West all spoke out about their misgivings (although Kane and Uslan would later recant their statements), and even Keaton expressed reservations until the director handed him the graphic novel of *The Dark Knight Returns* as a reference point for his intended direction.

'Taking someone like Michael and making him Batman supported the whole split personality idea,' said Burton in an interview with *Cinefantastique* in 1989. This, he felt, was the most interesting aspect of the character and the theme that had drawn him to the movie in the first place; in selecting his leading man, Burton believed that Keaton's 'everyman' qualities – as opposed to the typical, muscle-bound, macho action stars of the 1980s – would allow audiences to suspend their disbelief regarding to a character who opts to embark on a crusade against crime dressed as a giant bat. Furthermore, he was fully confident in the actor's ability to effectively convey the obsessive, driven nature of his protagonist. 'I wanted Michael from the start …' Burton told the *San Diego Union-Tribune* in 1989. 'There is something in his eyes, a dimension of feeling, even with the mask on.'

In an effort to placate the fan backlash, the producers brought in Bob Kane as project consultant and, with the leads secured, Burton set about assembling his supporting cast. Sean Young (*Blade Runner*, 1982) was initially hired as photojournalist and love interest Vicki Vale, although the actress was forced to pull out after breaking her arm rehearsing for a horse-riding scene and found herself replaced by former fashion model and Golden Globe-winner Kim Basinger (*The Natural*, 1984). Pat Hingle, traditionally known for his authority figure characters in films such as *Hang 'Em High* (1968), slipped comfortably into the role of Police Commissioner James Gordon, with Michael Gough – whose notable appearances included Hammer Film Productions' *Dracula* (1958) and *Phantom of the Opera* (1962) along with Sydney Pollack's Academy Award-winner *Out of Africa* (1985) – brought in to portray Bruce Wayne's trusted butler and confidant Alfred Pennyworth.

Another character to make the transition from page to screen was Harvey Dent, with Gotham's District Attorney undergoing a change in ethnicity in the form of Billy Dee Williams (*Star Wars:*

*Episode V – The Empire Strikes Back*, 1980), who signed up for the part on the understanding that he would return as Dent's criminal alter ego Two-Face in any potential sequels. Also cast as characters created specifically for the movie were former stand-up comic Robert Wuhl (*Good Morning, Vietnam*) and model Jerry Hall (*Topo Galileo*, 1987) as reporter Alexander Knox and mob girl Alicia Hunt, while crime boss Carl Grissom was brought to life by screen veteran Jack Palance, twice an Academy Award nominee (*Sudden Fear*, 1952, and *Shane*, 1953) who would eventually take home the Oscar at the third attempt when he was named Best Supporting Actor for his performance in the 1991 comedy *City Slickers*.

'Tim said in order to make this work, Gotham City has to be the third most important character in the movie,' recalled executive producer Michael Uslan. 'From the opening frame of the film, the audience must totally believe in Gotham City.' To realize his blueprint for Gotham, Burton approached celebrated production designer Anton Furst (*The Company of Wolves*, 1984), whose commitments to Stanley Kubrick's *Full Metal Jacket* (1987) and Neil Jordan's *High Spirits* (1988) had prevented an earlier collaboration with the director on *Beetlejuice*. Furst had regretted passing on the chance to work alongside Burton and was delighted to be given another opportunity to do so with *Batman*.

'Since no city was ever created by any one designer,' said Furst in *Batman: The Official Book of the Movie*, 'we felt it a good idea to go for a potpourri of styles, which would help us towards a sense of timelessness.' The Gotham City envisioned by Burton and Furst drew inspiration from classic cinematic cityscapes such as those created for Fritz Lang's *Metropolis* (1927), Ridley Scott's *Blade Runner* and Terry Gilliam's *Brazil* (1985), along with Bob Kane's original comic book sketches, which were in themselves influenced by the architecture of New York City. 'Gotham City is basically New York caricatured with a mix of styles squashed together,' explained Burton, 'an island of big, tall cartoon buildings textured with extreme designs.'

'We decided in the very early stages with the main *Batman* set, Gotham City, to construct it as a reality of its own,' Furst told *Film Review* in 1989. 'We weren't going to mix location and studio filming.' To house a set that would be the largest since *Cleopatra*, Burton convinced Warner Bros to let the shoot take place in Britain. Not only would this provide the necessary space and facilities at a reduced cost, but it also allowed for a greater deal of independence from the studio, along with a reprieve from the relentless media attention of the Hollywood press. *Batman* took over eighteen soundstages at Pinewood Studios – home to the *James Bond* and *Carry On* film series – and it was here that, armed with a $5.5m production budget, Furst and his team set about developing a sinister, noir-soaked vision of Gotham City.

Opting against the use of computer-generated

enhancements, Gotham was brought to life through the traditional method of combining physical sets with models and matte paintings. In addition to the construction of key sets such as the Batcave, the quarter-mile Broad Avenue and Gotham City Square, the Flugelheim Museum and the Monarch Theatre, detailed miniatures were created by visual effects supervisor Derek Meddings, who had shared a Special Achievement Award from the Academy for his work on Donner's *Superman*. Meanwhile a number of locations were also employed, with Acton Lane and Little Barford power stations doubling for the Axis Chemical Factory and Knebworth House and Hatfield House providing the exteriors for Wayne Manor. 'I envisaged Gotham the way I see it now at Pinewood,' enthused Bob Kane. 'They've got it, every building, every trash can, every brick.'

As well as taking on responsibility for the construction of Gotham City, Furst's role also incorporated the design of the Batmobile and Batwing. 'We didn't want to put [the Batmobile] into any particular period of time,' Furst informed *Empire* in 1989. 'In the end, we went into pure expressionism, taking the Salt Flat Racers of the 30s and the Stingray macho machines of the 50s. We wanted to get all the intimidation that comes out of Batman's image into the car.' Furst's designs were realized by special effects supervisor John Evans (*Raiders of the Lost Ark*) and his team of technicians, who built the vehicle in twelve weeks

using the frame of a Chevrolet Impala after tests on various Jaguars and Mustangs proved futile. Other contributions from Evans' department included the creation of Batman's vast array of gadgets, such as his grappling hook, Batarangs and iconic utility belt.

To compliment the 'timeless' look of Gotham City, Anton Furst worked with costume designer Bob Ringwood (*Empire of the Sun*, 1987) to develop a style that mixed modern fashions with those of the 1940s. However, there was further controversy within the fan community when it emerged that Ringwood's interpretation of the Batsuit would differ considerably from that of the comic book character. Instead of the distinguished grey and blue tights, Keaton's Batman would sport an all-black moulded body suit replete with fake muscles (thankfully producer Jon Peters' idea to endorse the costume with product placement was overlooked). Nevertheless, while initial fan response proved negative the new-look costume was met with enthusiastic approval from Bob Kane and director Tim Burton. Finally, responsibility for transforming Jack Nicholson into the Joker fell to make-up designer Nick Dudman, who had recently impressed with his work on *Willow* (1988).

*Batman* descended on Pinewood Studios for principal photography in October 1988 and, as had become customary with the film's development, the highly secretive twelve-week shoot continued to prove challenging for all involved. Having crossed the Atlantic to escape the prying eyes of the media, the production soon discovered that the British press were equally as voracious. A publicist was offered £10,000 to leak the first picture of the Joker and the police were called after two reels of footage was stolen from the set. Meanwhile speculation was rife that Jack Nicholson was dissatisfied with his director and was lobbying to have Burton removed from the picture. Behind the veil of secrecy, however, this was far from the truth; Burton had met his adversary not in Nicholson, who remained a staunch supporter of the young director throughout the shoot, but in producer Jon Peters.

Reluctant to fully entrust such a potentially lucrative franchise to an inexperienced director working on his first big-budget feature, Peters adopted a 'hands-on' approach and insisted on a number of rewrites to the script prior to filming. With preferred scribe Sam Hamm unable to contribute owing to a strike by the Writers Guild of America, the screenplay had passed through the hands of both Warren Skaaren (*Beetlejuice*) and Charles McKeown (*Brazil*), much to Burton's chagrin. Enforced rewrites continued into production and often occurred without the prior knowledge of the director, culminating with a change to the original ending that would have seen the Joker kill Vicki Vale before facing the wrath of a vengeful Dark Knight; instead, he would take her captive and climb to the top of Gotham Cathedral for the final showdown against Batman.

This new idea for the climax of *Batman* necessitated the construction of a 38ft model at a cost of $100,000 and Burton, who had argued against the changes, was left to admit on set to Nicholson that he had no idea about his character's motivation for climbing the cathedral steps. Eventually the actor grew tired of the persistent interference and confronted the producers while decked out in full Joker make-up. 'He was very angry and screaming, but with his face frozen in this smile,' recalled Peter Guber. 'It was kind of a surreal experience … and he was screaming at me and John: "I can't believe this film is ever going to see the light of day!"'

Despite Nicholson's sarcastic prediction – and an intense four-month shoot that Burton later described as the worst period of his life – filming wrapped on schedule and only marginally over budget. Burton retreated into post-production in February 1989, assembling the picture alongside notable British film editor Ray Lovejoy (*2001: A Space Odyssey*, 1968, and *The Shining*). However, Peters continued to exert his influence, raising concerns over Burton's decision to bring in composer Danny Elfman to produce the music for the film. Peters felt that Elfman, who had collaborated with Burton on both *Pee-Wee's Big Adventure* and *Beetlejuice* – and who would go on to score all of the director's movies except *Ed Wood* (1994) and *Sweeney Todd: The Demon Barber of Fleet Street* (2007) – would be out of his depth on such a big project, and wanted

Grammy Award-winning musician Prince to co-write the soundtrack.

'It was a rough thing, but Tim didn't have the power back then to call all the shots himself,' recalled Danny Elfman in an interview with MTV in 2010, 'I had major convincing to do on so many levels.' Facing up to the possibility that he could be removed from the project, Elfman composed a main theme that immediately impressed the producer, although Peters still insisted on the inclusion of two pieces of music by Prince, with the songs 'Partyman' and 'Trust' integrated into the soundtrack to accompany the Joker's crimes. While Prince's contributions would lead to a multi-million-selling soundtrack album, for the director it was an intrusion that instantly dated the movie and destroyed the timelessness that he had strived so hard to create.

The tampering of producer Jon Peters may have proven frustrating to some members of the cast and crew during the production of *Batman*, yet there was no denying his contribution as architect of the ensuing publicity campaign. In an effort to appease disenchantment within the Bat-community, Peters had assembled a thirty-second trailer at a cost of $400,000, which was screened to a select audience of *Batman* fans. Devoid of music, narration and titles, the short montage of scenes immediately sparked a buzz that spread rapidly through word of mouth. With it debuting in cinemas over the Christmas period, reports circulated that fans were purchasing movie tickets solely to catch a glimpse of the teaser trailer.

Capitalizing on the success of the trailer, Peters released an equally minimalist teaser poster featuring the yellow Bat-Insignia against a plain black background. Designed by Anton Furst, the poster quickly became a regular fixture on advertising billboards across America and over a thousand copies were reported stolen from bus shelters. Demand for Bat-merchandise soon reached an all-time high and any remaining hostility from the fan community was marginalized as Batmania went mainstream, gripping the public in anticipation of *Batman*'s release in the summer of 1989.

## RECEPTION

The ten-year struggle to bring the Dark Knight back to the screen ended on 23 June 1989 when Tim Burton's *Batman* opened on 2,194 screens across the United States. The response from the general movie-going public was phenomenal. *Batman* made $43.6m in its opening weekend, shattering the previous record of $29.4m which had been set by *Ghostbusters II* (1989) the week before, and went on to become the first film to break the $100m mark in ten days. By its third weekend it had dropped over fifty-five per cent to $19m, but despite a steady decline the film amassed a grand total of $251.2m in North America, making it the highest-grossing release of 1989. On the international front it earned a further

$160.15m for a world-wide haul of $411,348,924, second only to Steven Spielberg's *Indiana Jones and the Last Crusade* (1989) in terms of global box office. In Britain, *Batman* was instrumental in the creation of the 12 certificate, becoming the first title to receive that rating from the British Board of Film Classification when it hit UK cinemas on 11 August 1989, earning £2,058,159 in its opening weekend and £10,139,590 overall.

While *Batman's* success with the public was undeniable, the response from the fan community was less favourable, with a large proportion of comic book fans frustrated at the liberties taken by the filmmakers towards its source material. Among their concerns were the decision to have the Joker directly responsible for the murder of Bruce's parents (an idea incorporated by Burton and script rewriter Warren Skaaren during the Writers Guild of America strike), the fact that Alfred willingly reveals Bruce's secret identity by allowing Vicki Vale access to the Batcave, and Batman's liberal use of lethal force against his foes (however, it should perhaps be noted that the filmmakers had intended to take *Batman* back to his earliest roots and it wasn't until after the release of *Batman* #1 in 1940 that the Caped Crusader vowed never to take a life).

In terms of press reaction, a number of commentators felt that Tim Burton's take on *Batman* was overly dark and had too much focus on Nicholson's Joker, yet critical reception to the movie was generally positive. Industry bible

*Variety* praised the film, describing Nicholson's performance as 'a masterpiece of sinister comic acting', while in Britain *Empire* gave the movie four stars out of five in its review. Less impressed, however, was the respected American film critic Roger Ebert, who felt that *Batman* was a case of style over substance and made for depressing viewing, although he did have plenty of admiration for the filmmakers' interpretation of Gotham City.

Ebert's respect for *Batman's* impressive production design was shared by the Motion Picture Association of America, who honoured Anton Furst and Peter Young with the Oscar for Best Art Direction – Set Decoration at the 62nd Academy Awards in March 1990. Jack Nicholson received a Golden Globe nomination for Best Performance by an Actor in a Motion Picture – Comedy/Musical, and he was also nominated for Best Actor in a Supporting Role at the British Academy Film Awards, with *Batman* competing in a further five categories (Costume Design, Make-up, Production Design, Sound and Special Effects) without success. Elsewhere on the awards circuit, *Batman* was named Favourite Motion Picture and tied with *Steel Magnolias* (1989) for Favourite Dramatic Motion Picture at the People's Choice Awards, while Prince won a Brit Award for Best Soundtrack and both he and Danny Elfman received separate nominations at the Grammy Awards for their individual musical contributions.

In rising to the challenge of reintroducing a modern, darker take on the Caped Crusader, *Batman* achieved a level of success beyond all expectations. Complimenting the strong box-office returns were the producers' keen licensing deals, which generated an additional $750m in revenue from over 300 official tie-in products, the saturation of which led the *New York Observer* to describe *Batman* as 'less movie than a corporate behemoth'. Furthermore, it demonstrated to studios the potential for adapting pre-existing material and created a model to which all subsequent blockbusters have aspired, with an increased emphasis on promotional tie-ins, merchandizing and corporate partnerships, not to mention a greater focus on maximizing 'opening weekend' returns. Beyond that, it also brought *Batman* back into the public consciousness, with the character enjoying a spell of popularity not seen since the dizzying heights of early 1966, and Warner Bros were keen to exploit this by immediately pressing forward with their plans for a sequel.

# BATMAN RETURNS (1992)

**Release date:** 19 June 1992 (US); 10 July 1992 (UK)
**Certificate:** PG-13 (US); 12 (theatrical), 15 (home video) (UK)
**Running time:** 126 minutes
**Budget:** $80m (estimated)
**Global box office:** $266,822,354

## CAST

Michael Keaton (*Bruce Wayne/Batman*); Danny DeVito (*Oswald Cobblepot/The Penguin*); Michelle Pfeiffer (*Selina Kyle/Catwoman*); Christopher Walken (*Max Shreck*); Michael Gough (*Alfred Pennyworth*); Michael Murphy (*The Mayor*); Cristi Conaway (*Ice Princess*); Andrew Bryniarski (*Charles 'Chip' Shreck*); Pat Hingle (*Commissioner James Gordon*), Paul Reubens (*Mr Cobblepot*); Diane Salinger (*Mrs Cobblepot*).

## KEY CREW

Tim Burton (*Director*); Tim Burton, Denise Di Novi (*Producers*); Peter Guber, Jon Peters, Michael E. Uslan, Benjamin Melniker (*Executive Producers*); Ian Bryce (*Associate Producer*); Larry J. Franco (*Co-producer*); Sam Hamm, Daniel Waters (*Story*); Daniel Waters (*Screenplay*); Bob Kane (*Characters*); Danny Elfman (*Music*); Stefan Czapsky (*Cinematography*); Bob Badami, Chris Lebenzon (*Editing*); Bo Welch (*Production Design*), Bob Ringwood, Mary Vogt (*Costume Design*); Marion Dougherty (*Casting*).

## STORY

In the stuffy Cobblepot Manor, Mr and Mrs Cobblepot welcome their first-born son – a hideously deformed creature, of both body and mind. Driven to desperation, the wealthy couple abandon the child, sending him floating down the river in a basket, which drifts into the sewers before coming to a rest at the aquatic pavilion of the derelict Gotham Zoo.

Thirty-three years later, the citizens of Gotham City prepare for the holiday season amid rumours of a mysterious 'Penguin-man' living beneath their streets. Meanwhile, in the headquarters of Shreck Industries, the corrupt business magnate Max Shreck holds a meeting with the Mayor, hoping to gain support for the construction of a new power plant, despite the city having a surplus of energy. The Mayor refuses to grant approval, but before the debate can continue Shreck's son Chip arrives, informing the men that it is time to attend the lighting of the Christmas tree in Gotham Plaza.

While 'Gotham's own Santa Claus' Max Shreck makes his speech to the public, a giant Christmas present rolls into view and bursts open, with members of the notorious Red Triangle Circus Gang launching an attack on the gathering. The thugs attempt to kidnap Shreck but he manages to escape when Chip steps in to protect him. As chaos ensues, the Bat-Signal shines across Gotham, glaring through the window of Wayne Manor where the city's protector springs into action. Racing to the Plaza in the Batmobile, the Caped Crusader quickly repels the assault and rescues Shreck's timid secretary Selina Kyle from a mugger before rounding up the rest of the gang.

Having fled the violence, Max Shreck is captured by the Red Triangle Circus Gang and is taken to the Arctic World pavilion at Gotham Zoo, now home to the elusive 'Penguin' creature. The Penguin demands Shreck's assistance in orchestrating his re-emergence from the sewers, stating that he hopes to uncover the names of his parents and learn his true identity. The business mogul is reluctant at first until the Penguin provides incriminating evidence of his illegal dealings, with Shreck then agreeing to a partnership after devising a scheme he believes can be mutually beneficial.

Arriving back at her dreary apartment, Selina Kyle is greeted by the only company she has in her life – her cat, Miss Kitty – only to remember that she has forgotten to prepare a file for Shreck's upcoming meeting with Bruce Wayne. Heading back to the office, Selina learns that Shreck plans to suck energy from Gotham City and stockpile it in his new power plant, only to be interrupted by her boss. Hoping to cover his tracks, Shreck pushes the secretary out of a window, sending her hurtling to the snow-covered ground far below. As she lies motionless, a group of cats gather around Selina, breathing life back into her body. Suffering from amnesia, Selina returns home and undergoes a strange shift in personality, trashing her apartment and crafting herself a skin-tight black cat-suit, complete with razor-sharp claws. Taking to the streets, Selina rescues a young woman from a mugger before chastising the victim and introducing herself as Catwoman.

At a press conference, the Mayor attempts to reassure the public in light of the recent crime wave gripping the city when a member of the Red Triangle Circus Gang disrupts proceedings, stealing the Mayor's infant child and retreating into the sewers. He passes the baby over to the Penguin, who then emerges from the sewer with the infant and is proclaimed a hero, although Batman remains suspicious of his motives.

Aided by Max Shreck, the Penguin begins the search for his mother and father, visiting Gotham's hall of records and feverishly making notes as he wades through piles of birth certificates. Eventually he discovers his human name – Oswald Cobblepot – and visits the grave of his now-deceased parents, earning public sympathy by announcing that he has forgiven them for their decision to abandon him.

Bruce Wayne attends a meeting at Shreck Industries to discuss the power plant proposal, accusing the businessman of links to organized crime through his association with the Penguin. Much to Shreck's surprise, the meeting is interrupted by Selina Kyle, but the corrupt businessman is relieved to learn that she has no memory of their previous encounter. Selina escorts Bruce from the office while Shreck goes on to pay a visit to the Penguin, asking him to run

for mayor in order to gain approval for his power plant. Although reluctant at first, the Penguin comes around when he realizes the perks of the job and sets about discrediting the current mayor by stepping up the Red Triangle Circus Gang's reign of terror.

After battling with members of the gang that night, Batman confronts the Penguin outside Shreck's department store, with Cobblepot claiming to be surveying the chaos in a mayoral capacity. Catwoman then emerges from the department store as an explosion rips through the building. The Penguin flies away using a helicopter umbrella as the Dark Knight chases the femme fatale to a rooftop; during the confrontation, Catwoman teases Batman before sticking her claws into his torso, causing the Caped Crusader to instinctively knock her from the building into a passing sand truck. Later, as the Penguin launches his campaign to run for mayor, Catwoman pays him a visit in his office and suggests an alliance against Batman, with the pair then hatching a scheme to discredit the crime-fighter in the eyes of the public.

Selina Kyle attends Wayne Manor for a date with Bruce but their evening is cut short by a news report stating that Gotham's Ice Princess has been kidnapped. With the discovery of a bloody Batarang pointing towards Batman as the culprit, Bruce and Selina each make their excuses to leave, but it isn't long before they are reunited when the Caped Crusader locates the Ice

Princess, who is being held hostage on a rooftop by Catwoman and the Penguin. The Penguin unleashes bats from his umbrella, framing Batman for murder as the Ice Princess falls to her death with the police watching from below. Batman attempts to escape in the Batmobile, which has been tampered with by the Penguin's thugs, giving the villain control of the vehicle. As the Batmobile races through the city, the Penguin appears on a monitor and brags about his trickery to the Dark Knight, but Batman regains control of his car and manages to successfully evade the police.

With public confidence in Batman shattered, the Penguin addresses a crowd of voters only for his scheming to backfire as Batman takes control of the PA system, broadcasting a recording of the Penguin's boasts. Pelted with rotten vegetables, the Penguin retreats to the sewer and sets in motion his master plan – to round up and kill the first-born sons of Gotham while their parents attend a party thrown by Max Shreck. At the ball, Bruce Wayne and Selina Kyle discover each other's secret identities, but before they can start fighting the Penguin shows up with his thugs and takes Shreck hostage, imprisoning him in a giant bird cage at his Arctic World lair. The Dark Knight foils the plan to round up the first-born sons, causing the Penguin to swear revenge on the entire city by assembling an army of penguins equipped with rocket launchers, using a remote control to direct them towards Gotham Plaza.

As Batman races towards the Penguin's hideout in the Batskiboat, Alfred jams the villain's signal, causing the birds to stand down. The Penguin attempts to flee in his duck vehicle, surfacing to confront the Dark Knight in Gotham Zoo. The penguins unleash their missiles on the zoo as a flock of bats fly out of the Batskiboat, sending the Penguin hurtling down into the Arctic World pavilion far below. Inside the lair, Max Shreck escapes his holding cell and is confronted by Catwoman. Batman desperately tries to persuade Selina against killing her boss, tearing off his mask in an effort to talk her down. Seizing on the opportunity, Shreck shoots at Batman before unloading the rest of his ammunition into Selina, who counts down her remaining lives before grabbing hold of a power cable and leaning in for a kiss with Shreck. After a huge explosion, a wounded Batman sifts through the debris to find Shreck's charred remains, but Selina is nowhere to be found. Meanwhile a battered and bloody Penguin emerges from the pool and staggers towards his umbrella collection before collapsing, with a group of penguins then carrying his lifeless body down to a watery grave.

With Gotham's safety ensured, Bruce Wayne is driving home with Alfred when he spots a familiar shadow in an alleyway. Investigating, Bruce discovers Miss Kitty but there is no sign of Selina; however, high above on the rooftops, Catwoman looks on as the Bat-Signal shines out over the city once more.

## BRINGING BATMAN TO THE SCREEN

Even before *Batman* hit cinemas in the summer of 1989, Warner Bros were quietly confident that their big-screen reinvention of Bob Kane's Dark Knight Detective had the potential to spawn a lucrative film franchise. The studio were spending $20,000 a week to store Anton Furst's Gotham City sets at Pinewood Studios, which they aimed to use for a further two instalments, and when *Batman* went on to dominate at the box office it was inevitable that a sequel would soon follow. *Batman* scribe Sam Hamm was given the go-ahead to commence work on a first draft and there was increasing speculation that *Batman 2* would be fast-tracked into production for a May 1990 shoot.

While Warner Bros were eager to push on with their plans, director Tim Burton was less keen on an immediate return to Gotham City. The young filmmaker had endured a trying time on *Batman*, describing his experience as a 'nightmare', and was worn out from the pressures of his first big-budget studio production. Furthermore, Burton felt disconnected from *Batman*, leaving him unsure of what he could bring to a sequel; instead, he planned to return to more personal material for his fourth feature, realizing a project that had been gestating in his mind since childhood. Inspired by an image he had created of a man with scissors instead of hands, Burton contracted novelist Caroline Thompson (*First Born*,

1984) to develop a screenplay for *Edward Scissorhands* (1990), a fantasy romance about a socially excluded artificial man who finds himself living with a suburban American family after the death of his creator. Going into production at Twentieth Century Fox, the $20m project marked the first collaboration between Burton and actor Johnny Depp (*A Nightmare on Elm Street*, 1984), and also featured a supporting cast that included Winona Ryder (*Beetlejuice*), Dianne Wiest (*Hannah and Her Sisters*, 1986) and Anthony Michael Hall (*The Breakfast Club*, 1985), along with Burton's long-time idol Vincent Price, in what proved to be the veteran actor's final on-screen role.

Although Tim Burton was busy prepping *Edward Scissorhands* at Fox, progress continued on *Batman 2* as Sam Hamm delivered the first draft of the screenplay to Warner Bros. Taking the form of a direct sequel to the first movie, the script further explored a number of elements from *Batman*, such as Bruce Wayne's relationship with Vicki Vale and the reasons behind Jack Napier's murder of Bruce's parents. Furthermore, it also introduced the character of Dick Grayson, who had been removed from the screenplay of the first movie late in the pre-production stage. The central narrative for Hamm's *Batman 2* concerned a plot by the Penguin – whose name was altered from Oswald Cobblepot to that of 'Mr Boniface' – and Selina Kyle's Catwoman to steal artefacts from each of Gotham's 'Five Families', hoping to understand a map leading to a fortune in buried treasure by combining them together. After acquiring the map, the villains discover the treasure to be hidden in a cave beneath Wayne Manor, leading to a climactic showdown between Batman and the Penguin inside the Batcave, during which the criminal mastermind plummets down a crevice to his death.

'I would just keep looking at [*Batman*] and thinking it could have been better,' reflected Tim Burton, who found himself softening to the possibility of a second *Batman* movie in the early part of 1990. 'I hadn't done 100 per cent of what I wanted to do with that picture, and part of me felt that I wanted another chance at it.' Despite his departure to Fox, Warner Bros were keen to retain the services of a director with an emerging track record of profitability. A compromise was reached where Burton would agree in principle to return providing that the screenplay met with his approval, ensuring he could inject more of his own vision into the material and alleviating any concerns over studio interference. Keen to go for a completely new approach, Burton rejected Sam Hamm's script and turned instead to a young screenwriter who had been an early candidate to pen a proposed sequel to *Beetlejuice*.

'Tim had the attitude of "I dare you to make me want to make this movie",' said Daniel Waters, who received an Eddie Award for his first screenplay, *Heathers*, a dark teen comedy that had been brought to the screen in 1989 by *Edward Scissorhands* producer Denise Di Novi. After losing out to Jonathan Gems (*White Mischief*, 1987) for *Beetlejuice Goes Hawaiian*, Waters had followed *Heathers* with a co-writing credit on *The Adventures of Ford Fairlane* (1990) and he was busy working on *Hudson Hawk* (1991) in Italy when he received a call from Tim Burton for an initial discussion about *Batman 2*. 'He had some ideas, but he did not have a story … the only thing Tim knew was that he wanted the Penguin and Catwoman.'

Impressing the filmmaker with his vision for the script, Waters was brought in by Warner Bros to develop a new draft. To research the character, Waters immersed himself in the *Batman* universe and set about creating his own tale, jettisoning the majority of Sam Hamm's draft save for the alliance between Catwoman and the Penguin, the framing of Batman for murder and a handful of references to Vicki Vale and the Joker. Rather than a hunt for buried treasure, Waters devised a plot that would see the Penguin running for mayor of Gotham City, drawing parallels to the storyline of the episodes 'Hizzoner the Penguin' and 'Dizzonner the Penguin' from the second season of the 1960s *Batman* television series. Waters' initial 160-page draft also incorporated the character of Harvey Dent, who would end the film as Two-Face after being scarred in a climactic explosion. Robin also remained present at the behest of Mark Canton, then-Executive Vice President of Worldwide Motion Picture Production at Warner Bros, with the Boy Wonder re-envisioned as the leader of a juvenile gang.

*Edward Scissorhands* opened in December 1990 and went on to gross over $86m at the box office, giving Tim Burton his fourth consecutive hit. The filmmaker had already signed on with Disney to develop the stop-motion animation *The Nightmare Before Christmas* (1993) with fellow *The Fox and the Hound* animator Henry Selick as director, and as his stock had risen considerably since their initial deal, if Warner Bros wanted Burton to deliver a second *Batman* movie, this time it would have to be on his terms. To obtain his participation, the studio agreed to hand creative control of the project over to the filmmaker, who also took on the role of producer alongside Denise Di Novi, relegating Jon Peters and Peter Guber to nominal executive producer credits. The studio further affirmed their commitment to Burton by granting his request to film in California, despite spending a small fortune keeping *Batman*'s Gotham City sets in storage at Pinewood Studios.

Having secured Tim Burton, the next step for Warner Bros was to finalize a deal with Michael Keaton, who like the director had never been contracted to reprise his role as Bruce Wayne/Batman for any potential sequels. Similarly, the *Beetlejuice* star had no burning desire to don the cape and cowl once more, but Keaton was eventually swayed by the opportunity to work with Burton for a third time, along with a healthy pay increase that saw his *Batman* salary

doubled to a reported eight-figure sum. With both director and star confirmed to return, the film – which would eventually come to be referred to as *Batman Returns* – was officially moved into pre-production in early 1991, and this time there would be little doubt that it truly was 'A Tim Burton Film'.

Now that he had committed to the project, the first priority for Tim Burton was to perfect his narrative, with Daniel Waters setting out to revise the script based on feedback from the director. Given Burton's firm insistence on keeping the sequel distinct from the original, Waters was tasked with developing a new antagonist to fulfil the role of Harvey Dent; taking his place was a newly created character, the evil businessman Max Shreck (a reference to the German actor Max Schreck, star of the 1922 silent classic *Nosferatu, A Symphony of Horror*), who was originally conceived as the Penguin's 'normal' brother. Waters also revised the Robin character, transforming him from a juvenile gang member to a street-wise African-American garage mechanic known as 'The Kid'. As Waters set about refining the script and its characters, Burton began the search for actors to populate his latest vision of Gotham City.

Just as Jack Nicholson had been an obvious choice to portray the Clown Prince of Crime in *Batman*, given the size and stature of the Penguin – a character considered by Warner Bros to be the second most popular villain of the Rogues Gallery behind the Joker – Burton and Daniel Waters both had an inkling during the scripting stage that the part could eventually fall to the diminutive actor Danny DeVito (*Throw Momma from the Train*, 1987). Nevertheless, Burton also gave consideration to the possibility of casting screen icon and twice Academy Award-winner Marlon Brando (*On the Waterfront*, 1954, and *The Godfather*, 1972), a choice strongly opposed by *Batman* co-creator Bob Kane. Other names mentioned as potential candidates included John Candy (*Planes, Trains and Automobiles*, 1987), Bob Hoskins (*Who Framed Roger Rabbit?*, 1988) and Christopher Lloyd (*Back to the Future*), along with another double Oscar-winner in Dustin Hoffman (*Kramer vs Kramer*, 1979, and *Rain Man*, 1988). However, as anticipated, it was Danny DeVito who ultimately secured the role.

After graduating from the American Academy of Dramatic Arts in 1966, Danny DeVito made his screen debut as a thug in the little-known drama *Dreams of Glass* (1970) before going on to appear in a number of minor stage and screen roles, including a supporting turn in an off-Broadway production of *One Flew Over the Cuckoo's Nest*, a part he later reprised for the 1975 film version alongside Jack Nicholson. However, DeVito's real breakthrough came with his Emmy Award and Golden Globe-winning turn as Louie De Palma in the classic television comedy series *Taxi* (1978–83), a part that opened the door to a string of memorable comic roles in the likes of *Romancing the Stone* (1984), *The Jewel of the Nile* (1985), *Ruthless People* (1986) and *Twins* (1988), along with his directorial efforts *Throw Momma from the Train* and *The War of the Roses* (1989). Long rumoured to be the number one choice for the Penguin, DeVito was initially sceptical but accepted the role after a single meeting with Tim Burton, during which he was impressed by the director's take on the character.

While the casting of the Penguin proved straightforward, that was certainly not the case when it came to finding an actress to star as Catwoman, the feline felon who had made her first appearance in the comic book story 'The Cat' by Bill Finger, published in *Batman* #1 (Spring 1940). Unsurprisingly, a host of Hollywood actresses were thought to be in competition for the coveted part, including Ellen Barkin (*Switch*, 1991), Bridget Fonda (*The Godfather: Part III*, 1990), Jennifer Jason Leigh (*The Hitcher*, 1986), Madonna (*Dick Tracy*, 1990), Demi Moore (*Ghost*, 1990), Lena Olin (*Enemies: A Love Story*, 1989), Susan Sarandon (*Thelma & Louise*, 1991), Brooke Shields (*The Blue Lagoon*, 1980) and Debra Winger (*An Officer and a Gentleman*, 1982), along with Oscar-winners Cher (*Moonstruck*, 1987), Geena Davis (*The Accidental Tourist*, 1988), Jodie Foster (*The Accused*, 1988) and Meryl Streep (*Kramer vs Kramer* and *Sophie's Choice*, 1982).

Initially offered – and accepting – the role of Selina Kyle/Catwoman was Annette Bening, an actress who had made her screen debut in the

With the 1966 *Batman* series, executive producer William Dozier
planned to take full advantage of the boom in colour TV to recreate
a dynamic visual style unlike anything else on television. The show
itself would be presented as 'high camp'.

When asked about his approach to playing Batman, Adam West, pictured here with Burt Ward as Robin, said: 'With each script and new situation, I saw something funny in it. But I could never let the audience think that I thought it was funny'.

To secure Jack Nicholson's participation in the 1989 *Batman* film, the studio granted him one of the most lucrative contracts in Hollywood history; he received a $6m upfront salary and a percentage of the total box-office gross and merchandizing sales, a deal which is rumoured to have netted him between $50m and $75m in total.

When Michael Keaton was chosen for the role of Batman, alongside Golden Globe winner Kim Basinger as Vicki Vale, angry fans, who objected to the 'jokey' tone established by the television series, bombarded Warner Bros with over 50,000 letters of complaint.

After an initially cool reception from fans, Keaton proved to be a success as Batman and, in the 1992 film *Batman Returns*, his salary was doubled to a reported eight-figure sum.

1988 comedy *The Great Outdoors* before earning an Academy Award nomination for her supporting performance in Stephen Frears' crime thriller *The Grifters* (1990). Bening was forced to pull out of the film after falling pregnant, with Sean Young – Burton's original choice for Vicki Vale in *Batman* – then lobbying hard to win the part. After losing out to Kim Basinger when she suffered a broken arm during rehearsals for *Batman*, Young felt that she deserved a role in the sequel and turned up to the studio dressed in full Catwoman attire, confronting Warner Bros executive Mark Canton and demanding to speak to the director over his failure to cast her in the movie.

Young's efforts to secure the part of Catwoman would prove futile as Tim Burton chose to replace Annette Bening with the only other candidate he felt suitable for the role, the Golden Globe-winning actress Michelle Pfeiffer (*The Fabulous Baker Boys*, 1989), who signed on for a fee of $3m and a percentage of the gross. Beginning her career in 1979 with a number of small film and television appearances, Pfeiffer landed her first major role in 1982 with the musical sequel *Grease 2* before demonstrating her potential the following year with a well-received supporting turn in Brian De Palma's crime epic *Scarface* (1983). After tasting box-office success in 1987 alongside Jack Nicholson and fellow Catwoman contenders Cher and Susan Sarandon in *The Witches of Eastwick*, Pfeiffer then delivered a run of critically acclaimed performances that saw her contend for

Golden Globes over four consecutive years, receiving nominations for *Married to the Mob* (1988), *The Russia House* (1990) and *Frankie and Johnny* (1991) and taking home the award for *The Fabulous Baker Boys*, a role that also provided the actress with her second Oscar nomination after *Dangerous Liaisons* (1988).

To portray the ruthless business mogul Max Shreck, Burton turned to Christopher Walken, an actor whose intense performance in *The Deer Hunter* (1978) had been recognized with an Academy Award for Best Supporting Actor, and led to memorable roles in films such as *The Dead Zone* (1983), *A View to a Kill* (1985), *Biloxi Blues* (1988) and *King of New York* (1990). In terms of the supporting cast, Burton chose to retain the services of Michael Gough and Pat Hingle as Alfred Pennyworth and Police Commissioner James Gordon, while newcomers included Michael Murphy (*Manhattan*, 1979) as Gotham City's mayor and Andrew Bryniarski (*Hudson Hawk*) as Charles 'Chip' Shreck. Burton also took the opportunity to reunite with *Pee-Wee's Big Adventure* stars Paul Reubens and Diane Salinger for the small but pivotal roles of Mr and Mrs Cobblepot, after *Batman* television star Burgess Meredith was forced to decline an offer to cameo as the Penguin's father through ill health.

Another notable addition to the cast was that of Marlon Wayans, an up-and-coming comic actor who at the time was best known for being a member of the Wayans family, having made a brief appearance in brother Keenan Ivory Wayans' 1988 blaxploitation spoof *I'm Gonna Git You Sucka*. 'I got paid for almost being Robin. Actually, I was Robin,' explained Wayans in an interview with *The A.V. Club* in 1998. 'I got my wardrobe fitted and everything, and what happened was that there were too many characters, and they felt Robin wouldn't be of service.' The decision to remove the character of 'The Kid' would come late in the pre-production stage as Burton brought in screenwriter Wesley Strick (*Arachnophobia*, 1990) for uncredited rewrites on Daniel Waters' script. Along with the removal of the Boy Wonder, Strick's main focus was the development of the Penguin's master plan to kill Gotham's first-born sons, drawing inspiration from the biblical story of Moses as opposed to the studio's suggestions of freezing or warming the city.

'*Batman Returns* is not really a sequel to *Batman*. It doesn't pick up where the first film left off,' Burton would later explain in his foreword to *Batman Returns: The Official Movie Book*. 'The point was to make it all feel fresh and new. It was the only way I could envision the movie.' In an effort to differentiate between the movies, Burton chose to surround himself with an entirely different crew, save for a handful of collaborators such as regular composer Danny Elfman and costume designer Bob Ringwood, who would share wardrobe responsibilities with Mary Vogt (*The Naked Gun: From the Files of Police Squad!*, 1988), while *Batman* creator Bob Kane remained

nominally involved in the project as a creative consultant. Among the newcomers to the crew of *Batman Returns* were a number of Burton's *Edward Scissorhands* team, including director of photography Stefan Czapsky (*Last Exit to Brooklyn*, 1989) and Oscar-nominated production designer Bo Welch (*The Color Purple*, 1985). Another key addition was Stan Winston, the legendary visual effects and make-up maestro who had won an Academy Award for Best Visual Effects on *Aliens* (1986) and earned his fourth nomination with *Edward Scissorhands*. During the production of *Batman Returns*, Winston would add a further two Oscars to his collection, receiving Best Visual Effects and Best Make-up in recognition of his work on *Terminator 2: Judgement Day* (1991).

A core responsibility for production designer Bo Welch was to oversee the creation of a new Gotham City that would simultaneously match up to the quality of Anton Furst's celebrated designs while offering something 'fresh and new'. 'It's about oppression,' explained Welch on his approach to the visual style of the city, which drew inspiration from Russian, Teutonic and World's Fair architecture. 'It made sense to me that if a city is in desperate need of a hero and is rife with corruption, than it is decaying and it is decadent. So I tried to physically manifest some of those ideas.' To house the sets required for *Batman Returns*, Warner Bros devoted over half of their entire Burbank Studios lot – including their largest soundstage, Stage 16 – along with a section of their New York-style 'Hennessy Street' set, but the sheer scope of the project meant that extra space had to be hired from Universal Studios. Working seven days a week to meet the schedule, Welch and his team of 250 technicians constructed a number of sets including the Batcave, Wayne Manor, the Penguin's crumbling Gotham Zoo lair, a stretch of Gotham City rooftops running across two sound-stages and the enormous, 65 ft-high Gotham Plaza centrepiece, featuring giant sculptures, statues and a 35 ft Christmas tree. Many of these were painstakingly recreated in miniature form, with visual effects supervisor Michael Fink overseeing model work from respected visual effects studios such as Boss Films Studios (*Ghostbusters*), Stetson Visual Services (*Total Recall*, 1990) and 4-Ward Productions (*Terminator 2: Judgement Day*).

Other design considerations for Bo Welch included a number of key vehicles that would play important roles within the narrative. Retaining Anton Furst's sleek Batmobile design from the first movie – albeit with a series of modifications to include additional weaponry and the ability to transform into the streamlined Batmissile – *Batman Returns* would also see the Dark Knight debut a new ride in the form of a jet-powered hydrofoil known as the Batskiboat. Both the Batmissile and Batskiboat were built to full scale (the Batskiboat measuring 25 ft by 16 ft), with 4-Ward Productions also producing highly detailed

miniature versions. Meanwhile, more than a quarter of a century after he created the classic 1966 Batmobile, celebrated Hollywood car customizer George Barris returned to the *Batman* franchise, designing and constructing the sinister Red Triangle Circus Train.

Another aspect of the original movie that underwent a revamp for *Batman Returns* was Bob Ringwood's controversial Batsuit design, with Ringwood and Mary Vogt making a number of modifications to the rubber muscle suit at a cost of $100,000 in order to present a sleek, armour-like appearance. The cowl was adapted to strengthen its features, while a zipper was added to the pants of the 55 lb costume at the specific request of Michael Keaton. Working from initial concept sketches by Tim Burton, the duo were also responsible for producing Selina Kyle's slinky home-made Catsuit, creating over sixty costumes at a cost of $1,000 apiece in order to show its deterioration throughout the film. During the production, Michelle Pfeiffer would find herself vacuum sealed into the Catsuit, meaning that the actress could only perform for short periods at a time to avoid the risk of passing out.

In realizing the character of the Penguin, Tim Burton chose to present a vastly different interpretation from that of the bird-obsessed, umbrella-wielding criminal mastermind who had debuted in the comic book story 'One of the Most Perfect Frame-ups' by Bill Finger, published in *Detective Comics* #58 (December 1941). Based on sketches by Burton, the Penguin of *Batman Returns* took on a much more grotesque and deformed appearance, forcing Danny DeVito to undergo a complete physical transformation. Wearing a bodysuit designed to replicate the movements of human flesh, DeVito's appearance was further enhanced by prosthetic make-up created by Stan Winston, taking two hours to apply to the actor each day. DeVito was also required to use a combination of food colouring and mouthwash in order to replicate the black ooze that seeps from the Penguin's nose and mouth.

To recreate the Penguin's 'army', the filmmakers chose to employ a combination of techniques, incorporating the use of real penguins, actors in costume, computer-generated imagery and mechanical puppets. Six 40 lb emperor penguin suits were constructed to be occupied by little actors, while Boss Film Studios supplied CGI work and Stan Winston Studio engineered thirty remote-controlled robotic penguin puppets. Twelve king penguins and thirty African penguins were also brought in and compensated with their own refrigerated trailer, swimming pool and daily supply of ice and fresh fish. Despite this, the decision to use live penguins drew criticism from animal rights groups when it was discovered that prop rockets would be strapped to their backs for certain sequences.

After failing to make the predicted June starting date, *Batman Returns* officially commenced filming on 3 September 1991 under the fake working title 'Dictel'. Adopting the same shroud of secrecy as its predecessor, cast and crew members were required to sign non-disclosure agreements and carry photographic identification at all times. Warner Bros' strict security measures were so tight that even Hollywood star Kevin Costner was turned away from the set. However, a breach did occur midway through the production when a tabloid magazine published an unauthorized image of Danny DeVito in character as the Penguin, prompting the studio to hire a private investigator to uncover the source of the leak. Furthermore, while visitors were prevented from accessing the set, that didn't extend to representatives from the 130 official licensing partners of *Batman Returns* – including corporate giants such as Coca-Cola, Kenner Products and McDonald's – which once again proved to be a source of frustration for the director.

'The more money that's spent on a movie, the more people get involved and the more you have to deal with business that doesn't actually have anything to do with the filmmaking,' reflected Tim Burton in 2008. 'With [*Batman Returns*] I remember sitting with some people from McDonald's that wanted to know what the Penguin was going to look like, "Because we want to get our wrappers ready." And then I had to answer we had to make the film first and did not know yet what he was going look like. And the fact is that they weren't going to like the way he was going to look anyway. He doesn't really fit in the Happy Meal mode. You get a lot of things like that when you enter the bigger budget things and it's quite unpleasant.'

Coming through the 'nightmare' of *Batman* with his filmmaking reputation enhanced, Burton demonstrated an increased confidence when handling the demands of the sequel. Still, the sheer scale of the production took its toll on the director and what was originally planned as a four-month shoot soon stretched out to six. Principal photography eventually wrapped in February 1992, with *Batman Returns* coming in an estimated $10m over its initial budget of $55m, but the cameras would roll once again late in the post-production stage; as a response to confusion from test audiences over the fate of Selina Kyle, a new shot was composed featuring Catwoman looking out over Gotham City towards the Bat-Signal. With Michelle Pfeiffer unavailable through other commitments, a body double would stand in for the actress, with the brief sequence put together over the space of a single weekend and adding a further $250,000 to the film's burgeoning costs.

Having fallen behind schedule with the shoot, the filmmakers endured a hectic post-production phase in order to ensure that *Batman Returns* met its scheduled June release date. To assemble the cut Burton employed the Academy Award-nominated film editor Chris Lebenzon (*Top Gun*, 1986), who was assisted by music editor Bob Badami (*Star Trek II: The Wrath of Khan*, 1982), while Danny Elfman was forced to work twelve

hours a day, seven days a week in order to complete the musical score. Along with his orchestral pieces, Elfman also co-composed the song 'Face to Face', which was recorded by the British rock band Siouxsie and the Banshees and would feature during the masquerade ball sequence, in addition to the closing credits of the film.

In the run-up to the release of *Batman* in the summer of 1989, Warner Bros and their licensing partners had saturated the marketplace with promotional tie-ins and merchandise, generating a level of hype that ultimately overshadowed the movie itself. Keen to avoid making the same mistake with the sequel, the studio opted for a more reserved publicity campaign for *Batman Returns*. Apart from a pair of early teaser posters, it wasn't until February of 1992 that audiences got their first real look at the film with the arrival of the theatrical trailer. However, the marketing machine moved into top gear as the film's release date approached, with Warner Bros pumping $15m into a promotional blitz that included a flood of television, print and billboard advertisements, making *Batman Returns* one of the most anticipated movies of the year.

## RECEPTION

Director Tim Burton finally got the opportunity to deliver his unique and unrestricted vision for the Dark Knight when *Batman Returns* arrived in North American cinemas on 19 June 1992, enjoying immediate success with a record-breaking opening weekend of $45,687,711 from 2,644 screens. The film managed to retain top spot in the box-office chart for another two weeks but ultimately failed to replicate the stamina shown by *Batman*, finishing its domestic run with $162,831,698, the third-highest gross of the year behind *Aladdin* ($217m) and *Home Alone 2: Lost in New York* ($173m) and almost $90m less than that of its predecessor. This diminishing performance was matched in the international markets, where *Batman Returns* collected a further $103,990,656 for a world-wide box-office haul of $266,822,354, making it the sixth-biggest film of the year; it did, however, manage to surpass *Batman* on British soil, with an opening weekend of £4,307,045 propelling the film to a UK gross of £11,034,105.

Although *Batman Returns* proved unable to match the financial heights of its predecessor, publications such as *Time*, *Variety* and *The Washington Post* all praised the sequel as superior to the original, while *Empire* bestowed another four-star review, stating that 'Burton continues to capture the essence of the *Batman* legend and more importantly his audience's imagination.' The director was commended for his creativity, particularly towards his atmospheric interpretation of a murky and deteriorating Gotham City, but a number of commentators felt that Danny DeVito's Penguin was a poor substitute for the Joker and the film also came in for criticism due to the lack of humour and overly dark tone. 'The second

*Batman* film was – in my estimation – the *Batman* of the 1990s,' suggested executive producer Michael Uslan in an interview with *Batman-on-Film.com* in 2008. 'Almost soulless, very dark, almost vampiric … the best part for me was Michelle Pfeiffer as Catwoman.'

On the awards circuit, *Batman Returns* received Academy Award and BAFTA nominations for Best Visual Effects (Michael Fink, Craig Barron, John Bruno and Dennis Skotak) and Best Make-up (Ve Neill, Stan Winston) and also contended for five Saturn Awards, with Ve Neill and Stan Winston successful in the category of Best Make-up. Danny Elfman was honoured with a BMI Film Music Award and the film received further nominations at the Hugo Awards and the MTV Movie Awards; *Batman Returns* also marked the first time that the *Batman* franchise contested a Golden Raspberry Award – or 'Razzie' – with Danny DeVito pipped to the title of Worst Supporting Actor by Tom Selleck (*Magnum, P.I.*, 1980–8) for *Christopher Columbus: The Discovery*.

In what proved to be a rare and unusual turn of events, audiences reacted to *Batman Returns* with far less enthusiasm than that of the critics, with the film coming under fire for its increased levels of violence and suggestive sexual references. A backlash quickly built up against the movie, led by concerned parents who felt that the content was inappropriate for younger viewers. As a result of this, McDonald's made the decision to withdraw their Happy Meal promotion, bringing further negative publicity to the film. A large segment of the fan community also voiced frustrations over Burton's decision to push his dark artistic sensibilities to the forefront, resulting in a Batman character who kills as freely as his enemies, along with a Penguin far removed from the established continuity of the comic book. However, the response was not entirely negative and to this day *Batman Returns* remains the most divisive entry of the film franchise, with a number of fans proclaiming it to be the highlight of the series.

Despite making a significant profit on their investment of $80m – which was enhanced by a further $100m from video sales and rentals – Warner Bros were disillusioned by the overall reaction to *Batman Returns*. The sequel had failed to generate the same kind of excitement as *Batman* and had fallen some $144m short of its box-office haul, leaving it trailing *Aladdin* ($504.1m), *The Bodyguard* ($410.9m), *Home Alone 2* ($359m), *Basic Instinct* ($352.9m) and *Lethal Weapon 3* ($321.7m) in terms of the highest earners of 1992. Merchandizing sales were also down considerably from the summer of 1989, and to the studio it was clear that the parental backlash had severely impacted on their bottom line. If the franchise was to remain lucrative, then a fresh and lighter approach was needed for the third instalment.

# BATMAN FOREVER (1995)

**Release date:** 16 June 1995 (US); 14 July 1995 (UK)
**Certificate:** PG-13 (US), PG (cut), 12 (uncut) (UK)
**Running time:** 121 minutes
**Budget:** $100m
**Global box office:** $336,529,844

## CAST

Val Kilmer (*Bruce Wayne/Batman*); Tommy Lee Jones (*Harvey Dent/Two-Face*); Jim Carrey (*Edward Nygma/The Riddler*); Nicole Kidman (*Dr Chase Meridian*); Chris O'Donnell (*Dick Grayson/Robin*); Michael Gough (*Alfred Pennyworth*); Pat Hingle (*Commissioner James Gordon*); Drew Barrymore (*Sugar*); Debi Mazar (*Spice*); Elizabeth Sanders (*Gossip Gerty*); Rene Auberjonois (*Dr Burton*); Ed Begley Jr (*Fred Stickley*); John Favreau (*Assistant*); Dennis Paladino (*Boss Moroni*).

## KEY CREW

Joel Schumacher (*Director*); Tim Burton, Peter Macgregor-Scott (*Producers*); Michael E. Uslan, Benjamin Melniker (*Executive Producers*); Mitchell E. Dauterive (*Associate Producer*); Kevin J. Messick (*Co-producer*); Lee Batchler, Janet Scott Batchler (*Story*); Lee Batchler, Janet Scott Batchler, Akiva Goldsman (*Screenplay*); Bob Kane (*Characters*); Elliot Goldenthal (*Music*); Stephen

Goldblatt (*Cinematography*); Dennis Virkler (*Editing*); Barbara Ling (*Production Design*); Ingrid Ferrin, Bob Ringwood (*Costume Design*); Mali Finn (*Casting*).

## STORY

After breaking out of Arkham Asylum, the disfigured former District Attorney Harvey Dent embarks on an immediate return to his villainous ways as Two-Face, robbing the Second Bank of Gotham and taking a security guard hostage in the vault. The police assemble outside as Batman arrives on the scene, liaising with Commissioner Gordon and Dr Chase Meridian, a police psychologist who is immediately smitten by the allure of the Dark Knight. Batman successfully manages to rescue the hostage as Two-Face escapes by helicopter. Despite giving pursuit, the Caped Crusader is forced to abandon his efforts when Two-Face directs the helicopter to crash into Gotham's Statue of Justice before parachuting to safety.

The next day Bruce Wayne pays a visit to the electronics division of Wayne Enterprises where he is introduced to Edward Nygma, a lowly employee who is desperate to impress his idol with his latest invention, a remarkable device called 'the Box' that can manipulate brainwaves in order to broadcast television signals directly into the brain. Concerned by the implications of such technology, Bruce withdraws funding from the project, leaving an enraged Nygma to continue his work

in secrecy. Nygma is soon caught by his boss, Fred Stickley, and attacks his superior, using him as a test subject for the Box. During the process Nygma discovers that the machine enables him to read Stickley's mind and acquire his intellect, before covering up his crime by staging a suicide.

As the police investigate Stickley's death, Bruce Wayne begins to receive anonymous riddles, prompting him to pay a visit to Dr Chase Meridian, who suspects that the sender has developed a psychotic fixation with the billionaire. Chase accepts an invitation from Bruce to accompany him to the Gotham Charity Circus, during which a performance of the Flying Graysons is interrupted by Two-Face and his gang. Two-Face threatens to detonate a bomb unless Batman reveals his true identity, and although Bruce tries he cannot make himself heard over the commotion of the crowd. A countdown activates as the Flying Graysons work to remove the bomb through an opening at the top of the tent, with the youngest son, Dick, just managing to throw it into the river before it detonates. In retaliation, Two-Face shoots down the cables supporting the Graysons and Dick returns to see his parents and brother lying motionless on the ground below.

Seeing echoes of his own personal tragedy, Bruce takes Dick on as his ward and hopes to assist him in overcoming his grief, but the young acrobat is consumed by a thirst for revenge. Helping Dick to move his belongings into Wayne Manor, Alfred notices a symbol on Dick's motorcycle helmet representing a robin – a nickname bestowed upon him by his older brother; when Dick asks Alfred to throw his Flying Graysons costume away, the butler opts instead to place it in a drawer, sure that 'Robin' will one day fly again. Meanwhile Ed Nygma has transformed himself into a supervillain known as the Riddler and forged an alliance with Two-Face. Together they launch a crime spree to raise capital, hoping to mass produce the Box for every home in Gotham, uncovering the identity of the Batman and giving them control over the entire city.

Intrigued by the secrecy over a locked door in Wayne Manor, Dick manages to gain access and makes a startling discovery as he finds himself in the legendary surroundings of the Batcave. Taking the Batmobile out for a drive, Dick stops to help a young woman but finds himself overcome by a gang of street punks, with the Dark Knight coming to his rescue. Dick is furious with Batman for failing to save his family and demands his help in tracking down Two-Face so that he can kill him. Bruce refuses, explaining that taking a life will only leave him consumed by vengeance, yet Dick is adamant that he will settle the score and have his revenge.

Attending a gala launch event for Nygmatech's new fully interactive holographic entertainment system, Bruce challenges Nygma over the ethics behind his invention. Nevertheless, he is tricked into trying the machine for himself, although the process is interrupted as Two-Face gatecrashes the

party, robbing the guests in the hope of luring Batman into a trap. Sure enough, Bruce soon changes into the Dark Knight and chases Two-Face underground, where he is left buried in sand after a giant gas explosion. This time it is Dick who comes to Bruce's aid, revealing himself as Batman's new partner and instructing Alfred to hang his Flying Graysons costume next to the Batsuit.

Aside from his troubles with Dick, Bruce has become embroiled in a love-triangle with Dr Chase Meridian and his Dark Knight persona, having fallen in love with the psychologist but fearing that she has her heart set on Batman. Bruce pays Chase a visit as his costumed alter ego and they kiss, only for her to say that she is thinking about someone else. Relieved, Bruce invites Chase over to Wayne Manor where he reveals his true feelings – and his secret identity. Unfortunately, the Riddler and Two-Face have also uncovered the truth after gaining access to his memories. Invading Wayne Manor, Two-Face shoots Bruce as the Riddler destroys the Batcave, with the duo leaving behind another riddle before they depart.

Regaining consciousness some time later, Bruce examines the clues left behind by the Riddler and solves the mystery, linking the crimes to Ed Nygma. Donning a prototype Batsuit, the Dark Knight is joined by his new partner, with Dick presenting himself as Robin in an armoured version of his Flying Grayson outfit. The Dynamic Duo set off for the Riddler's island hideout in the

Batboat and Batwing. Upon arrival the crime-fighters are separated, with Robin squaring off against Two-Face and falling captive after saving the murderer from plummeting to his death. Elsewhere, the Dark Knight makes his way through the hideout to confront the Riddler in his chamber, where he discovers Chase and Robin suspended in a trap designed to force him into a choice between Bruce Wayne and Batman.

Distracting his foe with a conundrum of his own, Batman is able to destroy the Riddler's machine, scrambling the villain's mind as Chase and Robin are released and plummet down a shaft towards the sea. The Dark Knight manages to rescue both of them using his grappling hooks, only for the trio to be ambushed by Two-Face, who tosses a coin to decide their fate. As it spins, Batman hurls a handful of coins into the air, causing Two-Face to lose his balance and tumble to his death on the rocks below. Later, Chase Meridian is called to Arkham Asylum with Ed Nygma claiming to know the secret identity of the Caped Crusader. Driven completely insane by his machine, Nygma announces himself as Batman, leaving Bruce Wayne free to continue the crusade against crime alongside his new partner, Robin, the Boy Wonder.

## BRINGING BATMAN TO THE SCREEN

Although *Batman Returns* proved to be one of the most financially successful films of 1992, the negative publicity stemming from a public backlash against director Tim Burton's $80m sequel left Warner Bros executives concerned over the direction of their tent-pole franchise. Its increasingly dark approach had upset a large section of the audience, severely impacting on merchandizing sales and causing friction between the studio and their corporate partners. For Warner Bros, there was little doubt that a complete overhaul was needed to ensure that the *Batman* series maximized its popularity with younger viewers and reached its full potential in terms of earnings.

Having grown weary of the pressures attached to the *Batman* series, director Tim Burton was also reconsidering his own position. Since *Batman Returns*, Burton had continued his producing partnership with Denise Di Novi on *The Nightmare Before Christmas* and was busy developing several future projects, including *Cabin Boy* (1994) and *Ed Wood*. Burton was also slated to direct the *Strange Case of Dr Jekyll and Mr Hyde* adaptation *Mary Reilly* (1996) for TriStar Pictures, yet he remained attached to the *Batman* franchise in an unofficial capacity and had already given early consideration to his plans for a proposed third outing. Developing an initial concept that placed its emphasis on the character of the Dark Knight and featured the Riddler as the sole antagonist, the filmmaker then met with the studio to discuss how they could take the franchise forward.

'After the first two movies I went in to talk about a third one with Warner executives,' recalled

Tim Burton in 2008. 'And I realized halfway through that meeting that they really did not want me to do it. And I wasn't sure if I was interested myself. So I think I made my contribution to the *Batman* legacy and I just naturally moved on to other things.' Bringing his directorial reign on the *Batman* series to an end after two successful motion pictures with a combined box-office gross in excess of $678m, Burton also withdrew from *Mary Reilly* and went on to helm *Ed Wood*, his acclaimed biopic of cult filmmaker Edward D. Wood, Jr (*Plan 9 from Outer Space*, 1959).

While he had chosen to vacate the director's chair on the third *Batman* movie, Tim Burton's involvement with the Dark Knight wasn't severed entirely as he agreed to remain attached in a producing capacity alongside Peter Macgregor-Scott, a British-born producer whose credits included *Cheech & Chong's Next Movie* (1980), *Revenge of the Nerds* (1984), *Under Siege* (1992) and *The Fugitive* (1993). Burton also found himself linked to a potential reunion with *Batman Returns* producer Denise Di Novi, screenwriter Daniel Waters and star Michelle Pfeiffer on a proposed *Catwoman* spin-off (SEE 'MISCELLANEOUS SPIN-OFFS'), but the main priority for Warner Bros was to recruit a filmmaker capable of breathing new life into the Caped Crusader by delivering an accessible blockbuster appealing primarily to the younger viewer.

In their search for a new director to steer the *Batman* franchise, Warner Bros cast their eyes towards John McTiernan – a filmmaker best known for popular action films such as *Predator* (1987), *Die Hard* (1988) and *The Hunt for Red October* (1990) – only for McTiernan to encounter scheduling conflicts due to his work on *Die Hard with a Vengeance* (1995). Also keen to try his hand at bringing a superhero to the screen was Sam Raimi, director of cult titles such as the *Evil Dead* trilogy (1981–92) and the superhero-inspired *Darkman* (1990); nevertheless, the studio felt that Raimi's style would clash with their hopes for a lighter take on *Batman* and opted instead to turn to a versatile and energetic filmmaker with a proven track record of tapping into pop culture.

Surviving the 'sex, drugs and rock'n'roll' movement of the 1960s, Joel Schumacher moved to Hollywood to fulfil his childhood ambition of making movies, starting out as a costume designer on the comedy-drama *Play It As It Lays* (1972). Schumacher extended his filmmaking experience throughout the remainder of the decade, working as a costume designer for Woody Allen on *Sleeper* (1973) and *Interiors* (1978), penning the screenplays for *Sparkle* (1976), *Car Wash* (1976) and *The Wiz* (1978), and gaining his first experience of directing with the TV movies *The Virginia Hill Story* (1974) and *Amateur Night at the Dixie Bar and Grill* (1979). Making his theatrical debut in 1981 with *The Incredible Shrinking Woman*, Schumacher followed this up with the ensemble comedy *D.C. Cab* (1983) and coming-of-age tale *St Elmo's Fire* (1985) before delivering a cult classic with the teen vampire movie *The Lost Boys* (1987).

The success of *St Elmo's Fire* and *The Lost Boys* opened the door for Joel Schumacher to further demonstrate his creativity in a range of genres. Along with the comedy *Cousins* (1989), thriller *Flatliners* (1990) and romance *Dying Young* (1991), Schumacher had earned acclaim for his most recent effort, the crime drama *Falling Down* (1993), and he was busy prepping an adaptation of John Grisham's *The Client* (1994) when the call first came in from Warner Bros with regards to the *Batman* franchise. 'I said to Warner that I wouldn't do a *Batman* movie unless Tim said that it was okay, because we're friends,' explained Schumacher in an interview with *The A.V. Club*. 'So I went to see him, and he said, "Please, please, I had a nervous breakdown during *Batman Returns* … I don't want to do another one."'

Securing a new director in Joel Schumacher, *Batman Forever* was given the green light in September 1993 and fast-tracked into production ahead of a scheduled release in the summer of 1995. Looking to avoid another origin story, the studio rejected Schumacher's initial idea of adapting Frank Miller's *Batman: Year One* in favour of continuing to exploit the stock of villains from the Rogues Gallery. With Schumacher busy putting the finishing touches to *The Client* – a film that would provide his biggest hit upon its release in July 1994, grossing $117.6m – the task of developing a story for Batman's third theatrical adventure fell to the husband-and-wife screenwriting team of Lee and Janet Scott Batchler.

Starting their writing career with teleplays for the crime series *The Equalizer* (1985–9) and Christian children's programme *McGee and Me!* (1989–92), the duo had recently established themselves in Hollywood following the sale of an action-adventure spec-script entitled *Smoke and Mirrors*, which was in development at Disney after selling for a seven-figure sum.

In keeping with Tim Burton's original vision for the third movie, the decision was made to retain the services of the Riddler, albeit with an accomplice in the form of Harvey Dent/Two-Face, Gotham's fallen District Attorney, who first joined the ranks of the underworld after being hideously disfigured by mobster Boss Moroni in the comic book story 'The Crimes of Two-Face' by Bill Finger, published in *Detective Comics* #66 (August 1942). Although the quota of villains was increased, the Batchlers' script looked to place a much greater focus on the psyche of the Dark Knight than its predecessors, with Bruce Wayne struggling to come to terms with his dual identity while his own journey to masked vigilante is mirrored by that of Dick Grayson, the future Boy Wonder. Also incorporated into the story for *Batman Forever* were a number of ideas considered for previous instalments, such as Robin driving the Batmobile and the villains gaining access to the Batcave, while the script also included several references to the events of *Batman* and *Batman Returns*, taking the form of a direct sequel to the earlier movies.

Looking to lighten the tone from *Batman Returns*, the Batchlers drew on the immediate post-war *Batman* comic book portrayal of the character for their tale, incorporating the elaborate traps and light-hearted approach of the 1940s and 1950s to inject colour into Burton's dark vision of Gotham City. However, Warner Bros still held reservations over the mature nature of some of the content, while Schumacher felt that the tone could be further 'lighted down' by increasing the 'comic' aspect of the material. To preside over a second draft, the director turned to Akiva Goldsman, an up-and-coming writer whose first screenplay, *Silent Fall* (1994), had led to a collaboration with Schumacher on *The Client*. Goldsman's draft removed several superfluous scenes and plot-strands but kept much of the story and structure that had been laid out by the Batchlers, with his main contributions being to polish the dialogue and increase the level of humour within the script.

With the screenplay in development, Schumacher met with Tim Burton's leading man, Michael Keaton, to discuss the next instalment in the *Batman* franchise. Like Burton, Keaton endured a number of frustrations on the first two movies, and while it had been assumed that he would reunite with his *Beetlejuice* director for a third outing the actor's interest had cooled following the change in stewardship. Reports suggested that Keaton was asking for a fee of $15m plus a share in the profits to reprise his role

as the Caped Crusader, whereas Schumacher was pushing towards the casting of a younger actor for the title role. As it happened, Keaton found himself disappointed by Schumacher's intended direction for the film and chose to withdraw from the project, ensuring that *Batman Forever* would truly represent a new direction for the series.

Much as Michael Keaton's casting had been preceded by fervent speculation back in 1988, the opening for Gotham's Dark Knight Detective would see a host of Hollywood actors linked to the coveted role. Names rumoured to be in contention for the part included the likes of Alec Baldwin (*The Hunt for Red October*), Dean Cain (*Lois & Clark: The New Adventures of Superman*, 1993–7), Johnny Depp and Tom Hanks (*Philadelphia*, 1993), while Schumacher presented a shortlist of his preferred candidates to the studio; among the four names were William Baldwin (*Backdraft*, 1991) and Ralph Fiennes (*Schindler's List*, 1993), along with original Batman contender Daniel Day-Lewis and Keaton's eventual successor, Val Kilmer (*Top Gun*).

A Los Angeles native, Val Kilmer began his career as a stage actor after graduating from New York's prestigious Julliard School. His first screen appearance came in 1984 when he received top billing in the Zucker–Abrahams–Zucker Second World War spoof *Top Secret!* Kilmer enjoyed another lead role in the comedy *Real Genius* (1985) but it was his supporting turn the following year as

Iceman in Tony Scott's blockbuster action hit *Top Gun* that first brought him widespread public recognition. The actor then went on to appear in several TV movies alongside feature films such as *Willow*, *Kill Me Again* (1989), *Thunderheart* (1992), *The Real McCoy* (1993) and *True Romance* (1993); he would also earn acclaim for his work as Jim Morrison in Oliver Stone's biopic *The Doors* (1991), and it was his recent performance as the legendary Old West gunslinger Doc Holliday in *Tombstone* (1993) that convinced Schumacher of his suitability for the cape and cowl. Kilmer accepted the role without even reading the screenplay, receiving a reported fee of $7m for his services.

'I wanted to play Two-Face; I thought it would have been a very unique thing to do,' revealed Billy Dee Williams, the actor who had portrayed Gotham City's District Attorney Harvey Dent in Tim Burton's *Batman*. 'I would have done something interesting with the character, there's no question about it. It's just too bad I didn't have the opportunity.' Having originally been drawn to the role on the understanding that he would return to menace the Dark Knight as Dent's alter ego Two-Face, Williams' contract was bought out by the studio, providing Schumacher with the opportunity to bring in his own replacement. In doing so, the director continued the tradition of casting an Academy Award-winning actor in a villainous role, reuniting with his leading man from *The Client*, Tommy Lee Jones, who had received an Oscar for Best Supporting Actor for his work in

*The Fugitive*, produced by Peter Macgregor-Scott.

A respected screen veteran with extensive film and television credits dating back to the early 1970s, Tommy Lee Jones first demonstrated his ability with a Golden Globe-nominated turn in *Coal Miner's Daughter* (1980) before receiving a Primetime Emmy Award for his work in the 1982 TV movie *The Executioner's Song*. An acclaimed supporting performance in *JFK* (1991) led to his first Oscar nomination and paved the way for Jones to feature in a host of subsequent titles, including *The Fugitive* and *Under Siege* (both produced by Peter Macgregor-Scott), along with Oliver Stone's *Heaven & Earth* (1993) and *Natural Born Killers* (1994). Initially sceptical of taking on the role of Two-Face, Jones was finally convinced to accept by his son and signed up to reunite with Schumacher, giving him the distinction of becoming the first actor to bring the murderous alter ego of Gotham's former District Attorney to the screen.

After being overlooked for the Clown Prince of Crime in favour of Jack Nicholson, Robin Williams was eager to torment the Dark Knight in the role of Dr Edward Nygma and, indeed, screenwriters Lee and Janet Scott Batchler had written the part of the Riddler with the former *Mork & Mindy* (1978–82) star in mind. However, his interest cooled in the wake of Tim Burton's departure and Williams reportedly declined Warner Bros' offer to star, leaving the studio to contemplate a diverse range of actors such as Matthew

Broderick (*Ferris Bueller's Day Off*, 1986), Brad Dourif (*One Flew Over the Cuckoo's Nest*), Steve Martin (*Planes, Trains and Automobiles*) and Damon Wayans (*The Last Boy Scout*, 1991). Also said to have been in contention was pop superstar Michael Jackson, who was already familiar with Schumacher having appeared as the Scarecrow in *The Wiz*, along with Mickey Dolenz of The Monkees, a rumoured favourite of Tim Burton during his brief period in charge of the project.

Despite strong competition, the task of following Frank Gorshin's celebrated turn as the Prince of Puzzles fell to Jim Carrey, an emerging comic actor who had just tasted box-office success with the hit comedy *Ace Ventura: Pet Detective* (1994). Starting out as a stand-up comedian in the late 1970s, Carrey quickly turned his attention to the screen, and after an unsuccessful audition for Joel Schumacher's ensemble comedy *D.C. Cab*, he appeared in supporting roles in the likes of *Peggy Sue Got Married* (1986) and *The Dead Pool* (1988) before co-starring with Damon Wayans in *Earth Girls Are Easy* (1988). Carrey then joined Wayans' sketch show *In Living Color* (1990–4) for its entire five-season run, bringing his unique comic talents to the masses and leading to his breakthrough role in *Ace Ventura*. Signing on for the role of the Riddler just weeks after *Ace Ventura's* release in February 1994, Carrey found himself elevated to superstar status with the arrival of *The Mask* and *Dumb and Dumber* later that year as the three films generated $706m in global box-office receipts, confirming his new-found standing as one of Hollywood's most bankable stars.

Initially cast as 'The Kid' – a.k.a. Robin – in Tim Burton's *Batman Returns*, Jim Carrey's *In Living Color* co-star Marlon Wayans went as far as the costume-fitting stage only to have his contract carried over to the next movie when it was decided to hold off on the character late in pre-production. Having missed out at the last minute for both of Tim Burton's *Batman* movies, the Boy Wonder would finally make his cinematic debut in the Warner Bros series under Joel Schumacher, but – as with the Caped Crusader – the new director's casting choice would differ from that of his predecessor: 'They put me in the third one, and when the third one came around, they got a new director on it and their vision of the project changed. They decided they wanted somebody white to play Robin,' explained Wayans in an interview with *The A.V. Club*. 'I was like, "Hey, as long as the check clears, baby."'

In casting Batman's fan-dividing side-kick Dick Grayson, Schumacher aimed to establish more of a big brother–little brother rapport between the Dynamic Duo, as opposed to the conventional father–son approach that typically defined their partnership. Embarking on their search for Robin, Warner Bros were said to have auditioned a number of potential Boy Wonders, including Matt Damon (*Mystic Pizza*, 1988), Jude Law (*Shopping*, 1994), Ewan McGregor (*Shallow Grave*, 1994),

Toby Stephens (*The Camomile Lawn*, 1992), Scott Speedman (*Net Worth*, 1995) and even *The Lost Boys* stars Corey Feldman and Corey Haim. However, it would ultimately come down to a choice between Leonardo DiCaprio (*What's Eating Gilbert Grape?*, 1993) and the eventual victor, Chris O'Donnell, an up-and-coming actor who was building a firm reputation with well-received performances in the likes of *Men Don't Leave* (1990), *Fried Green Tomatoes at the Whistle Stop Café* (1991), *Scent of a Woman* (1992), *School Ties* (1992) and *The Three Musketeers* (1993).

With a potential *Catwoman* spin-off ruling out an immediate return for Michelle Pfeiffer's Selina Kyle, a vacancy had arisen for a new love interest for Gotham's most eligible bachelor. Rather than drawing on the Caped Crusader's extensive list of comic book conquests, screenwriters Lee and Janet Scott Batchler chose to introduce an original character, the criminal psychologist Dr Chase Meridian, with Rene Russo (*Lethal Weapon 3*, 1992) winning the part early in pre-production when Michael Keaton was still expected to return. Nevertheless, the arrival of Val Kilmer in the lead role prompted a rethink and Schumacher instead turned to a younger actress, Nicole Kidman (*Billy Bathgate*, 1991), who secured the part amid competition from Linda Hamilton (*The Terminator*, 1984), Jeanne Tripplehorn (*Basic Instinct*, 1992) and Robin Wright (*The Princess Bride*, 1987).

Although *Batman Forever* represented a new take far removed from the creative vision of Tim Burton, Schumacher did choose to stick with two of his predecessor's casting choices in Michael Gough and Pat Hingle, both of whom signed on to continue in their roles as Alfred Pennyworth and Police Commissioner Gordon respectively. Joining the veteran duo in the supporting cast were Drew Barrymore (*E.T.: The Extra Terrestrial*, 1982) and Debi Mazar (*Goodfellas*, 1990) as Two-Face's villainous vixens Sugar and Spice, Ed Begley Jr (*St Elsewhere*, 1982–8) as Fred Stickley and Rene Auberjonois (*Star Trek: Deep Space Nine*, 1993–9) as Dr Burton. Having featured as an extra in *Batman Returns*, Elizabeth Sanders — wife of *Batman* creator Bob Kane — was also cast as reporter Gossip Gerty, while Dennis Paladino (*Silk Stalkings*, 1991–9) would give a screen debut to Boss Moroni, appearing briefly as the mobster originally responsible for scarring Harvey Dent in 'The Crimes of Two-Face'.

To ensure a fresh visual approach for the $100m-budgeted blockbuster, Schumacher assembled an entirely new crew, with only costume designer Bob Ringwood and creative consultant Bob Kane returning to their positions for a third time. Charged with bringing Schumacher's ideas to life was his *Falling Down* production designer Barbara Ling, who also happened to share credits with both members of the Dynamic Duo, having worked on *The Doors*, *Men Don't Leave* and *Fried Green Tomatoes*. Using 1930s New York as a starting point, Schumacher and Ling looked to update the colourful depiction of Gotham City from the 1940s and 1950s comic books by drawing on a range of early twentieth-century design styles and combining elements of Art Deco, Constructivism, Modernism and Futurism with the feel of modern Tokyo. Schumacher aimed to present Gotham as a neon-soaked metropolis awash with colour and filled with towering statues and imposing architecture, which would be realized through a combination of physical sets, locations, miniatures and an increasing emphasis on computer-generated imagery.

As with its immediate predecessor, *Batman Forever* was based primarily out of Warner Bros' Burbank Studios, California; however, with the latest movie requiring almost three times the number of sets as *Batman Returns*, an immediate priority for the studio was to secure additional space in order to meet the demands of the production. This came in the form of the 'Spruce Goose' Dome in Long Beach, California – former home to Howard Hughes' legendary flying boat, the Hughes H-4 Hercules – with the vast hangar housing a number of sets such as the 150 ft-long Wayne Enterprises complex, the similar-length Wayne Manor interior, Two-Face's lair and a multi-level Batcave rising over 60 ft in height. The remaining sets were constructed at the Burbank lot, including the Gotham City Hippodrome, police headquarters rooftops, abandoned Gotham Plaza subway station, Second Bank of Gotham vault, Chase Meridian's office and apartment inte-

riors and the 80 ft-wide lair of the Riddler, while a section of the studio's Hennessy Street set was once again converted into Gotham's bustling streets and alleyways.

Continuing his efforts to present a brand new vision of the Caped Crusader, Schumacher opted to abandon Anton Furst's version of the Batmobile in favour of a fanciful biomechanical design. Complete with protruding 'wing' fins, illuminated front and sides and jet exhaust – along with the ability to scale walls courtesy of a grapping hook – the Batmobile took four months to construct and featured a carbon-fibre chassis built around a Chevrolet 350 ZZS engine, giving the car a top speed well in excess of 100 mph. The 'organic' style of the Batmobile was also replicated throughout the Dark Knight's expanding arsenal of vehicles, which included a fully functioning jet-powered Batboat and redesigned Batwing. Built in miniature form by Academy Award-winning visual effects supervisor John Dykstra (*Star Wars: Episode IV – A New Hope*, 1977) and his team, the revamped Batwing also possessed the ability to transform into the Batsub, a vehicle which earned the distinction of being the first in the series to be rendered by CGI.

Sharing wardrobe responsibilities on *Batman Forever* with Ingrid Ferrin (*The Client*), costume designer Bob Ringwood was tasked with implementing director Joel Schumacher's most contentious design change – the addition of rubber nipples to the Batsuit. Hoping to 'sex up' the Dark

Knight's wardrobe, Schumacher drew inspiration from the depiction of the Greek gods and reverted to Ringwood's initial 'muscle suit' design, forgoing the armour of *Batman Returns* in favour of an increased emphasis on 'anatomical correctness'. While absent from Batman's alternative high-tech 'Sonar Suit', this organic look also carried over into the design for Robin's costume, which was itself influenced by the appearance of Tim Drake, the third Boy Wonder, who had made his first appearance in the comic book story 'Batman: Year Three – Different Roads' by Marv Wolfman, published in *Batman* #436 (August 1989).

To account for the demands of the production, Ringwood and his team created approximately forty duplicates of each suit, using the knowledge gained from the previous two movies to deliver lighter costumes with increased flexibility for the actors. Also falling under Ringwood's remit were the extravagant garments worn by the Riddler, Two-Face and the various thugs and street gangs, with Ferrin handling the contrasting fashions of Sugar and Spice and the sophisticated attire of the Gotham elite. Meanwhile, to complete his transformation into Two-Face, Tommy Lee Jones was required to undergo an intensive make-up process, designed by the then twice Academy Award-winning special effects make-up artist Rick Baker (*An American Werewolf in London*, 1981, and *Bigfoot and the Hendersons*, 1987). Consisting of several foam latex prosthetics, the make-up initially took four hours to apply to the actor, but this was even-

tually narrowed down to less than half of that time as refinements were made to the procedure.

In his search for a cinematographer to capture his bold and ambitious comic book visuals, Joel Schumacher enlisted Stephen Goldblatt (*The Prince of Tides*, 1991), an Academy Award-nominated director of photography known for his work on films such as *The Hunger* (1983), *Young Sherlock Holmes* (1985), *Lethal Weapon*, *Lethal Weapon 2* (1989), *Joe Versus the Volcano* (1990) and *The Pelican Brief* (1993). With principal photography commencing in September 1994, the bulk of *Batman Forever* was shot on Barbara Ling's extensive collection of sets but the production also employed a number of physical locations. The Nygmatech party at the Ritz Gotham Hotel was filmed inside the Pantages Theater in Hollywood (the exterior was provided by the National Museum of the American Indian in Lower Manhattan), with New York's Manhattan Bridge serving as the exterior for Two-Face's lair and the Riddler's 'Claw Island' created by combining shots of California's ARCO Refinery with a digitally enhanced view of Alcatraz Island. Other sites included the Los Angeles Theatre (used for the interior of Gotham City Excelsior Grand Casino) and the Webb Institute of Naval Architecture (doubling as Wayne Manor), while a section of Figueroa Street in Los Angeles was transformed into Gotham's Pan-Asia Town with the aid of 100 ft of Asian-style artificial store fronts and matte paintings, miniatures and computer-generated imagery courtesy of the special visual effects team.

Just as Tim Burton had been severely tested during his two ventures into Gotham City, Joel Schumacher also suffered a trying time on the set of *Batman Forever*. However, whereas Burton found himself at odds with his producers and the corporate mentality of the studio, Schumacher's source of frustration lay with his cast – specifically his leading man, Val Kilmer, whom the director accused of childish and petulant behaviour. Kilmer was alleged to have clashed with several members of the crew leading to a breakdown in communication between star and director, while Schumacher also said that he was tired of defending actors for their on-set behaviour, suggesting that Tommy Lee Jones had felt threatened by his on-screen partner-in-crime Jim Carrey.

Putting the somewhat temperamental shoot behind him, Schumacher worked with film editor Dennis Verkler – twice an Oscar nominee with *The Hunt for Red October* and *The Fugitive* – to assemble a rough-cut of *Batman Forever* running just short of two hours forty minutes. Despite a conscious effort to lighten the tone from *Batman Returns*, Warner Bros still felt that a number of scenes had the potential to cause distress to younger viewers. In an effort to avoid another financially damaging backlash, the studio chose to remove the offending material from the film, including the intended opening which would have featured Dr Burton discovering Two-Face's

Arkham escape with the chilling message "The Bat must die' etched in blood on his cell wall. Additional edits were made to improve pacing, with the running time brought down to two hours, while in Britain a further ninety-three seconds were trimmed to ensure a PG certificate from the BBFC, which consisted of twenty-nine cuts in total.

Completing Joel Schumacher's reinterpretation of the *Batman* series was an entirely new musical accompaniment courtesy of Elliot Goldenthal, a versatile composer whose previous credits included *Drugstore Cowboy* (1989), *Alien 3* (1992), *Demolition Man* (1993) and *Interview with the Vampire* (1994), which had earned him an Academy Award nomination for Best Music, Original Score. Unlike Tim Burton, who had tussled with producer Jon Peters over the inclusion of two Prince songs in the soundtrack to *Batman*, Schumacher would embrace the idea of incorporating contemporary pop music alongside Goldenthal's score, even going as far as to direct a new music video tie-in for 'Kiss from a Rose' by British soul artist Seal. Joining Seal on the soundtrack were R&B singer Brandy ('Where Are You Now?') and American rockers The Flaming Lips ('Bad Days') and The Offspring ('Smash It Up'), while Irish megastars U2 reportedly received a $500,000 advance for the main *Batman Forever* theme, 'Hold Me, Thrill Me, Kiss Me, Kill Me'.

Although a number of Warner Bros' corporate partners had been left underwhelmed by the promotional campaign for *Batman Returns*, the studio pushed ahead with an intensive marketing blitz for their latest venture. Despite McDonald's cancelling their *Batman Returns* Happy Meal promotion, a new deal was signed with the fast food giant and a fresh wave of action figures, toys and merchandise invaded stores in the months leading up to the film's release. Meanwhile the decision to go for a 'pop' soundtrack would prove invaluable to the marketing campaign, with the arrival of the hit singles 'Hold Me, Thrill Me, Kiss Me, Kill Me' and 'Kiss from a Rose' and the best-selling album tie-in *Batman Forever: Music from the Motion Picture* gaining widespread public attention for the film and helping to build anticipation in the weeks leading up to its release.

## RECEPTION

Having made the decision to take the *Batman* franchise in a new direction under Joel Schumacher, Warner Bros were confident that the latest instalment would appeal to their favoured target audience, and the studio's high expectations were met when *Batman Forever* opened in North America on 16 June 1995. Claiming a record opening weekend of $52,784,433 that stood until the release of *The Lost World: Jurassic Park* in May 1997, *Batman Forever* slipped to second place the following weekend but went on to become the second-highest grossing film of the year in North America behind *Toy Story* with a final domestic haul of $184,031,112, over $20m more than that of *Batman Returns*.

Even more pleasing to the studio was the response from the international markets, where *Batman Forever* earned an additional $152,498,032 for a total world-wide haul of $336,529,144, making it the sixth-biggest hit of the year behind *Die Hard with a Vengeance* ($366.1m), *Toy Story* ($362m), *Apollo 13* ($353.5m), *GoldenEye* ($352.2) and *Pocahontas* ($346.1m). On 14 July *Batman Forever* arrived in Britain, where it continued the trend of outperforming its predecessor, setting a franchise high of £4,703,430 with its opening weekend and going to on prove the most popular instalment of the franchise with a strong four-month run that saw it earn £20,037,254.

While *Batman Forever* enjoyed undeniable success with the general public, it did come under fire from fans who struggled with Joel Schumacher's new direction; criticism was levelled towards the light-hearted, over-the-top and cartoonish approach, while Schumacher's design choices were also questioned, particularly the saturation of neon lighting and his decision to introduce nipples to the heroes' costumes. This – along with numerous lingering shots of buttocks and codpieces – led *Chicago Sun-Times* columnist Garry Willis to accuse the director of injecting a homoerotic subtext into the material, mirroring the accusations of psychiatrist Fredric Wertham in his 1954 book *Seduction of the Innocent*.

As with audiences, *Batman Forever* received a mixed reception from critics, with Britain's *Empire* magazine suggesting that 'Schumacher's spin of the black-suited vigilante is as flawed as it is brilliant, as messy as it is impressive,' a view echoed by *Variety* reviewer Brian Lowry, who wrote that the third movie 'succeeds on some basic levels while coming up short in others'. Opinion was split over the film's visual style and increased levels of humour, yet there was a general consensus surrounding the increasingly commercial direction of the series and the fact that Schumacher's first outing suffered from a thin and uneven script that placed spectacle over story. In terms of the cast, Val Kilmer was generally praised for his portrayal of the Dark Knight but a number of reviewers felt that the performances of Jim Carrey and Tommy Lee Jones were too over-the-top, with the latter's interpretation of Two-Face described as a cheap imitation of Jack Nicholson's Joker.

Along with its financial success, *Batman Forever* found itself competing for a host of prestigious awards and became the first film in the series to be nominated for three Oscars, competing for Best Cinematography (Stephen Goldblatt), Best Effects, Sound Effects Editing (John Leveque and Bruce Stambler) and Best Sound (Donald O. Mitchell, Frank A. Montaño, Michael Herbick and Petur Hliddal). The Academy of Science Fiction, Fantasy & Horror Films nominated *Batman Forever* for four Saturn Awards (Best Costumes, Best Make-up, Best Special Effects and Best Fantasy Film), while it also received six nominations at the MTV Movie Awards (Best Villain – Jim Carrey and Tommy Lee Jones; Best Movie Song – 'Kiss from a Rose' and 'Hold Me, Thrill Me, Kiss Me, Kill Me'; Most Desirable Female – Nicole Kidman; and Most Desirable Male – Val Kilmer) and Elliot Goldenthal contended for Grammy Award for Best Instrumental Composition Written for a Motion Picture or for Television. Seal received a BMI Award for Most Performed Song from a Film, with Elliot Goldenthal and U2 winning ASCAP Awards for Top Box Office Films and Most Performed Songs from Motion Pictures respectively. The Brit Awards honoured *Batman Forever* with Best Soundtrack, while U2's 'Hold Me, Thrill Me, Kiss Me, Kill Me' also competed for two further gongs – the Golden Globe for Best Original Song – Motion Picture and the Razzie Award for Worst Original Song.

'*Batman Forever*, no question about it, was the Dick Sprang, Batman and Robin, Bill Finger-written stories of the 40s and 50s,' reflected executive producer Michael Uslan in an interview with *Batman-on-Film.com*. 'Batman and Robin jumping across the keys of giant typewriters and having this amazing, grotesque Rogues Gallery of supervillains.' For Warner Bros, this light-hearted approach had proved to be a recipe for fiscal success; keen to exploit this, the studio contacted Joel Schumacher about an immediate sequel, fast-tracking this through production to arrive in cinemas in June 1997 and leading to the darkest period of the Caped Crusader's screen history.

## BATMAN & ROBIN (1997)

Release date: 20 June 1997 (US); 27 June 1997 (UK)
Certificate: PG-13 (US); PG (UK)
Running time: 125 minutes
Budget: $125m
Global box office: $238,207,122

### CAST

Arnold Schwarzenegger (*Dr Victor Fries/Mr Freeze*); George Clooney (*Bruce Wayne/Batman*); Chris O'Donnell (*Dick Grayson/Robin*); Uma Thurman (*Dr Pamela Isley/Poison Ivy*); Alicia Silverstone (*Barbara Wilson/Batgirl*); Michael Gough (*Alfred Pennyworth*); Pat Hingle (*Commissioner James Gordon*); John Glover (*Dr Jason Woodrue*); Elle Macpherson (*Julie Madison*); Vivica A. Fox (*Ms B. Haven*); Vendela K. Thommessen (*Nora Fries*); Elizabeth Sanders (*Gossip Gerty*); Jeep Swenson (*Bane*).

### KEY CREW

Joel Schumacher (*Director*); Peter Macgregor-Scott (*Producer*); Michael E. Uslan, Benjamin Melniker (*Executive Producers*); Mitchell E. Dauterive (*Associate Producer*); William M. Elvin (*Co-producer*); Akiva Goldsman (*Screenplay*); Bob Kane (*Characters*); Elliot Goldenthal (*Music*); Stephen Goldblatt (*Cinematography*); Dennis Virkler (*Editing*); Barbara Ling (*Production Design*); Ingrid Ferrin, Robert Turturice (*Costume Design*); Mali Finn (*Casting*).

### STORY

Batman and Robin respond to a break-in at the Gotham Museum of Art only to find it covered in ice at the hands of a new villain, Mr Freeze, who is there to steal a valuable diamond to power his high-tech armoured suit. After battling his gang, the Dynamic Duo pursue Mr Freeze as he makes his escape but are unable to prevent him from taking the diamond, with Batman having to end the chase to defrost Robin after the Boy Wonder falls victim to Freeze's ray gun.

Elsewhere, the brilliant botanist Dr Pamela Isley is conducting animal–plant experiments with a new drug called Venom under Dr Jason Woodrue in South America. However, Woodrue has other ideas for the drug, using it to turn a feeble convict into a hulking super-soldier known as Bane, whom he plans to sell on to the highest bidder. Isley is shocked to learn the truth behind Woodrue's experiments and confronts him in her laboratory, where Woodrue lashes out at his assistant and pushes a shelf of chemicals over her, causing Isley to sink into the earth. Mutated by the toxins in the soil, Isley later rises as the seductive Poison Ivy, sealing Woodrue's fate with a toxic kiss; setting fire to the laboratory, Poison Ivy notices that Woodrue has been funded by Wayne Enterprises and departs with Bane for Gotham City.

At the Batcave, Bruce and Dick investigate Mr Freeze and learn that he was once Dr Victor Fries, a Nobel Prize-winning biologist who planned to cryogenically freeze his terminally ill wife Nora as he attempted to find a cure for her disease, the mysterious MacGregor's Syndrome. Accidentally slipping into the cryo-solution, Fries was left dependent on a diamond-powered cryogenic suit for survival while his wife was declared missing, presumed dead. Unbeknown to the Dynamic Duo, Nora survived and is being held in suspended animation at Mr Freeze's hideout, with the villain plotting to freeze the entire city, holding Gotham to ransom in order to finance the remainder of his research and revive his true love.

Along with the threat from Mr Freeze, a rift is beginning to emerge between Batman and Robin, with the Boy Wonder accusing his partner of a lack of trust – an opinion shared by Alfred. Meanwhile Wayne Manor gets a new visitor as Alfred's orphaned niece, Barbara Wilson, arrives on a break from studying computer sciences at Oxbridge Academy. Accepting an invitation from Bruce to stay as their guest, Barbara sees that Alfred is trying to contact his brother Wilfred in India. She soon deduces that her uncle is hiding an illness, with the butler having contracted the first stage of MacGregor's Syndrome, while Dick also notices the teenager sneaking out of Wayne Manor each night on a motorcycle to take part in illegal street races.

Bruce Wayne attends the unveiling of a Wayne Foundation-donated telescope at Gotham Observatory with his girlfriend, Julie Madison. There he is confronted by Pamela Isley, who suggests a proposal to save the environment that would lead to the death of millions due to cold and hunger. When Bruce rejects her recommendations, Isley loses her temper and threatens a plant uprising on Gotham, only for the crowd to laugh at her predictions, stating that Batman and Robin will protect them. Bruce invites Isley to meet the crime-fighters at a charity auction hosted by the Dynamic Duo in support of Gotham Botanical Gardens, where they plan to ensnare Mr Freeze with the lure of an auction for a prize diamond, the Heart of Isis.

Later that night the city's elite gather at the charity ball in a rooftop botanical garden. Poison Ivy shows up and seduces Batman and Robin with a love dust, sparking a bidding war between the partners over the temptress until Mr Freeze crashes the party. Shaking off the effects of the potion, Batman and Robin engage Mr Freeze and his men and successfully apprehend the villain, who is then sent to Arkham Asylum for his crimes. Despite their victory, Bruce and Dick both remain besotted with thoughts of Poison Ivy, pushing them further apart as a team. Meanwhile, as Dick uncovers the truth behind Barbara's nocturnal activities, he also learns of Alfred's sickness. Bruce realizes that Mr Freeze may offer the only hope of saving Alfred's life, but the crime-fighters soon receive word that the criminal has escaped imprisonment in Arkham with help from Poison Ivy and Bane.

Arriving at Freeze's hideout to find it occupied by the police and the Dynamic Duo, Poison Ivy tells Mr Freeze to go and recharge his suit while she retrieves Nora. Ivy and Bane attack Batman and Robin, turning the partners on each other once again, before double-crossing her own partner-in-crime by deactivating his wife's storage tank. Framing Batman for Nora's death, Ivy tricks Mr Freeze into unleashing a new Ice Age upon the world, giving control of the planet back to Mother Nature.

Hoping to distract Batman and Robin while Mr Freeze makes preparations to unleash his scheme using the reflective power of Gotham Observatory's new telescope, Poison Ivy steals Commissioner Gordon's keys and sends Robin a signal to lure the Boy Wonder to his doom. Batman is able to convince his partner that Ivy is trying to play them against one another and they set their own trap, but it backfires and they become entangled in her deadly plants. Meanwhile, Barbara hacks into a secret message intended for her Uncle Wilfred and discovers the secrets held beneath Wayne Manor. Suiting up as Batgirl, she comes to the rescue of the Dynamic Duo and defeats Poison Ivy, imprisoning her in the petals of a giant plant.

Having learnt of Mr Freeze's diabolical plan, Batman, Robin and Batgirl race to the Gotham Observatory as the villain begins the process of turning the city into a frozen wasteland. Upon arrival, Robin and Batgirl come under attack from Bane but manage to defeat the brute by severing the tubes delivering Venom into his body, causing

him to revert to his original state. Batman is also successful in besting Mr Freeze in hand-to-hand combat, although the telescope is destroyed in the process. Batgirl manages to use her computer skills to reposition satellites, deflecting the sun's rays to thaw the city.

With Mr Freeze lying defeated, Batman reveals the details behind Poison Ivy's double-cross and explains that Nora has survived and will be transferred to the lab at Arkham Asylum to allow him to continue his work. In exchange, Mr Freeze redeems himself by providing Batman with an experimental cure for MacGregor's Syndrome. Transferred to Arkham, Mr Freeze promises to make life a living hell for his new cell-mate Poison Ivy, while back at Wayne Manor Alfred makes a full recovery. Bruce and Dick also reaffirm their partnership, gaining a new full-time addition to the team when Barbara decides to stay on and fight crime alongside the Dynamic Duo as Batgirl.

## BRINGING BATMAN TO THE SCREEN

In light of what were perceived to be disappointing financial returns for Tim Burton's *Batman Returns*, Warner Bros made the bold decision to reinvent the *Batman* franchise for the third entry in their lucrative feature film series, bringing in *The Lost Boys* director Joel Schumacher to deliver a 'lighter' take on the Dark Knight with *Batman Forever*. Despite faring less favourably with critics and fans than both of its predecessors, *Batman*

*Forever* enjoyed a record-breaking $52.8m opening weekend, which was more than enough to convince the studio that they had stumbled upon the formula for financial success.

Eager to capitalize on the renewed box-office potential of their biggest property, executives at Warner Bros immediately commissioned a sequel to be fast-tracked through production for release in June 1997. Responsibility for the fourth instalment was passed to *Batman Forever* producer Peter Macgregor-Scott, bringing an end to Tim Burton's involvement with a franchise he had launched so successfully back in 1989. Although Burton would reunite with Warner Bros the following year for the ultimately aborted Man of Steel reboot *Superman Lives*, the task of continuing the *Batman* saga now lay firmly on the shoulders of his replacement, Joel Schumacher.

After tackling directorial duties on his first big-budget summer blockbuster, Joel Schumacher chose to follow his Gotham City adventure with a second John Grisham adaptation for Warner Bros, reuniting with *The Client* and *Batman Forever* screenwriter Akiva Goldsman for the legal thriller *A Time to Kill* (1996). Assembling an ensemble cast that included Sandra Bullock (*Speed*, 1994), Matthew McConaughey (*Boys on the Side*, 1995), Samuel L. Jackson (*Pulp Fiction*, 1994), Kevin Spacey (*The Usual Suspects*, 1995) and Ashley Judd (*Heat*, 1995), Schumacher was busy with pre-production on *A Time to Kill* in August 1995

when he accepted an offer to helm the Caped Crusader's fourth outing, *Batman & Robin*.

As far as Warner Bros were concerned, there was but one creative mandate for *Batman & Robin*, which was best exemplified by the film's promotional tagline of 'More Heroes … More Villains … More Action …' However, as Schumacher would come to discover, the main emphasis of the fourth movie was to maximize its marketing potential at every available opportunity: 'With *Batman & Robin*, everybody got really greedy. They wanted more toys, more machines in the movie, to make it more for kids,' admitted the director in an interview with Nathan Rabin of *The A.V. Club* in 2003. 'Adults think kids are too scared of *Batman*, so we had to make it more kid-friendly, make it funnier, make it lighter.'

With the studio adamant that the next movie be ready for release in the summer of 1997, Schumacher and Akiva Goldsman developed a story for *Batman & Robin* during the pre-production phase of *A Time to Kill*. Drawing inspiration from the camp tone of the *Batman* television series, Goldsman amplified the over-the-top action and light-hearted humour of *Batman Forever*, crafting a plot that saw the Dynamic Duo struggling to hold their crime-fighting partnership together as they battled to save Gotham from the combined threat of the maniacal scientist Mr Freeze, eco-terrorist Poison Ivy and her chemically enhanced super-soldier henchman, Bane. Meanwhile, sticking to the 'More …' directive, Goldsman also ice-related gags and one-liners, further increasing the 'campy' tone of the screenplay.

While Mr Freeze had previously tormented the Dynamic Duo as a Special Guest Villain in three episodes of the *Batman* television series, *Batman & Robin* marked the live-action debut for his partner-in-crime: Dr Pamela Isley, a.k.a. Poison Ivy, the botanical temptress who made her first appearance in the comic book story 'Beware of Poison Ivy!' by Robert Kanigher, published in *Batman* #181 (June 1966). After she came to Schumacher's attention with an early supporting turn as the goddess Venus in *The Adventures of Baron Munchausen* (1988), the honour of being the first person to bring Poison Ivy to the screen fell to Academy Award nominee Uma Thurman (*Pulp Fiction*). Having broken out as a leading lady with starring roles in the likes of *Henry & June* (1990), *Mad Dog and Glory* (1993), *Even Cowgirls Get the Blues* (1993) and *The Truth About Cats & Dogs* (1996), Thurman was reported to have secured the part of *Batman & Robin's* femme fatale amid competition from Demi Moore (*Ghost*), Julia Roberts (*Pretty Woman*, 1990), Nicollette Sheridan (*Knots Landing*, 1979–93) and Sharon Stone (*Basic Instinct*).

Increasing the female contingent of *Batman & Robin* was Alicia Silverstone, an up-and-coming young actress who made her feature film debut as a 16-year-old in *The Crush* (1993) before being thrust firmly into the spotlight with appearances in three Aerosmith music videos and the hit comedy *Clueless* (1995). Silverstone was cast as Batgirl, although rather than drawing on the established Barbara Gordon continuity of the comic book series and 1960s television series, she would adopt a newly created alter ego, that of Alfred Pennyworth's niece, Barbara Wilson. Further female additions came in the shape of two supermodels, with Vendela K. Thommessen making her feature film debut as Nora Fries and Elle Macpherson (*Sirens*, 1994) securing the part of Bruce Wayne's newest girlfriend, Julie Madison – a former comic book fiancée of the billionaire playboy who first debuted in 'Batman Versus the Vampire' by Gardner Fox, published in *Detective Comics* #31 (September 1939), becoming Bruce's first love interest. Meanwhile Vivica A. Fox (*Independence Day*, 1996) also signed on to appear as Mr Freeze's assistant, Ms B. Haven, for a brief, single-day cameo.

To heighten the challenge facing the Dynamic Duo in *Batman & Robin*, the filmmakers also chose to incorporate a revised version of Bane, the popular supervillain who made his first appearance in 'Vengeance of Bane' by Chuck Dixon, published in *Batman: Vengeance of Bane* #1 (January 1993) before quickly earning a reputation as 'The Man who Broke the Bat' in the classic *Batman: Knightfall* story arc. Retaining nothing of the character's personality, traits or back-story save for his Venom-enhanced physique, Schumacher turned to 6 ft 4 in, 400 lb professional wrestler Jeep Swenson (*No Holds Barred*, 1989) to portray the hulking

*Forever* enjoyed a record-breaking $52.8m opening weekend, which was more than enough to convince the studio that they had stumbled upon the formula for financial success.

Eager to capitalize on the renewed box-office potential of their biggest property, executives at Warner Bros immediately commissioned a sequel to be fast-tracked through production for release in June 1997. Responsibility for the fourth instalment was passed to *Batman Forever* producer Peter Macgregor-Scott, bringing an end to Tim Burton's involvement with a franchise he had launched so successfully back in 1989. Although Burton would reunite with Warner Bros the following year for the ultimately aborted Man of Steel reboot *Superman Lives*, the task of continuing the *Batman* saga now lay firmly on the shoulders of his replacement, Joel Schumacher.

After tackling directorial duties on his first big-budget summer blockbuster, Joel Schumacher chose to follow his Gotham City adventure with a second John Grisham adaptation for Warner Bros, reuniting with *The Client* and *Batman Forever* screenwriter Akiva Goldsman for the legal thriller *A Time to Kill* (1996). Assembling an ensemble cast that included Sandra Bullock (*Speed*, 1994), Matthew McConaughey (*Boys on the Side*, 1995), Samuel L. Jackson (*Pulp Fiction*, 1994), Kevin Spacey (*The Usual Suspects*, 1995) and Ashley Judd (*Heat*, 1995), Schumacher was busy with pre-production on *A Time to Kill* in August 1995

when he accepted an offer to helm the Caped Crusader's fourth outing, *Batman & Robin*.

As far as Warner Bros were concerned, there was but one creative mandate for *Batman & Robin*, which was best exemplified by the film's promotional tagline of 'More Heroes … More Villains … More Action …' However, as Schumacher would come to discover, the main emphasis of the fourth movie was to maximize its marketing potential at every available opportunity: 'With *Batman & Robin*, everybody got really greedy. They wanted more toys, more machines in the movie, to make it more for kids,' admitted the director in an interview with Nathan Rabin of *The A.V. Club* in 2003. 'Adults think kids are too scared of *Batman*, so we had to make it more kid-friendly, make it funnier, make it lighter.'

With the studio adamant that the next movie be ready for release in the summer of 1997, Schumacher and Akiva Goldsman developed a story for *Batman & Robin* during the pre-production phase of *A Time to Kill*. Drawing inspiration from the camp tone of the *Batman* television series, Goldsman amplified the over-the-top action and light-hearted humour of *Batman Forever*, crafting a plot that saw the Dynamic Duo struggling to hold their crime-fighting partnership together as they battled to save Gotham from the combined threat of the maniacal scientist Mr Freeze, eco-terrorist Poison Ivy and her chemically enhanced super-soldier henchman, Bane. Meanwhile, sticking to the 'More …' directive, Goldsman also managed to work an incarnation of the Batgirl character into the story, which much like Yvonne Craig's introduction to the 1960s TV series – was designed primarily to broaden the appeal, particularly with teenagers.

By the turn of the year *Batman & Robin* was gearing up for pre-production, with principal photography on the $125m blockbuster scheduled to commence in August 1996. The immediate priority was to secure the film's eponymous heroes, and while Chris O'Donnell's return as Robin was assured, that was far from the case when it came to the Dark Knight. Having endured a strained relationship with Val Kilmer on the set of *Batman Forever*, Joel Schumacher went on to describe the actor as 'childish' and 'impossible', stating that he had no desire to work with the star for a second time. Further complicating matters was Kilmer's decision to sign on to *The Saint* (1997), for which his commitments would run until mid-July, leaving little in the way of preparation time for a second outing as the Caped Crusader. In February 1996 it was confirmed that Kilmer would not be reprising his role in *Batman & Robin*, with the studio opting instead to find a new actor to don the iconic cape and cowl: 'He sort of quit, we sort of fired him,' Schumacher told *Entertainment Weekly* in the wake of Kilmer's departure. 'It probably depends on who's telling the story.'

Despite rumours that Warner Bros were keen on casting David Duchovny, star of the popular sci-fi series *The X-Files* (1993–2002), the honour of becoming the studio's third Batman – and the sixth overall – eventually fell to another actor who had recently shot to fame through his work in a hit television show. The nephew of singer Rosemary Clooney and actor José Ferrer (a contender for the part of the Joker in the 1960s TV series), George Clooney made a handful of early appearances before gaining his first major role in the short-lived sitcom *E/R* (1984–5), but it would be ten years before a different emergency room setting propelled the actor into the limelight and finally opened the door to Hollywood.

Spending the best part of a decade guest starring in the likes of *The Facts of Life* (1979–88), *Murder, She Wrote* (1984–96) and *Roseanne* (1988–97) – along with low-budget features such as *Combat Academy* (1986), *Return to Horror High* (1987) and *Return of the Killer Tomatoes!* (1988) – Clooney eventually enjoyed his mainstream breakthrough when he was cast as Dr Doug Ross in the hugely successful medical drama *ER* (1994–2009). With his career kickstarted by *ER*, Clooney then went on to explore his feature aspirations with the vampire thriller *From Dusk Till Dawn* (1996), which brought him to the attention of Joel Schumacher as a potential Batman candidate. Becoming convinced of the actor's suitability after sketching a cowl over his face in a newspaper advertisement, Schumacher then approached Clooney, who signed on as the next incarnation of the Dark Knight for a reputed fee of $10m.

For their interpretation of *Batman & Robin*'s primary antagonist, Mr Freeze – the long-serving *Batman* villain who had debuted as Mr Zero in 'The Ice Crimes of Mr Zero!' by Dave Wood, published in *Batman* #121 (February 1959) – Joel Schumacher and Akiva Goldsman initially drew upon elements of the Emmy Award-winning *Batman: The Animated Series* episode 'Heart of Ice' (SEE 'THE DARK KNIGHT IN THE DC ANIMATED UNIVERSE'). However, this characterization underwent a dramatic transformation when Schumacher chose to portray the molecular biologist-turned-supervillain as 'big and strong like he was chiselled out of a glacier'. With early contenders such as Patrick Stewart (*Star Trek: The Next Generation*, 1987–94) and Academy Award-winners Anthony Hopkins (*The Silence of the Lambs*, 1991) and Ben Kingsley (*Ghandi*, 1982) ruled out by this change in vision, there was but one man for the job – Arnold Schwarzenegger, the former bodybuilder and seven-times Mr Olympia whose screen successes in the 1980s had led him on a path to international superstardom.

After moving from his native Austria in pursuit of the American Dream, Arnold Schwarzenegger achieved iconic status in the world of bodybuilding before setting his sights on Hollywood. Receiving his first credit as Arnold Strong in *Hercules in New York* (1970), Schwarzenegger went on to earn a Golden Globe for Best Acting Debut in a Motion Picture with a supporting turn in *Stay Hungry* (1976) before enjoying a further career boost with the bodybuilding docudrama *Pumping Iron* (1977). Nevertheless, his true breakthrough came in the early 1980s, with a starring role in the hit box-office fantasy *Conan the Barbarian* (1982) leading to a sequel, *Conan the Destroyer* (1984), along with the first of three appearances in what became his signature role – that of an unstoppable killing machine from the future in James Cameron's classic 1984 action sci-fi *The Terminator*.

Epitomizing the 'macho' image of the 1980s, Arnold Schwarzenegger rose to become the highest paid actor in Hollywood with a string of hit action titles such as *Commando* (1985), *Predator*, *The Running Man* (1987) and *Total Recall* (1990), while successfully exploring more family-friendly material with the popular comedies *Twins* and *Kindergarten Cop* (1990). In 1991 he reunited with James Cameron for *Terminator 2: Judgement Day*, which pulled in a career high of $519.8m in global box-office receipts, before continuing his run of success with *Last Action Hero* (1993), *True Lies* (1994) and *Junior* (1994). As Joel Schumacher's preferred candidate for Mr Freeze, Arnold Schwarzenegger would receive a reported $25m in exchange for his services, with rival action star Sylvester Stallone (*Rocky*, 1976) and wrestling legend Hulk Hogan (*Suburban Commando*, 1991) said to have been the director's second and third choices respectively. Schwarzenegger's arrival also led to extensive script rewrites from Akiva Goldsman, who accommodated his casting by peppering Mr Freeze's dialogue with a stream of ice-related gags and one-liners, further increasing the 'campy' tone of the screenplay.

While Mr Freeze had previously tormented the Dynamic Duo as a Special Guest Villain in three episodes of the *Batman* television series, *Batman & Robin* marked the live-action debut for his partner-in-crime: Dr Pamela Isley, a.k.a. Poison Ivy, the botanical temptress who made her first appearance in the comic book story 'Beware of Poison Ivy!' by Robert Kanigher, published in *Batman* #181 (June 1966). After she came to Schumacher's attention with an early supporting turn as the goddess Venus in *The Adventures of Baron Munchausen* (1988), the honour of being the first person to bring Poison Ivy to the screen fell to Academy Award nominee Uma Thurman (*Pulp Fiction*). Having broken out as a leading lady with starring roles in the likes of *Henry & June* (1990), *Mad Dog and Glory* (1993), *Even Cowgirls Get the Blues* (1993) and *The Truth About Cats & Dogs* (1996), Thurman was reported to have secured the part of *Batman & Robin's* femme fatale amid competition from Demi Moore (*Ghost*), Julia Roberts (*Pretty Woman*, 1990), Nicollette Sheridan (*Knots Landing*, 1979–93) and Sharon Stone (*Basic Instinct*).

Increasing the female contingent of *Batman & Robin* was Alicia Silverstone, an up-and-coming young actress who made her feature film debut as a 16-year-old in *The Crush* (1993) before being thrust firmly into the spotlight with appearances in three Aerosmith music videos and the hit comedy

*Clueless* (1995). Silverstone was cast as Batgirl, although rather than drawing on the established Barbara Gordon continuity of the comic book series and 1960s television series, she would adopt a newly created alter ego, that of Alfred Pennyworth's niece, Barbara Wilson. Further female additions came in the shape of two supermodels, with Vendela K. Thommessen making her feature film debut as Nora Fries and Elle Macpherson (*Sirens*, 1994) securing the part of Bruce Wayne's newest girlfriend, Julie Madison – a former comic book fiancée of the billionaire playboy who first debuted in 'Batman Versus the Vampire' by Gardner Fox, published in *Detective Comics* #31 (September 1939), becoming Bruce's first love interest. Meanwhile Vivica A. Fox (*Independence Day*, 1996) also signed on to appear as Mr Freeze's assistant, Ms B. Haven, for a brief, single-day cameo.

To heighten the challenge facing the Dynamic Duo in *Batman & Robin*, the filmmakers also chose to incorporate a revised version of Bane, the popular supervillain who made his first appearance in 'Vengeance of Bane' by Chuck Dixon, published in *Batman: Vengeance of Bane* #1 (January 1993) before quickly earning a reputation as 'The Man who Broke the Bat' in the classic *Batman: Knightfall* story arc. Retaining nothing of the character's personality, traits or back-story save for his Venom-enhanced physique, Schumacher turned to 6ft 4in, 400lb professional wrestler Jeep Swenson (*No Holds Barred*, 1989) to portray the hulking brute. Meanwhile John Glover (*Gremlins 2: The New Batch*, 1990) – who had earlier voiced the Riddler in *Batman: The Animated Series* (SEE 'THE DARK KNIGHT IN THE DC ANIMATED UNIVERSE') – was cast as Dr Jason Woodrue, a minor DC villain who first appeared in 'Master of the Plant World!' by Gardner Fox, published in *Atom* #1 (July 1962).

In rounding out his supporting cast, Schumacher once again retained the services of Michael Gough as Alfred Pennyworth and Pat Hingle as Police Commissioner Gordon, giving the screen veterans the distinction of being the only two actors to have appeared in all four instalments of the series. Elizabeth Sanders also reprised her role as Gossip Gerty from *Batman Forever*, while her husband Bob Kane continued to serve as consultant to the project. This familiarity also extended behind the camera, with over 60 per cent of the *Batman Forever* crew returning for the sequel, including key collaborators such as production designer Barbara Ling, cinematographer Stephen Goldblatt, visual effects supervisor John Dykstra, film editor Dennis Virkler and composer Elliot Goldenthal. Ingrid Ferrin continued to serve as costume designer and was aided this time by Robert Turturice (*Clean and Sober*), bringing an end to Bob Ringwood's involvement with the *Batman* franchise after contributing to each of Warner Bros' previous movies.

With just a five-month break between fulfilling their responsibilities on *Batman Forever* and commencing pre-production on *Batman & Robin*, production designer Barbara Ling and her team of artists, model makers, set designers and technicians worked around the clock to realize Joel Schumacher's unrestrained vision of Gotham City. For Schumacher and Ling, the goal was to increase the scope of the city and its environments, a feat they would accomplish by intensifying the luminous, neon-soaked approach of *Batman Forever*, delivering a garish architectural style that the production designer later described as 'World's Fair on ecstasy'.

Much like the previous instalment, the majority of the sets for *Batman & Robin* were housed at Warner Bros' Burbank Studios, along with neighbouring Universal Studios and the 'Spruce Goose' Dome in Long Beach, California. Previously visited locations such as the Batcave and Wayne Manor were completely redesigned in order to increase their scale, while new additions included interiors for the 75 ft-high Gotham Observatory, the Project Gilgamesh laboratory, Poison Ivy's Blossom Street Turkish Baths lair, Mr Freeze's Snowy Cones Factory hideout and the jungle-themed Rooftop Botanical Garden, which stretched across two soundstages on the Warner Bros lot. Another key construction was the Gotham Museum of Art, a gigantic set measuring 200 ft long by 150 ft wide and decorated with a number of large statues including a full-size model of a brachiosaurus. Adding to the challenge facing Ling and her team was the need for several of the sets – including the Museum of Natural History –

to appear in a 'frozen' state, a feat accomplished by covering the area in a reflective polyester film, which was then coated with a clear polyurethane substance to create a hard, artificial ice-like surface.

Having featured in both *Batman Returns* and *Batman Forever*, Warner Bros' celebrated Hennessy Street set was once again transformed into a stretch of Gotham City exteriors, this time serving as the Soho district, while a 300 ft-long bridge was also constructed in a shipyard next to the Vincent Thomas Bridge in San Pedro, Los Angeles. As with its predecessors, the Gotham of *Batman & Robin* was further enhanced by the use of matte paintings and painstakingly recreated miniatures, along with a sharp increase in the use of computer-generated imagery, both in its realization of the city and for elaborate visual effects such as Poison Ivy's rapidly growing plants and Mr Freeze's deadly Freeze Gun. *Batman & Robin* would also become one of the first films to incorporate highly detailed 'digital stuntmen', using a combination of motion capture technology and CGI provided by the visual effects and computer-animation specialists Pacific Data Images.

Similarly to *Batman Forever*, the wardrobe department of *Batman & Robin* found themselves charged with designing multiple outfits for the heroes, with Batman, Robin and Batgirl each receiving colour-coordinated 'advanced armoured suits' in addition to their regular attire. 'George wanted a new Batsuit,' stated Joel Schumacher

during pre-production on *Batman & Robin*. 'He did fit into Val's, but he likes to say that the codpiece had to be made bigger.' Joking aside, the director ignored the heavy criticism towards the 'anatomically correct' costumes of *Batman Forever*, retaining the rubber nipples on three of the Dynamic Duo's suits and taking things a step further with an 'anatomically exaggerated' approach that saw the heroes' codpieces enlarged to near-comical proportions; coupled with Schumacher's fascination for lingering crotch and buttock shots, this led to further accusations of homosexual innuendo upon the film's eventual release.

In terms of the costumes themselves, a number of changes were made to the 'traditional' design of the basic Batsuit for *Batman & Robin*: dropping the yellow background of the Bat-Insignia and straying from the established black colour scheme in favour of a blue–black tint. Robin's suit also received a radical overhaul with a new look heavily influenced by the comic book appearance of Dick Grayson as Nightwing, while a late change to the Batgirl costume saw the character's customary cowl design replaced by a domino mask. Manufactured from a refined latex foam material, the light-weight costumes offered much greater mobility than earlier outfits, with the resulting loss in durability meaning that up to fifty duplicates of each suit were required to satisfy the demands of the production.

While the costumes of Poison Ivy and Bane retained a similar look to those of their comic book counterparts, Mr Freeze's high tech cryogenic body armour received a complete refurbishment. Working from initial concept sketches by Mariano Diaz, four versions of the Freeze Suit were constructed from hand-pounded aluminium. Each weighed 45 lb and consisted of more than twenty separate pieces, which were then used to create moulds for fifteen fibreglass replicas. Adding to the challenge of realizing the suit were the intricate electronics of the design, with each costume containing a circuit of approximately 2,500 neon-blue LED lights powered by batteries inside a backpack. Owing to the complex nature of the final product, five technicians were required to be present on set at all times in order to assist Arnold Schwarzenegger in assembling and removing the suit, and a special chair was also built to allow the actor to rest comfortably between takes.

Completing Arnold Schwarzenegger's transformation into the diabolical Mr Freeze was the make-up design of Jeff Dawn, a regular Schwarzenegger collaborator who had worked with the star on fourteen previous films and received the Academy Award for Best Make-up on *Terminator 2: Judgement Day*. The punishing process was complicated by Schwarzenegger's reluctance to shave his head for the role, with the need to apply a prosthetic latex bald cap adding over an hour to the already lengthy procedure. From here, Dawn coated the actor's face with an acrylic metallic silver paint and enhanced his features with a darker shade of blue. Texture was added by airbrushing blue and white acrylic paint, with opalescent contact lenses used to give Schwarzenegger's eyes a yellow glow. Coupled with the application of the Freeze Suit, Schwarzenegger would suffer an exhausting six hours of preparation each day, while Jeep Swenson was also required to undergo two and a half hours of make-up as Bane, with several layers of tattoo ink airbrushed directly on to the actor's impressive physique to give the impression of Venom surging through his veins.

Leading the Dynamic Duo's ever-increasing fleet of vehicles was a completely modified Batmobile, with Barbara Ling taking influence from classic automobiles such as the Delahane 165 and Jaguar D-Type to present the iconic car as a single-seat, convertible roadster. Created by custom fabrication specialists TFX and measuring almost 30 ft in length, the Batmobile was built around a Chevy 350 ZZ3 engine and featured elongated fins, six flame exhaust pipes, a high-gloss paint job and a significant increase in internal lighting, with pulsating red, blue, yellow and orange LED lights built into the chassis. Given the shift to a single-seat Batmobile, the Boy Wonder would also find himself gaining a new mode of transportation for *Batman & Robin*, adopting the name of Tim Drake's modified sports coupe, the Redbird, for a custom-built motorcycle consisting of a reinforced carbon-fibre chassis and single cylinder 605 cc Rotax motor.

Along with the Batmobile and Redbird, customizers TFX were responsible for crafting three completely original and fully functional 'ice-themed' designs for use by the heroes in the film's climactic third act – Batman's snowmobile-inspired Bathammer, Robin's Batsled hovercraft and Batgirl's low-slung Batblade motorcycle. Also falling under their remit was the realization of Mr Freeze's tank-like Freezemobile, an armoured vehicle measuring 26ft in length and 9ft in height; powered entirely by electricity, the chassis of the Freezemobile was made from carbon fibre coated in foil and took nine weeks to construct. The finished product was capable of reaching speeds of 50mph – an impressive feat given its enormous frame.

Although Warner Bros initially planned for principal photography on *Batman & Robin* to commence in August 1996, the demanding pre-production phase meant that the film was running a month behind schedule when cameras eventually started rolling on 12 September. The shoot itself proved equally as frantic, with the majority of the cast and crew working twelve hours a day, seven days a week in order to meet the rapidly approaching release date. Adding to the difficulties was the need to work around George Clooney's schedule for *ER*, while the star also suffered ankle ligament damage late in the production during a lunchtime game of basketball, forcing him to complete the last two weeks of filming wearing a cast. However, Schumacher

somehow managed to overcome these obstacles and brought the *Batman & Robin* shoot to a close at the end of January 1997, two weeks earlier than anticipated.

Having revitalized the earning potential of the franchise with *Batman Forever*, Warner Bros were happy to grant Schumacher a much greater degree of independence with *Batman & Robin*, allowing him the freedom to fully exert his creative vision. Still, as a result of the overly toyetic and family-friendly approach, there was a growing discontent among the cast and crew with regards to the movie's tone, with John Glover later stating that Schumacher's instructions during the shoot were to treat the material as if it were a cartoon. 'It just felt like everything got a little soft the second time,' reflected Chris O'Donnell on his second outing as the Boy Wonder in *Batman & Robin*. 'On *Batman Forever*, I felt like I was making a movie. The second time, I felt like I was making a kid's toy commercial.'

Regardless of these concerns, Warner Bros were confident that Joel Schumacher would deliver another success, particularly with a hot cast that included 'man of the moment' George Clooney alongside a proven box-office superstar in Arnold Schwarzenegger. Impressed by the dailies of their latest effort, the studio made the brash decision to green light a fifth instalment while cameras were still rolling on *Batman & Robin*. This led to a major change in post-production, with Schumacher opting to remove Julie

Madison's death scene at the hands of Poison Ivy in order to bring the character back for the next instalment. Meanwhile a number of Batgirl scenes were also edited out owing to Alicia Silverstone having put on weight during filming, forcing Schumacher to publicly defend the actress after she was heavily criticized by the media for her weight gain.

The promotional campaign for *Batman & Robin* kicked off in February 1997 when *Entertainment Tonight* unveiled the official trailer, giving fans their first look at George Clooney's Dark Knight. Adopting a light-hearted, humorous approach, the trailer immediately set the tone for the latest instalment and met with a negative reaction from members of the *Batman* fan community, many of whom were already disappointed with Schumacher's previous take on the Caped Crusader. Undeterred, the studio embarked on their customary marketing blitz, unleashing a flood of official merchandise, action figures, and promotional tie-ins. Among these were three themed amusement attractions – the $15m 'Batman & Robin: The Chiller' roller-coaster at Six Flags Great Adventure and identical 'Mr Freeze' rides at Six Flags Over Texas and Six Flags St Louis – although technical difficulties delayed the official opening of the three rides until the following year. *Batman & Robin* also spawned an official soundtrack album, with five songs from the movie – The Smashing Pumpkins' 'The End is The Beginning is The

End', R. Kelly's 'Gotham City', Goo Goo Dolls' 'Lazy Eye', Moloko's 'Fun for Me' and Underworld's 'Moaner' – joined by a selection of tracks 'inspired by the motion picture'.

Despite a $15m marketing investment from Warner Bros, subsequent trailers did little to appease the mounting concerns of the Bat-community towards *Batman & Robin* and many fans took to the internet to voice their opinion. Central to this was the Texas-based film buff and self-confessed geek Harry Knowles, founder of *AintItCoolNews.com*, an increasingly popular movie website that was earning a reputation for delivering insider information from its network of 'spies'. Posting a series of negative *Batman & Robin* reviews based on early preview screenings, Knowles came under fire from Joel Schumacher and the studio, with the filmmaker accusing him of generating a negative buzz around the film with his 'yellow journalism'. Nevertheless, as far as the studio were concerned, the internet held little influence and it would be the general movie-going public that ultimately decided the fate *Batman & Robin*.

## RECEPTION

Pushed through an incredibly tight production schedule, Joel Schumacher's camp homage to the 1960s television show hit North American cinemas on 20 June 1997. Defying a growing wave of pessimism, *Batman & Robin* took first place at the box office in its debut weekend, pulling in

$42,872,605 for the third-highest opening of the year. Still, this was more than $10m below the opening haul of *Batman Forever* (and almost $3m down on *Batman Returns*). With negative word of mouth spreading like wildfire the film suffered a horrendous 63.3 per cent drop in its second weekend, slipping to third in the chart. *Batman & Robin* spent just three more weeks in the top ten – less than any of its predecessors – and went on to set a new low for the franchise, collecting a domestic gross of just $107,325,195.

Despite failing to recuperate its production budget during its North American run, *Batman & Robin* did enjoy some success in the international markets, overtaking *Batman Returns* as it went on to generate a further $130,881,927 in receipts. However, a combined world-wide gross of $238,207,122 fell far short of Warner Bros' lofty expectations, placing the $140m sequel fifteenth in the list of the highest-grossing films of the year and giving the studio their lowest ever return on a *Batman* movie. Although the platinum-selling soundtrack album and an additional $58.5m in rental receipts helped to push the sequel further into the black, the atrocious response to the film would see Joel Schumacher adopt Bane's reputation as 'the man who broke the Bat'.

'No matter how bad you have heard this is, nothing can prepare you for the sheer glorious travesty of the 200-megaton bomb of a film that this is,' wrote Harry Knowles in his review of *Batman & Robin* on *AintItCoolNews.com*. 'This film is so bad, so awful, so vanity ridden with horrible over the top performances, that nothing I can say can prepare you for it.' Although *AintItCoolNews.com* bore the brunt of Joel Schumacher's frustrations over the film's dismal reception, Knowles' damning verdict was echoed by the majority of fans and critics, with *Batman & Robin* coming in for near-universal derision. Although Uma Thurman received praise from the likes of *The New York Times* and *Variety*, many reviewers were stinging in their criticism and attacked almost every aspect of the film, condemning *Batman & Robin* for its weak script, poor dialogue, over-the-top performances, constant attempts at humour and excessively toyetic approach. Its reputation diminished even further over time, with *Batman & Robin* coming to feature as a regular contender for the title of the worst superhero movie, and in 2010 readers of *Empire* took things one step further by voting *Batman & Robin* as the clear victor in a poll to find 'The 50 Worst Movies Ever Made'.

Given the poor response towards *Batman & Robin*, there was little surprise when the sequel became the first instalment of the series not to contend for an Academy Award. The film did receive some industry recognition, competing without success for three Saturn Awards (Best Costumes, Best Make-up, Best Fantasy Film), while Chris O'Donnell and Uma Thurman were named Best Supporting Actor and Best Supporting Actress – Sci-Fi at the Blockbuster

Entertainment Awards. Elliot Goldenthal received an ASCAP Award for Top Box Office Films, having previously collected the honour for *Batman Forever*, and Alicia Silverstone was presented with a Blimp Award for Favourite Movie Actress at the Kids' Choice Awards. Silverstone was also declared Worst Supporting Actress by the Golden Raspberry Awards, giving *Batman & Robin* its only victory from a total of eleven Razzie nominations, including Worst Picture, Worst Director, Worst Screenplay, Worst Remake or Sequel, Worst Screen Couple – George Clooney and Chris O'Donnell, Worst Supporting Actor – Chris O'Donnell, Worst Supporting Actor – Arnold Schwarzenegger, Worst Supporting Actress – Uma Thurman, Worst Original Song – 'The End is The Beginning is The End', and Worst Reckless Disregard for Human Life and Public Property.

In their review of *Batman & Robin*, *Empire* wrote that the fourth instalment was a 'camp end to a dreadful era for Schumacher at the helm of the *Batman* franchise', and many were in agreement that the director had brought the Dark Knight to his knees. The studio had already negotiated a deal with Schumacher to develop a fifth feature but by October 1997 George Clooney was expressing doubts over the future of the franchise, stating that *Batman & Robin* could have 'killed' the franchise. As it happened, Clooney was almost right. Warner Bros had released four films in the eight years since Tim Burton first brought their version of the Dark Knight to the screen and in the aftermath of *Batman & Robin* – it would take another eight for them to bring him back.

# Batman on hiatus (1997–2003)

When Warner Bros first handed Tim Burton the responsibility of bringing Bob Kane's Dark Knight Detective to the big screen, not even the studio could have predicted that the relatively unproven director would go on to launch one of the most successful movie franchises of all time. Burton's *Batman* became the template for future summer blockbusters, kick-starting a multi-billion-dollar franchise and leading to one of the most sustained periods of popularity in the character's history. After leading the series down a dark path with *Batman Returns*, Burton handed the reins over to fellow director Joel Schumacher, who followed up the hugely popular *Batman Forever* with the much-maligned fourth instalment, *Batman & Robin*, an overly commercialized offering which looked to have steered the series to a disastrous conclusion.

Although the latest movie had been financially successful, its hostile reception left Warner Bros facing a major dilemma, having already given Joel Schumacher the go-ahead to develop a fifth entry while cameras were still rolling on *Batman & Robin*. With *Batman Forever* and *Batman & Robin* scribe Akiva Goldsman passing on the opportunity to write the screenplay for the Caped Crusader's next cinematic adventure, Warner Bros hired scriptwriter Mark Protosevich as his replacement in late 1996. As with *Batman & Robin*, the initial plan was to fast-track the film through production for release in the summer of 1999, with Schumacher set for a return to Gotham City alongside stars George Clooney, Chris O'Donnell and Alicia Silverstone.

Entitled *Batman Triumphant*, Protosevich's screenplay incorporated another of Batman's long-standing adversaries as the primary antagonist – Dr Jonathan Crane, a.k.a. the Scarecrow, a mentally unstable psychologist who made his first appearance in the comic book story 'Riddle of the Human Scarecrow' by Bill Finger, published in *World's Finest* #3 (Fall 1941). Also featuring in the script was Harley Quinn – the popular female side-kick of the Joker, created by Paul Dini and

Bruce W. Timm for *Batman: The Animated Series* (SEE 'THE DARK KNIGHT IN THE DC ANIMATED UNIVERSE') – albeit with her back-story being revised to that of Jack Napier's daughter. Meanwhile, the inclusion of the Scarecrow also provided the studio with an opportunity to resurrect the most popular villain of the Rogues Gallery, with the Clown Prince of Crime returning to torment the Caped Crusader in the form of a fear gas induced hallucination.

Despite the fact that *Batman & Robin* was yet to arrive in cinemas, the rumour-mill soon went into overdrive in terms of potential casting for *Batman Triumphant* as the likes of Steve Buscemi (*Fargo*, 1996), Robert Englund (*A Nightmare on Elm Street*), Jeff Goldblum (*Jurassic Park*, 1993), Ewan McGregor and even 'shock jock' radio personality Howard Stern (*Private Parts*, 1997) were all rumoured to be under consideration for the Scarecrow. Jack Nicholson was thought to be open to a second outing as the Joker, while Madonna and Playboy model-turned-presenter Jenny McCarthy (*Singled Out*, 1995–7) were among the names mentioned in connection with Harley Quinn. There was also talk that two other villains would make brief appearances, with Schumacher allegedly interested in casting Mark Linn-Baker (*Perfect Strangers*, 1986–93) and Martin Short (*Mars Attacks!*, 1996) for the roles of Dr Kirk Langstrom/Man-Bat and Dr Jervis Tetch/The Mad Hatter respectively.

'I believe I actually killed [the *Batman* franchise] off,' said George Clooney in October 1997, just months after the arrival of *Batman & Robin*. 'I think my character was uninteresting, and I think that in many ways, that may have been my fault. I don't think they'll do another *Batman* movie now.' Regardless of who was to blame for *Batman & Robin*, it was clear that the series was in urgent need of a fresh approach if there was to be any chance of regaining its credibility. Despite presenting a darker take on the material – with Batman rumoured to be framed for the murder of Batgirl by Man-Bat in the first act – Protosevich's script remained a direct sequel to the earlier movies, and when George Clooney confirmed that he would not be reprising his role as the Dark Knight, Warner Bros briefly considered a replacement before making the decision to cease development on *Batman Triumphant*.

Following the cancellation of *Batman Triumphant*, fans would suffer a stream of constant and often unsubstantiated rumours surrounding the possible future direction of the series. Talk of Michael Keaton and Clint Eastwood being approached to star as an aging Bruce Wayne for an adaptation of *The Dark Knight Returns* proved unfounded, but Joel Schumacher was turning his attention to another of Miller's classic story arcs. Almost a year after the release of *Batman & Robin*, the director met with Warner Bros to discuss the possibility of taking the Caped Crusader back to basics with a cinematic interpretation of

*Batman: Year One*, widely regarded as one of the greatest *Batman* stories ever told. However, while executives were intrigued by the potential of a prequel, they were already giving strong consideration to an original proposal courtesy of the screenwriting duo of Lee Shapiro and Stephen Wise.

'During an unrelated pitch at Warner Bros, we – my writing partner, Stephen Wise, one of the creative execs, Greg Silverman, and myself – got onto the topic of *Batman*,' explained Lee Shapiro, discussing the origins of *Batman: DarKnight* in an interview with *Batman-on-Film* in July 2005. 'We pitched an idea to return the story franchise to its dark roots, which they liked, but what really hooked them was our concept of including the Man-Bat as one of the antagonists.' First introduced in the comic book story 'Challenge of the Man-Bat!' by Frank Robbins, published in *Detective Comics* #400 (June 1970), Dr Kirk Langstrom's hideous winged alter ego had featured briefly in a draft of *Batman Triumphant* alongside the Scarecrow, whose experiments into fear served as the catalyst for Langstrom's transformation in *Batman: DarKnight*.

Set several years after the events of *Batman & Robin*, *Batman: DarKnight* adopted a much darker tone than that of Schumacher's previous entries and saw Bruce Wayne coming out of self-imposed retirement to clear his name when Batman is blamed for Man-Bat's reign of terror. Delivering the first draft of their script in late 1998,

Shapiro and Wise were left waiting on a response as the franchise underwent a restructure behind the scenes. Joel Schumacher vacated the director's chair, with Warner Bros executive Jeff Robinov taking on overall responsibility for the series and opting to pass on *Batman: DarKnight* in mid-2000. With the Caped Crusader no closer to a cinematic return, Robinov then went on to instigate a renewed push to resurrect the *Batman* franchise for the new millennium, giving the go-ahead for two projects to move into development simultaneously.

Turning to the small screen for inspiration, Warner Bros decided to explore the possibility of developing a live-action adaptation of *Batman Beyond*, a futuristic take on the Dark Knight featuring an elderly Bruce Wayne reluctantly handing over the mantle of the Bat to teenager Terry McGinnis. In August 2000 the studio announced that DC Animated Universe regulars and *Batman Beyond* co-creators Alan Burnett and Paul Dini had signed on to pen a screenplay alongside director Boaz Yakin (*Remember the Titans*, 2000), with further creative input from cyberpunk novelist Neal Stephenson (*Cryptonomicon*, 1999). As work commenced on the script, fans' hopes for the Dark Knight's big-screen return received a further boost when it was revealed that a second project was about to go into development, with the studio following up on an idea initially proposed by Joel Schumacher back in 1993.

Just weeks after news of the *Batman Beyond* feature, Warner Bros announced that up-and-coming filmmaker Darren Aronofsky – director of the acclaimed independent features π (1998) and *Requiem for a Dream* (2000) – had signed on to helm an adaptation of Frank Miller's classic *Batman* storyline, *Year One*, with Miller himself tackling scriptwriting duties. First published in *Batman* #404–7 in 1987, *Year One* was a noir-infused reinterpretation of the Dark Knight's origin, detailing Batman's early exploits and the formation of his partnership with Gotham's only honest cop, the future Commissioner James Gordon. Aronofsky appeared to be a popular choice to handle the revered material, with fan approval boosted by the addition of Miller, whose prior screenwriting credits included the sci-fi sequels *RoboCop 2* (1990) and *RoboCop 3* (1993). The creative partnership also strongly appealed to the studio, who chose to pass on the script for *Batman Beyond* in favour of Aronofsky's new interpretation of the Dark Knight – a vision that would take the character further from his established continuity than ever before.

'It's *somewhat* based on Frank Miller's novel … but it's going to be very different than anything in *Year One*, and anything you've seen,' explained Darren Aronofsky in December 2000. 'Toss out everything you can imagine about Batman! Everything! We're starting completely anew.' Aronofsky's proposed changes became the subject of hot debate the following year when *AintItCoolNews.com* posted an alleged script review of the first draft, the legitimacy of which quickly came under question. Describing the script as an urban crime drama similar in tone to *The French Connection* (1971), the review was highly critical and suggested a radical departure from established continuity, with Gordon's role reduced to that of an alcoholic serial adulterer and a number of key characters completely re-envisioned, including a heroin-smuggling Penguin and 'jive-talking' Alfred.

Regardless of the authenticity of *AintItCool News.com's* script review, Darren Aronofsky and Frank Miller spent considerable time working on subsequent drafts, leaving fans to speculate over potential casting choices for the Dark Knight. While the likes of Ben Affleck (*Pearl Harbor*, 2001), Christian Bale (*American Psycho*, 2000), Brendan Fraser (*The Mummy*, 1999) and Josh Hartnett (*The Faculty*, 1998) were all linked to the role, a lack of progress raised fears that *Year One* had slipped into development hell. By the end of the year it was increasingly clear that Warner Bros held serious reservations about the project and the studio finally brought a halt to *Year One* in mid-2002, opting instead to move forward on a pitch from *Se7en* (1995) screenwriter Andrew Kevin Walker that would have brought DC Comics' two biggest superheroes together for *Batman vs Superman* (SEE 'ABORTED SPIN-OFFS').

Following the collapse of *Year One*, details emerged that seemed to add credence to the earlier script review and highlighted the dilemma that Warner Bros had faced with the project. Aronofsky's plan was to reinvent the *Batman* mythos, with the orphaned Bruce Wayne disappearing after the murder of his parents, only to be raised in a seedy part of town by a garage mechanic called Big Al. Growing up surrounded by pimps, prostitutes and low-lifes, Bruce develops an intense anger that he unleashes on the criminal element of Gotham City in the guise of the 'Bat-Man'. Teaming up with a suicidal Jim Gordon to root out corruption, Bruce's quest for revenge sees him take down the corrupt Police Commissioner Loeb before reclaiming his place as heir to the Wayne family fortune. A mature and violent vigilante tale, Aronofsky's take on *Year One* ultimately proved far too dark for Warner Bros, offering little opportunity for merchandizing tie-ins and running the risk of sparking a backlash that could have left the franchise damaged beyond all repair.

With *Batman vs Superman* collapsing just weeks after the project was first announced, there appeared to be little hope of an end to the Caped Crusader's screen exile. Rumours circulated that filmmaking siblings Andy and Larry Wachowski (*The Matrix*, 1999) had declined an offer to tackle the fifth instalment, but with the launch of the hugely successful *Harry Potter* film series providing Warner Bros with another lucrative revenue stream, the studio felt confident in taking their time to ensure that the Dark Knight's return was handled correctly. In late 2002 a pitch was rejected from *Buffy the Vampire Slayer* (1997–2003) creator Joss Whedon that took the form of a new origin story and featured an original 'Hannibal Lecter'-type villain. Despite passing on Whedon's concept, the studio were extremely keen to present Batman with a new beginning – a vision they shared with Christopher Nolan, an emerging British film director who signed on to the franchise in January 2003.

# The Christopher Nolan era

## BATMAN BEGINS (2005)

Release date: 15 June 2005 (US); 16 June 2005 (UK)
Certificate: PG-13 (US); 12A (theatrical), 12 (DVD) (UK)
Running time: 140 minutes
Budget: $150m
Global box office: $372,710,015

### CAST

Christian Bale (*Bruce Wayne/Batman*); Michael Caine (*Alfred Pennyworth*); Liam Neeson (*Henri Ducard/Ra's al Ghul*); Katie Holmes (*Rachel Dawes*); Morgan Freeman (*Lucius Fox*); Gary Oldman (*Sgt James Gordon*); Cillian Murphy (*Dr Jonathan Crane/The Scarecrow*); Tom Wilkinson (*Carmine Falcone*); Ken Watanabe (*Ra's al Ghul decoy*); Rutger Hauer (*William Earle*); Mark Boone Junior (*Detective Flass*); Larry Holden (*District Attorney Finch*); Colin McFarlane (*Police Commissioner Loeb*); Richard Brake (*Joe Chill*); Tim Booth (*Victor Zsasz*).

### KEY CREW

Christopher Nolan (*Director*); Larry J. Franco, Lorne Orleans, Charles Roven, Emma Thomas (*Producers*); Michael E. Uslan, Benjamin Melniker (*Executive Producers*); Cheryl A. Tkach (*Associate Producer*); David S. Goyer (*Story*); Christopher Nolan, David S. Goyer (*Screenplay*); Bob Kane (*Characters*); James Newton Howard, Hans Zimmer (*Music*); Wally Pfister (*Cinematography*); Lee Smith (*Editing*); Nathan Crowley (*Production Design*), Lindy Hemming (*Costume Design*); John Papsidera, Lucinda Syson (*Casting*).

### STORY

Playing in the grounds of his stately home with his childhood friend Rachel Dawes, a young Bruce Wayne falls down a well where he is attacked by a colony of bats, leaving him with a deep-rooted fear of the creatures. Following an evening at the opera with his parents, Thomas and Martha Wayne, Bruce's life takes a dramatic turn when his mother and father are gunned down before his eyes by the mugger Joe Chill. Years later, Bruce drops out of Princeton and returns to Gotham as a young man, aiming to avenge his parents by shooting Chill at his parole hearing. However, Bruce is robbed of the opportunity for revenge when Chill is gunned down in a mob hit to prevent him testifying against the crime lord Carmine Falcone.

After revealing his plan to kill Joe Chill to Rachel – now an intern for District Attorney Carl Finch – Bruce is lectured on the difference between justice and revenge and decides to confront Falcone directly, only to find himself severely unprepared; taking a beating from Falcone's men, Bruce decides to disappear from Gotham. Stowing away on a cargo ship, he travels the world in order to develop an understanding of the criminal mind and gain the necessary skills to wage a war on crime. Eventually this path sees Bruce arrested for theft of Wayne Enterprises property and he is thrown into a Bhutanese prison. There he is visited by a man calling himself Henri Ducard, who offers Bruce a chance at salvation courtesy of Ra's al Ghul, the head of a mysterious organization known as the League of Shadows.

Released from prison, Bruce is told to collect a rare blue flower and carry it to the top of the mountain, a journey that takes him to the temple of Ra's al Ghul. Here, Bruce undergoes a period of intense training under Ducard, confronting his guilt over the death of his parents and learning to control his fear, turning it into a weapon against his enemies. Nevertheless, Bruce refuses to carry out his final test – the execution of a murderer – with Ducard asserting that unless he kills the man he is unfit to lead the League of Shadows in their mission, the destruction of Gotham City. Bruce refuses, duelling with Ra's al Ghul

and setting fire to the temple; the ensuing confrontation sees Ra's killed by falling debris, with Bruce saving an unconscious Ducard from the blaze before making his return to Gotham City on a flight with his trusted family butler, Alfred Pennyworth.

Arriving back home to find Gotham under the grip of Carmine Falcone, Bruce reintroduces himself into society while secretly enacting his plan to bring justice to the city. Assigning himself to the Applied Sciences division of Wayne Enterprises, Bruce strikes up a friendship with Lucius Fox, a former board member unjustly demoted by CEO William Earle. Acquiring a number of prototype materials from Fox – who prefers to remain oblivious as to their usage – Bruce constructs an armoured bodysuit, taking on the form of a bat in order to strike fear into the hearts of his enemies by becoming more than just a man. With the help of Alfred, he converts the cave beneath Wayne Manor into his base of operations and establishes contact with Sgt James Gordon, one of the few honest cops in the city, hoping to gain support in his quest to restore Gotham City to its former glory.

Having completed his preparations, Bruce sets out to confront Carmine Falcone for the second time as the crime lord visits Gotham's docks to oversee a drug shipment into the city. Striking from the shadows, Bruce makes quick work of Falcone's men before revealing to the mobster his striking new persona – the masked vigilante,

Batman. Falcone tries to flee but is easily over-powered by the Dark Knight, who drapes him across a search-light at police headquarters, projecting a bat-like image across the night sky. Batman then saves Rachel from an assassination attempt and provides her with the leverage needed to secure a conviction against Falcone. The mobster is arrested, although he is subsequently transferred to Arkham Asylum, being declared insane by the corrupt psychiatrist Dr Jonathan Crane.

Investigating the drugs seized from Falcone, the police notice a strange new substance, which – unbeknown to them – is a powerful hallucinogenic fear toxin that Falcone has been bringing into the city on behalf of Dr Crane. In Arkham, as the mob boss threatens to expose Crane's fear experiments on his patients, Crane sprays him with the drug, bringing out a sinister mask and introducing himself as the Scarecrow before tormenting Falcone to insanity. Elsewhere, Batman gains intelligence from the corrupt police detective Flass and traces the drugs to an address in the Narrows section of Gotham City where he also comes face to face with the Scarecrow; infected by the nerve agent, Batman is dowsed in petrol and set alight, only barely managing to escape by throwing himself out of a window onto the rain-soaked streets below.

Waking two days later, Bruce Wayne is given an antidote to the toxin developed by Lucius Fox, who is later fired from Wayne Enterprises by William Earle after he discovers that a microwave emitter has been stolen from the company. Meanwhile Jonathan Crane summons Rachel Dawes to Arkham Asylum, where he reveals his plan to contaminate Gotham's water supply with his nerve agent. Since it is harmful only in vapour form, Crane intends to unleash the toxin upon the population using the microwave emitter and sprays Rachel with the drug, only for Batman to arrive on the scene. The Dark Knight rescues Rachel and escapes Arkham, taking her to the Batcave in the Tumbler, a prototype military vehicle supplied by Lucius Fox. Batman administers the antidote and provides Rachel with a further two vials, one for Sgt Gordon and one to mass produce for the population.

Hosting a birthday party at Wayne Manor, Bruce is confronted by Henri Ducard, who reveals his true identity as Ra's al Ghul and explains his scheme to drive Gotham into self-destruction using the Scarecrow's fear toxin. Bruce tricks his guests into leaving the party and fights with Ra's as his henchmen set fire to Wayne Manor, with Bruce only narrowly managing to escape the blaze with the aid of Alfred. Meanwhile the League of Shadows instigate a breakout at Arkham Asylum and unleash the fear toxin on the Narrows, leaving Rachel and Gordon as the only two people not affected. As the police prepare to close off the Narrows, Batman joins the fight against the inmates, revealing his secret identity to Rachel before setting off to prevent Ra's al

Ghul from transporting the microwave emitter along the city's monorail to the central water hub beneath Wayne Tower, which would allow him to contaminate the entire population of Gotham.

Boarding the monorail, Batman engages in combat with Ra's al Ghul while Gordon uses the Tumbler's weapon systems to destroy a section of the tracks, preventing the microwave emitter from reaching Wayne Tower. Batman eventually defeats Ra's and escapes using his grappling hook, leaving his former mentor to perish as the train car runs out of track and crashes to the ground. With the people of Gotham safe from the threat of the League of Shadows, Bruce Wayne gains control of Wayne Enterprises and installs Lucius Fox as CEO, but his happiness is short-lived when Rachel explains that she cannot be with him while he continues his crusade on crime. Later, Batman visits the newly promoted Lieutenant Gordon at police headquarters; expressing concerns over escalation, Gordon reveals that a new costumed villain has emerged and hands Batman a Joker playing card, which the Dark Knight promises to investigate.

## BRINGING BATMAN TO THE SCREEN

'The studio had decided that they wanted to try and revive the *Batman* franchise and had been working on it for a number of years,' said Charles Roven, the American film producer and co-founder of Atlas Entertainment (later part of Mosaic Media Group), the production company behind films such as *Twelve Monkeys* (1995), *Three Kings* (1999) and *Scooby-Doo* (2002). 'When Jeff Robinov came on as president of production, and with Alan Horne there, they sort of focussed in on a desire to create an origination story.' Sharing this preference towards a fresh retelling of the Dark Knight's origins was up-and-coming English director Christopher Nolan, the man whose creative vision would ultimately serve to revive the fortunes of the ailing film franchise.

Undergoing his filmmaking education with a series of 16mm shorts during his days as a student at University College London, Christopher Nolan graduated to feature films with his ultra low-budget, self-financed debut, *Following* (1998). A neo-noir thriller (which, coincidentally, featured a brief shot of a *Batman* sticker on the front door of the protagonist), *Following* was shot guerrilla-style on a part-time basis over the space of a year, and while it was well received on the festival circuit the film made little impact at the box office when it received a limited release in North America. For his next feature, Nolan collaborated with younger brother Jonathan on an idea about a man suffering from short-term memory loss while searching for his wife's killer; released in 2000 to financial success, *Memento* was an inventive, non-linear psychological thriller that earned a host of plaudits including Academy Award nominations for Best Editing (Dody Dorn) and Best Original Screenplay (Christopher Nolan,

Screenplay; Jonathan Nolan, Story) and it has since gone on to achieve cult status.

After demonstrating his talent with *Memento*, Nolan's next film saw him directing Academy Award-winning actors Al Pacino (*Scent of a Woman*), Robin Williams and Hilary Swank (*Boys Don't Cry*, 1999, and *Million Dollar Baby*, 2004) in *Insomnia* (2002), a remake of the 1997 Norwegian film of the same name. Distributed by Warner Bros, the $46m psychological thriller proved a hit for the studio, earning over $113m at the global box office, and leading to further acclaim for the filmmaker. It was enough to convince Warner Bros to invite Nolan to pitch his concept for a new take on the *Batman* franchise and, with executives impressed by his ideas for a complete overhaul of the series, Nolan was officially announced as director on the $150m-budgeted reboot on 27 January 2003. Although the appointment was met favourably within the Bat-community there remained a degree of apprehension, with weary fans still suffering from a string of disappointments as previous revivals failed to get off the ground.

'The creative mandate was really to do something fresh and original and if it wasn't, I wouldn't have gotten involved with the project,' reflected Nolan in 2005. 'For me, what that became was my desire to do something we hadn't seen before – a superhero story told in a realistic fashion.' Joined on the project by his wife and producing partner Emma Thomas, Nolan's first task was to secure a writer capable of juggling this 'realistic'

approach while delivering an exciting story that would stay true to the rich history of the *Batman* mythos and, perhaps most importantly, repair the damaged reputation of the franchise after *Batman & Robin*. To do so he turned to a screenwriter with extensive experience adapting comic book titles, and one who had been a key figure in the current resurgence of the superhero movie.

David S. Goyer received his first credit in 1990 as screenwriter of the Jean-Claude Van Damme actioner *Death Warrant*, and after a number of low-budget, straight-to-video affairs he enjoyed his first taste of the comic book movie with *The Crow: City of Angels* (1996), a sequel to the hit 1994 adaptation of James O'Barr's acclaimed underground series. His breakthrough came two years later when he penned screenplays for the cult sci-fi thriller *Dark City* (1998) and the Marvel adaptation *Blade* (1998), the success of which laid the foundations for a fresh wave of superhero films such as *X-Men* (2000), *Spider-Man* (2002), *Daredevil* (2003), *Hulk* (2003) and *X2: X-Men United* (2003). Meanwhile Goyer's comic credentials continued to expand with scriptwriting duties on the TV movie *Nick Fury: Agent of S.H.I.E.L.D.* (1998), the theatrical sequel *Blade II* (2002) and an unproduced adaptation of Marvel's *Doctor Strange*, in addition to a run as writer of the DC Comics title *JSA*.

'Frankly, as much as I love *Batman*, I don't know if I would have been interested in writing it for anyone else,' said Goyer, who officially signed

1999) as Bruce's loyal butler and father figure, Alfred Pennyworth, after fellow Oscar-winner Anthony Hopkins declined the opportunity. Caine was soon joined by another Academy Award-winning actor when Morgan Freeman (*Million Dollar Baby*) joined the cast as Lucius Fox, the Wayne Enterprises executive who had debuted in the comic book story 'Dark Messenger of Mercy' by Len Wein, published in *Batman* #307 (January 1979).

After Chris Cooper (*American Beauty*, 1999) rejected an approach to portray Police Sgt James Gordon, Gary Oldman (*Leon*, 1994) won the role ahead of two former Batman candidates, Dennis Quaid and Kurt Russell, who had been linked to Gordon since the very first rumblings of a *Batman* prequel in the late 1990s. Finally, completing the Dark Knight's allies was *Dawson's Creek* actress Katie Holmes, who fought off competition from Sarah Michelle Gellar (*Buffy the Vampire Slayer*) and Rachel McAdams (*The Hot Chick*, 2002) for the part of Rachel Dawes, a newly created character who would serve as a love interest to Bruce Wayne while providing Batman with a sympathetic figure in the District Attorney's office, a role fulfilled by Harvey Dent in *Year One*.

Just as speculation had been rife over the casting of Batman, so too were the incessant rumours surrounding possible villains, not to mention the actors thought to be in contention for the coveted roles. However, while the likes of Paul Bettany (*A Beautiful Mind*, 2001), Russell Crowe (*Gladiator*, 2000), Robert De Niro (*Raging Bull*, 1980), Christopher Eccleston (*Shallow Grave*), John Malkovich (*In the Line of Fire*, 1993), Viggo Mortensen (*The Lord of the Rings*, 2001–3) and even rock musician Marilyn Manson were all mooted as possibilities, Nolan would first turn to an actor who had left a lasting impression on the director during his audition for Batman.

'Just to get to work with Chris even for the [Batman screen-test] was amazing and then, I don't know, he saw something in it that he thought maybe he could use for the other characters,' said Cillian Murphy, the up-and-coming Irish actor who had recently made the transition to Hollywood after enjoying his career breakthrough on Danny Boyle's well-received British horror *28 Days Later*. Cast in December 2003, it was a further three months before Murphy's character was confirmed as Dr Jonathan Crane, a.k.a. the Scarecrow, a villain who had first been pinpointed as an antagonist for the Caped Crusader back in 1996 when Mark Protosevich was hired to script the potential *Batman & Robin* sequel, *Batman Triumphant*.

Joining Murphy as the film's primary antagonist was another Irish actor, Liam Neeson, whose turn as the title character in Sam Raimi's 1990 superhero film *Darkman* had led to an Academy Award-nominated performance in *Schindler's List* and recent big-budget efforts such as *Star Wars: Episode I – The Phantom Menace* (1999) and *Gangs of New York* (2002). Neeson was officially cast in

Screenplay; Jonathan Nolan, Story) and it has since gone on to achieve cult status.

After demonstrating his talent with *Memento*, Nolan's next film saw him directing Academy Award-winning actors Al Pacino (*Scent of a Woman*), Robin Williams and Hilary Swank (*Boys Don't Cry*, 1999, and *Million Dollar Baby*, 2004) in *Insomnia* (2002), a remake of the 1997 Norwegian film of the same name. Distributed by Warner Bros, the $46m psychological thriller proved a hit for the studio, earning over $113m at the global box office, and leading to further acclaim for the filmmaker. It was enough to convince Warner Bros to invite Nolan to pitch his concept for a new take on the *Batman* franchise and, with executives impressed by his ideas for a complete overhaul of the series, Nolan was officially announced as director on the $150m-budgeted reboot on 27 January 2003. Although the appointment was met favourably within the Bat-community there remained a degree of apprehension, with weary fans still suffering from a string of disappointments as previous revivals failed to get off the ground.

'The creative mandate was really to do something fresh and original and if it wasn't, I wouldn't have gotten involved with the project,' reflected Nolan in 2005. 'For me, what that became was my desire to do something we hadn't seen before – a superhero story told in a realistic fashion.' Joined on the project by his wife and producing partner Emma Thomas, Nolan's first task was to secure a writer capable of juggling this 'realistic'

approach while delivering an exciting story that would stay true to the rich history of the *Batman* mythos and, perhaps most importantly, repair the damaged reputation of the franchise after *Batman & Robin*. To do so he turned to a screenwriter with extensive experience adapting comic book titles, and one who had been a key figure in the current resurgence of the superhero movie.

David S. Goyer received his first credit in 1990 as screenwriter of the Jean-Claude Van Damme actioner *Death Warrant*, and after a number of low-budget, straight-to-video affairs he enjoyed his first taste of the comic book movie with *The Crow: City of Angels* (1996), a sequel to the hit 1994 adaptation of James O'Barr's acclaimed underground series. His breakthrough came two years later when he penned screenplays for the cult sci-fi thriller *Dark City* (1998) and the Marvel adaptation *Blade* (1998), the success of which laid the foundations for a fresh wave of superhero films such as *X-Men* (2000), *Spider-Man* (2002), *Daredevil* (2003), *Hulk* (2003) and *X2: X-Men United* (2003). Meanwhile Goyer's comic credentials continued to expand with scriptwriting duties on the TV movie *Nick Fury: Agent of S.H.I.E.L.D.* (1998), the theatrical sequel *Blade II* (2002) and an unproduced adaptation of Marvel's *Doctor Strange*, in addition to a run as writer of the DC Comics title *JSA*.

'Frankly, as much as I love *Batman*, I don't know if I would have been interested in writing it for anyone else,' said Goyer, who officially signed on to the project in March 2003. '[Nolan] was going to be telling a story in a way that it seems like the story should have been told, but for some reason no one had ever approached *Batman* that way.' Goyer was also drawn towards the prospect of tackling a reboot, which would not only free the film of the constraints set by previous instalments but would also provide an opportunity for the Batman character to take centre-stage for the first time in Warner Bros' series. 'We wanted to create a character in Bruce Wayne who had a lot of complexity and darkness within him and within his life experience, just like the bad guys do,' producer Charles Roven would later explain, 'and show exactly how close we are as humans to being both good and bad.' However, unlike Burton's 1989 retelling, Nolan and Goyer's take on the character's origin would be one that was firmly rooted in the established continuity of the comic book.

First detailed by writer Bill Finger in a two-page story entitled 'The Legend of the Batman – Who He Is and How He Came to Be', published in *Detective Comics* #33 (November 1939), Batman's beginnings were expanded upon by Finger in 'The Origin of the Batman' in *Batman* #47 (June 1948) but it wasn't until 1987 that DC Comics revamped the story for modern audiences with the release of Frank Miller's *Year One*. This classic story arc was highly influential on Goyer and Nolan's script, particularly with regard to the emerging relationship between the Dark Knight

and Sgt James Gordon, and the inclusion of characters such as Carmine Falcone, Police Commissioner Loeb and Detective Flass. This would also be true of their depiction of Gotham as a city rife with corruption, which would provide the perfect setting to explore the genesis of the grim avenger.

Along with *Year One*, the screenwriting duo also drew upon elements of Denny O'Neil and Dick Giordano's 'Batman: The Man Who Falls' (published in *Secret Origins*, 1989), which explored Bruce's training and development as he travelled the globe in preparation for his return to Gotham, along with the acclaimed thirteen-issue limited series *Batman: The Long Halloween* (December 1996–December 1997) by writer Jeph Loeb and artist Tim Sale. 'DC and Warner Bros were great. They just embraced it,' recalled David Goyer on the freedom afforded to him and Nolan during the development of their story. 'It was actually the best experience I've ever had working with a studio, because they truly trusted us and just said, "You guys know what you are doing and we are going to let you run with it".'

With Nolan and Goyer busy on the screenplay, a wave of optimism swept through the fan community and speculation soon began as to who would be the actor to replace George Clooney as the Dark Knight in a project that was being referred to as *Batman: Intimidation Game*. Early rumours suggested that Warner Bros were keen on Ashton Kutcher, star of the popular teen sitcom *That 70's Show* (1998–2006) and host of MTV's *Punk'd* (2003–7), while David Boreanaz (*Angel*, 1999–2004), Josh Hartnett and *Memento* star Guy Pearce were also said to be in contention. A definitive shortlist soon emerged and early in September eight actors auditioned for the role, including Eion Bailey (*Band of Brothers*, 2001), Henry Cavill (*The Count of Monte Cristo*, 2002), Billy Cudrup (*Almost Famous*, 2000), Hugh Dancy (*Black Hawk Down*, 2001), Jake Gyllenhaal (*Donnie Darko*, 2001), Joshua Jackson (*Dawson's Creek*, 1998–2003) and Cillian Murphy (*28 Days Later*, 2002). While Gyllenhaal was said to have been a particular favourite of David Goyer, the role was eventually secured by Christian Bale, an actor who first came under consideration for the cape and cowl during the development of Darren Aronofsky's *Year One* project.

'What I see in Christian is the ultimate embodiment of Bruce Wayne,' said Nolan in a press release confirming Bale's casting on 11 September 2003. 'He has exactly the balance of darkness and light that we were looking for.' Bale first came to attention as a 13-year-old when he starred in the acclaimed Steven Spielberg war drama *Empire of the Sun*. Although he went on to enjoy a number of appearances in films such as *Little Women* (1994) and *Velvet Goldmine* (1998), it wasn't until his turn as Patrick Bateman in Mary Harron's controversial adaptation of *American Psycho* that the actor firmly established his Hollywood credentials. This elevated Bale to leading-man status

with roles in the likes of *Laurel Canyon* (2002), *Reign of Fire* (2002) and *Equilibrium* (2002), while he also established a reputation for his intense approach and devotion to his work. At the time of his casting, the actor had lost over 60 lb in weight for his previous project, *The Machinist* (2004), and had to undergo a strict, three-month training regime to physically prepare him for the role of the Dark Knight.

'With *Superman*, you can really look at Christopher Reeve and the way that he played it, and he's become the defining Superman, but I don't feel like that ever happened with Batman before,' said Bale on his aspirations for the film. 'In this movie we're making it much more character-based. We want to understand the pain, the anger, the guilt that [Bruce] went through, the obsession and the fanaticism that he must have to maintain those feelings through to adulthood. There is this constant conflict of his rage and his need for vengeance with the fact that he has the philanthropy learned from his father, and the need to uphold his father's good work, but frankly, he wants to kill. He wants to kill but he's having to rein himself in constantly, because Batman never kills.'

Having found his leading man, Christopher Nolan turned his attention to assembling a supporting cast and firmly stated his ambitions by securing the twice Academy Award-winner Michael Caine (Best Supporting Actor – *Hannah and Her Sisters*, 1986, and *The Cider House Rules*,

1999) as Bruce's loyal butler and father figure, Alfred Pennyworth, after fellow Oscar-winner Anthony Hopkins declined the opportunity. Caine was soon joined by another Academy Award-winning actor when Morgan Freeman (*Million Dollar Baby*) joined the cast as Lucius Fox, the Wayne Enterprises executive who had debuted in the comic book story 'Dark Messenger of Mercy' by Len Wein, published in *Batman* #307 (January 1979).

After Chris Cooper (*American Beauty*, 1999) rejected an approach to portray Police Sgt James Gordon, Gary Oldman (*Leon*, 1994) won the role ahead of two former Batman candidates, Dennis Quaid and Kurt Russell, who had been linked to Gordon since the very first rumblings of a *Batman* prequel in the late 1990s. Finally, completing the Dark Knight's allies was *Dawson's Creek* actress Katie Holmes, who fought off competition from Sarah Michelle Gellar (*Buffy the Vampire Slayer*) and Rachel McAdams (*The Hot Chick*, 2002) for the part of Rachel Dawes, a newly created character who would serve as a love interest to Bruce Wayne while providing Batman with a sympathetic figure in the District Attorney's office, a role fulfilled by Harvey Dent in *Year One*.

Just as speculation had been rife over the casting of Batman, so too were the incessant rumours surrounding possible villains, not to mention the actors thought to be in contention for the coveted roles. However, while the likes of Paul Bettany (*A Beautiful Mind*, 2001), Russell Crowe (*Gladiator*, 2000), Robert De Niro (*Raging Bull*, 1980), Christopher Eccleston (*Shallow Grave*), John Malkovich (*In the Line of Fire*, 1993), Viggo Mortensen (*The Lord of the Rings*, 2001–3) and even rock musician Marilyn Manson were all mooted as possibilities, Nolan would first turn to an actor who had left a lasting impression on the director during his audition for Batman.

'Just to get to work with Chris even for the [Batman screen-test] was amazing and then, I don't know, he saw something in it that he thought maybe he could use for the other characters,' said Cillian Murphy, the up-and-coming Irish actor who had recently made the transition to Hollywood after enjoying his career breakthrough on Danny Boyle's well-received British horror *28 Days Later*. Cast in December 2003, it was a further three months before Murphy's character was confirmed as Dr Jonathan Crane, a.k.a. the Scarecrow, a villain who had first been pinpointed as an antagonist for the Caped Crusader back in 1996 when Mark Protosevich was hired to script the potential *Batman & Robin* sequel, *Batman Triumphant*.

Joining Murphy as the film's primary antagonist was another Irish actor, Liam Neeson, whose turn as the title character in Sam Raimi's 1990 superhero film *Darkman* had led to an Academy Award-nominated performance in *Schindler's List* and recent big-budget efforts such as *Star Wars: Episode I – The Phantom Menace* (1999) and *Gangs of New York* (2002). Neeson was officially cast in the role of Henri Ducard, a mentor figure created by Batman scriptwriter Sam Hamm in the comic book story 'Citizen Wayne', published in *Detective Comics* #599 (April 1989); in actuality the character of Ducard would act as cover for Ra's al Ghul, the international terrorist and centuries-old supervillain who had been introduced to the comic book line by Denny O'Neil and Neal Adams in 'Daughter of the Demon', a story that appeared in *Batman* #232 in June 1971. To preserve the ruse, Ken Watanabe (*The Last Samurai*, 2003) was announced as Ra's al Ghul, although his character would ultimately be revealed as a decoy.

'I felt very strongly that we should use characters that hadn't been depicted in the films before and I felt that, in the case of the Scarecrow and Ra's al Ghul, that they were two really great villains that hadn't been used,' explained David Goyer with regards to the choice of foes from the Rogues Gallery. 'Ra's al Ghul is a unique *Batman* villain because although his goals are certainly perverted, he is more realistic as a character, while the Scarecrow is unique because it allowed us the opportunity to depict a villain who is truly scary and frightening. Because Chris and I wanted to tell a story about fear and overcoming fear, the Scarecrow seemed like a no-brainer.'

Also joining the ensemble cast was Tom Wilkinson (*The Full Monty*, 1997) as mob boss Carmine Falcone, along with Mark Boone Junior (*Memento*) and Colin McFarlane (*Chunky Monkey*, 2001) as fellow *Year One* characters Detective Arnold Flass and Police Commissioner Gillian B. Loeb. Cult actor Rutger Hauer (*The Hitcher*) signed on as William Earle, CEO of Wayne Enterprises, while further appointments included Larry Holden (*Insomnia*) as District Attorney Carl Finch, Linus Roache (*Hart's War*, 2002) and Sara Stewart (*The Winslow Boy*, 1999) as Thomas and Martha Wayne, and Richard Brake (*Cold Mountain*, 2003) as hitman Joe Chill. Meanwhile, the film would also feature another familiar face from the Rogues Gallery as Tim Booth, lead singer of the English rock band James, was approached for a brief cameo as Victor Zsasz, the deranged serial killer who made his first appearance in 'The Last Arkham: Part I' by Alan Grant, published in *Batman: Shadow of the Bat* #1 (June 1992).

In order to turn his concepts for the Dark Knight into a reality, Nolan turned to production designer Nathan Crowley; earning his first credit with a junior art department role on *Hook* (1991), Crowley had climbed the ladder on titles such as *Braveheart* (1995), *Mystery Men* (1999) and *Mission: Impossible II* (2000) before collaborating with Nolan on *Insomnia*. Their first task was to design a living, breathing Gotham City worthy of its illustrious history: 'The way that we approached Gotham … was to look at interesting geographical features of different cities of the world,' explained Nolan in an interview with *IGN.com* in 2005. Unlike the Gothic designs of Tim Burton's films or the neon-soaked, futuristic vision of Joel

Schumacher, Nolan would strive for realism with his depiction of Gotham and drew inspiration from elements of New York City, Chicago and Tokyo, along with Hong Kong's Kowloon Walled City, which would influence the style of Gotham's slum-like area, the Narrows. 'We wanted something that reflects the reality of a large modern city which is a tremendous variety of architecture.'

Towards the end of 2003 Nolan was joined on the project by another of his regular collaborators, cinematographer Wally Pfister, who had first met the director during the Sundance Film Festival in 1999. Having developed his skills on a host of low-budget horrors and erotic thrillers throughout the 1990s, Pfister went on to work with Nolan on both *Memento* and *Insomnia*, while his recent credits included *Laurel Canyon* and *The Italian Job* (2003). With the crew assembled, the production set up camp at the celebrated Shepperton Studios in Surrey, England – home to classics such as *The Third Man* (1949), *The Omen* (1976), *Alien* (1979), *Gandhi* (1982) and *A Passage to India* (1984) – to complete the pre-production phase of Warner Bros' fifth *Batman* movie.

At Shepperton, Crowley oversaw the construction of a vast Batcave set that was 250 ft high, 120 ft wide and 40 ft high and also included a waterfall that was powered by twelve pumps circulating 12,000 gallons of water per minute. Despite the epic scale of the Batcave, this would be dwarfed by an enormous city set that began construction inside Cardington Hangar in Bed-

fordshire in February 2004; at 900 ft long, 240 ft wide and 160 ft high, the hangar would house the largest indoor set ever assembled. It contained the Narrows section of Gotham City, Arkham Asylum, the monorail legs and a number of assorted streets, buildings and roads, which would then be mixed with location shooting to present a fully realized, sprawling metropolis. 'My main task was to make you not question Gotham and that's very difficult when you're building sets because naturally with all the finishes and the way things are aged, there's not generations of change on sets, so they're always going to feel a bit fake,' Crowley told Paul Wares of *Batman-on-Film.com* during a set visit in January 2005. 'Really we needed to then introduce tonnes of locations and I think most *Batman* films haven't used the amount of locations that we've used and that gives me the reality … I'm using real architecture from Chicago, I'm using real streets from London. What we had to build out here is bits that we can't find on location or we have stunt work to do.'

Another of Crowley's objectives was the development of a new look Batmobile, one that saw a dramatic shift from the fanciful designs of the previous movie incarnations towards the tank-like approach of *The Dark Knight Returns*. Working to a set of strict specifications (including the ability to accelerate from 0 to 60 mph in five seconds, reach speeds in excess of 100 mph, handle turns at speed *and* jump 30 ft through the air) Crowley began the process by 'kitbashing', using parts of other models to create a one to twelve scale replica that was then used as a reference point for the carving of a full-size Styrofoam model. A test frame was then built and tweaked to perfection, before the military-inspired Tumbler was ready for construction. In all, five fully operational Tumblers were engineered at a cost of approximately $250,000 each. These included a jet version, fitted out with a working jet engine fuelled by six propane tanks, an electric-powered version, featuring a sliding roof to allow easy access for the actors, in addition to two lightweight dummy models and a 6ft miniature that was used for scenes of the vehicle flying between buildings.

'There are certain things that you have to have. You have to have the suit, you have to have the Batmobile and there's only so far you can push it,' said Nathan Crowley on the iconography of the Caped Crusader. 'I think the Batmobile we could [push], because it had dated itself so sufficiently that we could start from scratch. We had to start from scratch because everyone's fed up with it, I don't think anyone's fed up with the Batsuit.' Tasked with creating a practical and realistic interpretation of the Batsuit that eschewed the rubber-nipple excesses of the Joel Schumacher era was the experienced costume designer Lindy Hemming. In addition to credits on all four of Pierce Brosnan's Bond movies, Hemming had also tackled other big-budget blockbusters such as *Lara Croft: Tomb Raider* (2001) and *Harry Potter and the Chamber of Secrets* (2002), while her work

on Mike Leigh's period drama *Topsy-Turvy* (1999) had seen her honoured with an Academy Award.

In terms of the Batsuit, key requests from Nolan included increased mobility, particularly around the head and neck, along with a matte colour scheme and an increased emphasis on the cape as a method of concealment. To achieve the specifications, Hemming and her team created a life cast of Christian Bale that was used to create moulded latex sections for the calves, knees, legs, arms, torso, spine and cowl. These sections were then glued to a neoprene undersuit, while the cape was engineered from an electrically flocked nylon parachute silk sprinkled with a fine dust, a process employed by the British Ministry of Defence to minimize night-vision detection. Owing to the complexity of the costume and its seamless design, three crew members were needed to dress Christian Bale, and approximately forty Batsuits would be used throughout the production.

On 3 March 2004, Jeff Robinov, President of Production at Warner Bros, announced that filming was underway on Christopher Nolan's *Batman Begins*. Starting out in Iceland at the Vatnajökull glacier – which doubled as the Himalayas and the exteriors to Ra's al Ghul's temple – the shoot would last until September and take in a number of locations across the UK, along with exterior filming in Chicago. Key sites employed in England included Mentmore Towers country house in Buckinghamshire (Wayne Manor), Coalhouse Fort (the Bhutanese prison) and Tilbury Docks in

Essex, along with a number of London locations such as the National Institute for Medical Research (Arkham exterior), St Pancras Station and the Abbey Mills Pumping Stations (Arkham interiors), University College London (City of Gotham State Courts interiors) and the Farmiloe Building (Gotham City Police Station interiors). Across the pond in Chicago, the majority of the main chase sequence was filmed around Lower Wacker Drive and the Amstutz Expressway, along with other exterior sites such as the Chicago Board of Trade Building (Wayne Enterprises), the Jewelers' Building (City of Gotham State Courts) and the Franklin Street Bridge.

Although Nolan had preferred traditional visual effects techniques and stunt work as opposed to computer-generated imagery, certain digital enhancements were employed during the post-production stage, including an establishing shot of a sunrise over Gotham City, a number of monorail shots and the majority of the bats seen in the final film. As the visual effects work was being completed, Nolan set about assembling the film with Lee Smith (*Master and Commander: The Far Side of the World*, 2003). An Academy Award-nominated Australian film editor and regular collaborator of fellow countryman Peter Weir, Smith had started out as a sound designer in the late 1970s and had extensive credits in both fields, working on films such as *Dead Calm* (1989), *RoboCop 2*, *The Piano* (1993), *The Truman Show* (1998) and *Buffalo Soldiers* (2001). Meanwhile Nolan also

invited the Academy Award-winning German-born composer Hans Zimmer (Best Original Music Score – *The Lion King*, 1994) to create the score, with Zimmer then working in collaboration with James Newton Howard (*The Sixth Sense*, 1999). Together the two composers – who had amassed an astonishing fifteen Oscar nominations between them – produced two hours and twenty minutes of music that incorporated electronic elements in addition to a ninety-piece orchestra.

Unlike prior instalments in the series, *Batman Begins* progressed smoothly through its production, with Nolan managing to avoid the studio pressures and interference that had plagued his predecessors. Furthermore, it was also generating excitement within the Bat-community, and while the redesigned Batmobile received a mixed reaction, a genuine sense of excitement was starting to build for the Dark Knight's much-anticipated return to the big screen. On 28 July 2004 a well-executed teaser trailer was released, emphasizing Bruce's story and culminating with a brief glimpse of Bale as Batman. This was followed by a series of character images released through the official website as filming wrapped and *Batman Begins* entered post-production.

The year 2004 had proven to be memorable for both *Batman* fans and Warner Bros, who had finally managed to overcome the self-inflicted hurdles laid out back in the summer of 1997 with the release of *Batman & Robin*. Bringing the year to a close with a new theatrical trailer and a teaser poster featuring a silhouetted Batman against a dark, sepia-toned background, the studio marketing machine kicked into overdrive in the early part of 2005; along with a steady supply of official images and alternative poster designs, a second theatrical trailer arrived in cinemas in April and, while anticipation levels never quite reached the heights of the summer of 1989, there was a growing sense of confidence both behind the scenes and within the fan community that *Batman Begins* really would mark a new beginning for the Dark Knight Detective.

## RECEPTION

After an abundance of failed projects and an eight-year absence, the Dark Knight finally returned to the big screen when *Batman Begins* hit North American cinemas on Wednesday 15 June 2005. Arriving on 3,858 screens (over 900 more than *Batman & Robin* had opened on back in 1997), *Batman Begins* took first place in the box-office chart and had amassed $72,896,986 by the end of its first weekend, of which $48,745,440 came from the Friday to Sunday period. This three-day haul was described by industry commentators *BoxOfficeMojo.com* as 'strong but unimpressive by today's instantaneous blockbuster standards', and just fell short of the franchise's record opening of $52.78m set by *Batman Forever* back in 1995. Nevertheless, the film retained pole position in its second weekend, adding another $27,589,389 on its way to a total domestic gross of $205,343,774,

making it the eighth-highest grossing film of 2005 in North America and second only to Tim Burton's first outing in terms of the biggest domestic earners of the *Batman* franchise.

In Britain, *Batman Begins* took first place in the box-office chart in its opening weekend with £4,427,802 (including £856,317 from Thursday previews), but neither that nor its combined haul of £16,101,589 was enough to dethrone *Batman Forever* as the most successful entry of the series on UK soil. However, the film did manage to outperform *Batman Forever* in the international markets overall where it set a franchise high with combined foreign receipts of $167,366,241. In all, *Batman Begins* was the ninth-biggest film of 2005 (a year led by *Harry Potter and the Goblet of Fire* with $895.9m), and its worldwide gross of $372,710,015 gave Warner Bros their best return on a *Batman* film since the 1989 original.

Along with a solid financial run, the critical reception given to *Batman Begins* was generally positive, with particular appreciation shown towards the film's realistic approach, strong characterization and dramatic storytelling, along with Nolan's direction and the performance of Christian Bale in the dual role of Bruce Wayne and Batman. Roger Ebert was full of admiration in the *Chicago Sun-Times*, giving the film four stars out of four, while *Empire* magazine wrote in their five-star review that *Batman Begins* 'delivers the full noir with a side order of dementia', and lauded the film for revitalizing the DC series and putting them back on an even footing with rival comics house Marvel. Despite this, some critics were left underwhelmed by the film's pacing, its climactic action sequence and the chemistry between Bale and Katie Holmes, while *Variety* also voiced concerns that *Batman Begins* could be too dark thematically for younger viewers.

On the awards circuit *Batman Begins* became the first instalment since *Batman Forever* to contend for an Oscar as director of photography Wally Pfister received a nomination for Best Achievement in Cinematography, losing out to Dion Beebe for *Memoirs of a Geisha* (2005). The film challenged in three categories at the BAFTA Awards (Best Achievement in Special Visual Effects, Best Production Design and Best Sound) and became the fourth consecutive *Batman* film to receive a Razzie nomination, with Katie Holmes competing against eventual winner Paris Hilton (*House of Wax*, 2005) for Worst Supporting Actress at the Golden Raspberry Awards. *Batman Begins* also received recognition from the Academy of Science Fiction, Fantasy & Horror Films, who bestowed three Saturn Awards upon the film (Best Actor – Christian Bale, Best Writing – Christopher Nolan and David S. Goyer, and Best Fantasy Film), while Christian Bale also received an MTV Award for Best Hero.

Although *Batman Begins* may not have quite delivered the mainstream financial success expected of contemporary blockbusters, there was no denying that Christopher Nolan had been entirely successful in his aim of delivering a fresh and original take on Bob Kane's classic character. The film was extremely well received by the fan community and became a big hit on DVD, where it banked an additional $125m in sales as word began to spread that Warner Bros had finally banished the ghost of *Batman & Robin*. 'You've got to put credit where credit is due. And the credit goes on the arms, shoulders, and legs of Chris Nolan. This guy is a genius,' declared executive producer Michael Uslan in an interview with *Batman-on-Film.com* in November 2005. 'What Chris has accomplished is that he has elevated the comic book movie to a new, higher, platform. It is at the highest place it has ever been.'

Nolan's gritty and realistic approach towards *Batman Begins* went on to herald a new trend in Hollywood thinking, with the film subsequently cited as an influence on a host of projects including *Casino Royale* (2006), *Iron Man* (2008), *The Incredible Hulk* (2008), *Star Trek* (2009), *Terminator Salvation* (2009), *X-Men Origins: Wolverine* (2009) and *X-Men: First Class* (2011). However, the legacy of *Batman Begins* would soon be overshadowed by Nolan's second venture into Gotham City as the director delivered a follow-up that completely redefined the 'comic book movie' and achieved a level of success beyond all expectation.

# THE DARK KNIGHT (2008)

**Release date:** 18 July 2008 (US); 24 July 2008 (UK)
**Certificate:** PG-13 (US); 12A (theatrical), 12 (DVD) (UK)
**Running time:** 152 minutes
**Budget:** $185m
**Global box office:** $1,001,921,825

## CAST

Christian Bale (*Bruce Wayne/Batman*); Aaron Eckhart (*Harvey Dent/Two-Face*); Heath Ledger (*The Joker*); Michael Caine (*Alfred Pennyworth*); Maggie Gyllenhaal (*Rachel Dawes*); Gary Oldman (*Lt James Gordon*); Morgan Freeman (*Lucius Fox*); Eric Roberts (*Sal Maroni*); Cillian Murphy (*Dr Jonathan Crane/The Scarecrow*); Chin Han (*Lau*); Nestor Carbonell (*Mayor Garcia*); Colin McFarlane (*Police Commissioner Loeb*); Anthony Michael Hall (*Mike Engel*); Michael Jai White (*Gambol*); Ritchie Coster (*The Chechen*); Monique Gabriela Curnen (*Ramirez*); Ron Dean (*Wuertz*); William Fichtner (*Bank Manager*).

## KEY CREW

Christopher Nolan (*Director*); Christopher Nolan, Lorne Orleans, Charles Roven, Emma Thomas (*Producers*); Kevin De La Noy, Thomas Tull, Michael E. Uslan, Benjamin Melniker (*Executive Producers*); Jordan Goldberg (*Associate Producer*); Philip Lee (*Line Producer*); Christopher Nolan, David S. Goyer (*Story*), Christopher Nolan, Jonathan Nolan (*Screenplay*); Bob Kane (*Characters*); James Newton Howard, Hans Zimmer (*Music*); Wally Pfister (*Cinematography*); Lee Smith (*Editing*); Nathan Crowley (*Production Design*), Lindy Hemming (*Costume Design*); John Papsidera (*Casting*).

## STORY

The criminals of Gotham City are running scared, fearful of falling prey to the masked vigilante known as Batman. Mob operations have come under increasing pressure from Lieutenant James Gordon's Major Crimes Unit (MCU), while newly elected District Attorney Harvey Dent has vowed to stamp out corruption and smash organized crime. However, for crime lords such as Sal Maroni, there is a much more pressing concern – a spate of bank robberies targeting mob funds orchestrated by the Joker, a psychotic criminal whose jagged facial scars are hidden beneath a layer of grotesque clown make-up.

In a parking garage, a drug deal between the Chechen and Gotham's sole remaining supplier, Dr Jonathan Crane, is interrupted by a group of Batman impersonators who have taken to the streets after being inspired by the Dark Knight's exploits. The Chechen flees as Crane and his men battle the impostors until the real Batman arrives on the scene, tussling with a pack of Rottweiler dogs before subduing Crane, his gang and the impersonators. Batman then meets with Lt

Gordon in the vault of the Gotham National Bank, where the two allies discuss the Joker before conversation turns to Harvey Dent – specifically, whether the 'White Knight of Gotham' can be trusted to join them in their efforts against the underworld.

Sharing this interest in the new District Attorney – and his girlfriend, Rachel Dawes – is Batman's alter ego Bruce Wayne. As Bruce and Alfred discuss the possibility of a bright future for Gotham under Dent, the DA's hopes of securing a conviction against Sal Maroni fall apart when the star witness changes his testimony, allowing the gangster to walk free. Following the court appearance, Lt Gordon pays Dent a visit, hoping to secure search warrants against five banks suspected of holding mob money. Harvey grants Gordon the warrants, but not before voicing his distrust that Gordon's unit is filled with corrupt cops – earning him a certain nickname within MCU – and demanding to meet with the Batman. Dent does get an opportunity to meet with Bruce Wayne later that evening, during which the billionaire becomes impressed by the DA's determination to clean up Gotham and offers to throw a lucrative fundraiser.

Suspecting a Chinese investment company of laundering mob money, Bruce invites the chairman, Lau, to submit a proposal for a joint venture with Wayne Enterprises, providing him with access to Lau's books. His suspicions are confirmed and Lau later assembles a meeting between the city's crime lords; appearing via a television set, Lau explains that MCU are carrying out raids after locating their funds but he has already taken precautions by withdrawing the money, moving it to a secure location before flying to Hong Kong. The Joker interrupts proceedings, stating that Batman will track Lau; instead, he suggests tackling the real problem, offering to kill the Dark Knight for half of their combined funds and leaving behind his Joker card when his proposal is rejected.

Frustrated by the failure of the operation to seize the mob's money, Harvey Dent activates the Bat-Signal and is joined on the roof of police headquarters by Lt Gordon and the Dark Knight. Together they form an alliance to bring down the city's remaining gangs, with Batman promising to locate Lau and bring him back to Gotham. Bruce accompanies Lucius Fox to Hong Kong on business and, with the aid of a high frequency sonar device created by Fox, Batman is able to snatch Lau from his office and return him to the city.

After Rachel interrogates Lau, he refuses to reveal the location of the money but offers to give up his clients in exchange for immunity. Having gathered their funds together, Dent is confident he can bring conspiracy charges against all of the various criminal factions and Lt Gordon subsequently oversees the arrest of 549 of the city's mobsters, delivering a stunning victory for the White Knight. In their desperation, the crime lords agree to the Joker's earlier proposal and soon the homicidal anarchist has invaded the airwaves, broadcasting a home video recording in which he brutally murders one of the Batman impersonators. The Joker promises more deaths unless the Dark Knight comes forward and reveals his true face.

At the Harvey Dent fundraiser, Bruce explains to Rachel that he believes Batman's time is drawing to a close as Harvey takes on the mantle of the city's hero. Later, as Harvey proposes to Rachel, the Joker gatecrashes the party, leading an assassination attempt on his life; Bruce renders Harvey unconscious, moving him to a secure location before changing into his Batsuit and confronting the Joker, who then throws Rachel out of a broken window. Batman leaps from the building and manages to save Rachel's life, but the case against Gotham's crime lords disintegrates when the police are unable to prevent Commissioner Loeb and Judge Surillo from falling victim to the Joker's hit squads.

The next day the Joker disguises himself as a police officer in order to get close to Mayor Garcia at a memorial service for Commissioner Loeb. The Joker shoots at the Mayor, only for Lt Gordon to jump in front of the shot and catch the bullet in the chest; with Gordon pronounced dead, the Joker manages to escape in the ensuing pandemonium, while Dent captures one of his goons and discovers that Rachel is next on his hit list. Rachel goes to stay in Bruce's penthouse for protection as Batman confronts Sal Maroni, hoping to secure information on the Joker's whereabouts. After being dropped from a fire-escape, a defiant Maroni tells Batman that – unlike the Joker – he is restricted by his 'rule', and that if the Dark Knight wants to bring an end to the killing he will need to cave in to the Joker's demands.

Desperate to find information on the Joker, Harvey Dent interrogates the captured thug and threatens to kill him, letting the decision come down to fate with a flip of his father's lucky coin. With the coin landing 'good heads' up, Dent tosses it for a second time but it is caught by Batman, who berates the DA for jeopardizing all of their prosecutions by crossing the line. Batman instructs Dent to call a press conference and later explains to Rachel that he has no choice but to reveal his identity. However, the next day Harvey pleads with the public not to give in to the Joker and – realizing that the city needs Batman – he declares himself to be the masked vigilante. Stunned by the turn of events, Rachel leaves a note for Bruce with Alfred as Harvey is led away in handcuffs.

Transporting Harvey into custody, the police escort comes under attack by the Joker and his henchmen, with Batman in hot pursuit in the Tumbler. The Joker fires an RPG at Batman, who emerges from the wreck of the Tumbler on the Batpod and continues to make chase, eventually causing the Joker's truck to flip over. The Joker is apprehended by Lt Gordon, having faked his own death as part of a ruse to ensnare the villain, and he is taken into custody at police headquarters.

The Mayor arrives, congratulating Gordon and promoting him to Police Commissioner, but the celebrations are short-lived when they receive word that Harvey Dent is missing.

After Gordon unsuccessfully interrogates the Joker, he hands proceedings over to Batman. The Dark Knight learns that Harvey and Rachel have been taken to separate locations across the city, with the Joker supplying both addresses as part of a twisted game to make him choose between the two. Batman sets off to rescue Rachel but instead finds Harvey Dent, the Joker having deliberately switched locations. Batman is able to save Dent, although the District Attorney suffers severe burns to one side of his body, but the police are too late to prevent Rachel from perishing, arriving just as a fireball tears through the building. The Joker also manages to escape police custody, taking Lau hostage and ultimately setting fire to the accountant along with all of the mob's money.

With Bruce in mourning over Rachel, Alfred reads her note and – seeing that she was going to marry Harvey – he later destroys it to avoid further heartbreak. Rachel's death has also driven a hospitalized Harvey Dent to the brink of madness, with the DA demanding that Commissioner Gordon address him by his MCU nickname, Harvey Two-Face, before revealing the shocking extent of his injuries. Meanwhile, the Joker threatens to blow up a city hospital, and with evacuations underway he adopts a nurse disguise to pay Dent a visit. Deflecting responsibility for

Rachel's death, the Joker convinces Harvey to exact revenge on Batman, Gordon, Sal Maroni and the crooked cops who sold him out. Dent opts to let chance decide the Joker's fate, and when the coin falls in his favour the Clown Prince of Crime is free to carry out his threat of blowing up the building.

Stepping up his campaign of terror, the Joker declares his plan to unleash chaos on Gotham, claiming to have rigged all of the bridges and highways with explosives. As the public attempt to flee, the Joker reveals that he has planted explosives on two ferries, one containing regular citizens and the other hardened criminals; each has the option to destroy the other at the touch of a button, but if neither vessel makes a decision, he will detonate both at midnight. At Wayne Enterprises, Lucius Fox discovers that Batman has used his sonar technology to create a highly advanced spy network, and despite his reservations over the machine he agrees to help the Dark Knight locate the Joker, tracking him to a skyscraper construction site.

Entering the construction site, Batman takes on the Joker's henchmen and confronts his nemesis, only to be beaten down with a steel pipe. The Joker restrains Batman and waits as midnight approaches, confident that one of the ferries will destroy the other; however, his prediction ultimately proves misguided, and before the Joker can detonate the explosives he is caught in the face by spikes from Batman's gauntlet. Refusing to break his rule not to kill, Batman catches the

Joker with his grappling hook as he falls from the building, leaving the villain dangling upside down as the Joker reveals his ace in the hole – Harvey Two-Face.

Driven to insanity by the Joker, Two-Face has embarked on a bloody path of revenge, slaying the corrupt police detective Wuertz, mob boss Sal Maroni and his driver, before coercing Detective Ramirez into luring Commissioner Gordon's wife and children into a trap. Two-Face contacts Gordon and demands he meet him at the site of Rachel's death, where he beats down the Police Commissioner. Taking Gordon's son hostage as Batman arrives, Two-Face flips his coin to determine Batman's fate and shoots him in the chest. He then judges himself, with the coin landing in his favour, before moving on to Gordon. Before he can catch the coin, Two-Face is tackled by Batman and he is thrown from the side of the building, plunging to his death as the Dark Knight clings on to Gordon's son.

Standing beside the broken body of Gotham's White Knight, Commissioner Gordon fears that by shattering Harvey's incorruptible image, the Joker has been victorious. However, to preserve Harvey's reputation and the hope he offered Gotham, Batman takes responsibility for Two-Face's crimes himself, convincing Gordon to launch a manhunt against him. As the Bat-Signal is destroyed, Batman finds himself a fugitive from justice, serving as a silent guardian – Gotham's watchful protector, the Dark Knight.

## BRINGING BATMAN TO THE SCREEN

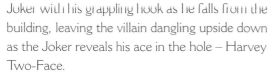

'Chris [Nolan] originally said that he would do one and just the one,' *Batman Begins* screenwriter David S. Goyer told the audience at the San Diego Comic-Con International in July 2004. Although cameras were still rolling on director Christopher Nolan's reboot, questions were already being asked about the possibility of a sequel, yet understandably the filmmakers remained non-committal at such an early stage: 'The notion was that after our film was finished, we could then go off and if Chris or Warner Bros wanted to play with subsequent films they could then reintroduce the pantheon of villains.'

While talk of a sequel may have been a little premature at that point, as the release date drew nearer there was a growing confidence within the camp that *Batman Begins* would successfully manage to reignite the ailing franchise. 'Chris and I both felt that Bruce, as Batman, initially thought that this would be a job with an end – that he could fix Gotham, obliterate the Batman character and everything would run smoothly from there on in,' suggested Christian Bale, teasing the potential for future instalments at WonderCon in February 2005. 'He kind of becomes trapped because he's started something – it causes escalation.' This 'escalation' would come in the shape of two popular villains who, unlike the Scarecrow and Ra's al Ghul, had already made their debut in Warner Bros' feature film series: 'The next one would have Batman enlisting the aid of [James] Gordon and [Harvey] Dent in bringing down the Joker,' Goyer told *Premiere*, confirming that he had developed a story which was heavily inspired by the limited series *Batman: The Long Halloween* and would span a further two films, culminating with the origin of Two-Face: 'In the third, the Joker would go on trial, scarring Dent in the process.'

Hopes for a sequel were confirmed in June 2005 when *Batman Begins* opened atop the North American box-office chart, going on to become the second-highest grossing instalment in the series with world-wide receipts of $372.7m. Furthermore, it had been well received by fans and critics alike and its closing scenes left audiences buzzing with anticipation for the introduction of Batman's arch-nemesis, the Joker. However, while star Christian Bale had signed a three-picture deal as the Dark Knight, that was not the case with Christopher Nolan. 'We're waiting for Chris Nolan to declare himself,' admitted *Batman Begins* producer Charles Roven in an interview with *Sci Fi Wire* in August 2005. 'The studio owns the franchise and they can do without any of us, but it was a spectacular experience with Chris so we hope it will happen again with him.'

As it happened, Nolan would declare his intentions to return to the *Batman* franchise just two months later, but only after reuniting with *Batman Begins* stars Christian Bale and Michael Caine for a cinematic adaptation of Christopher Priest's 1995 novel *The Prestige*. A Victorian-era

mystery centring on two feuding magicians, *The Prestige* first came to the director's attention back in 2000, with Nolan and younger brother Jonathan then working on the screenplay intermittently over a five-year period. Bale would share top billing in the resulting film with Hugh Jackman, another superhero-fan favourite from his turn as Wolverine in Twentieth Century Fox's *X-Men* and *X2: X-Men United*, while other additions to the cast of the $40m production included Piper Perabo (*Coyote Ugly*, 2000), Rebecca Hall (*Starter for 10*, 2006), Scarlett Johansson (*Lost in Translation*, 2003), Andy Serkis (*The Lord of the Rings*), Ricky Jay (*Magnolia*, 1999) and David Bowie. Shot between January and April 2006 and released that October, *The Prestige* went on to gross $109.6m and received Academy Award nominations for Best Art Direction (Nathan Crowley, Art Direction; Julie Ochipinti, Set Decoration) and Best Cinematography (Wally Pfister).

The fact that Nolan was preoccupied with work on *The Prestige* did little to deter the internet fan community from passionate speculation over the sequel, nor did it prevent a host of top Hollywood talent from vying for positions within the cast. Among the diverse range of names reported to have expressed their interest in the coveted role of the Joker were Academy Award-winner Adrien Brody (*The Pianist*, 2002), Steve Carell (*The 40-Year-Old Virgin*, 2005), Lachy Hulme (*The Matrix Revolutions*, 2003) and Sam Rockwell (*Confessions of a Dangerous Mind*,

2002) along with former Rogues Gallery candidates Paul Bettany and Robin Williams. Actors linked to Gotham's District Attorney Harvey Dent included Josh Lucas (*Hulk*), Ryan Phillippe (*Cruel Intentions*, 1999), Liev Schreiber (*The Manchurian Candidate*, 2004) and *The Prestige* star Hugh Jackman, while there was also talk of Oscar-winner Philip Seymour Hoffman (*Capote*, 2005) featuring in cameo as a British arms dealer by the name of Oswald Cobblepot, a.k.a. the Penguin.

Working behind the scenes, Christopher Nolan had already informed Warner Bros' President of Production Jeff Robinov of his plans for the continuation of the *Batman* saga prior to starting *The Prestige*. Taking time out from Gotham City to direct his fifth feature, Nolan tasked younger brother Jonathan with turning his and David Goyer's ideas into a fully fledged screenplay. 'It felt like a very easy job – one of the easiest I've had because [Chris and David] nailed it right out of the gate with this incredible story,' reflected Jonathan on the process of developing the script. 'With *Batman Begins* and how the story and characters were already set up so well, it was just very easy to take that story and those characters and move forward.'

During post-production on *The Prestige*, *Batman* fans received the news they had been clamouring for on 31 July 2006 when Warner Bros announced that Christopher Nolan was officially set to return for the hotly anticipated follow-up to *Batman Begins*. Unlike rumoured titles such as *Batman Attacks*, *Batman Continues*, *Batman Escalation* and *Batman Strikes*, it would go by the moniker of *The Dark Knight* – becoming the first Batman feature not to incorporate the hero's name directly within its title – and while the news was accompanied by the expected confirmation of Christian Bale's return, that was certainly not the case with Nolan's casting choice for the Joker. 'Our challenge in casting the Joker was to find an actor who is not just extraordinarily talented but fearless,' said Christopher Nolan as he revealed the actor who would bring his incarnation of the Clown Prince of Crime to the screen. 'Watching Heath Ledger's interpretation of this iconic character taking on Christian Bale's Batman is going to be incredible.'

Having made a number of television appearances in his native Australia (including a short stint in 1997 on the popular soap *Home and Away*), Heath Ledger made the shift to Los Angeles where he enjoyed his first taste of Tinseltown with a starring role in the teen comedy *10 Things I Hate About You* (1999). After supporting turns in *The Patriot* (2000) and *Monster's Ball* (2001), Ledger starred in the medieval action-adventure *A Knight's Tale* (2001) and went on to headline films such as *Ned Kelly* (2003), *The Sin Eater* (2003) and *The Brothers Grimm* (2005), but it was his most recent role, a critically acclaimed performance in *Brokeback Mountain* (2005), which truly demonstrated his ability and saw him lauded with Academy Award, Golden Globe and BAFTA nominations for Best Actor.

'Unlike Batman, who I wanted very much to explore his origin and where he came from, with heroes it's just different,' revealed Christopher Nolan in an interview with *Batman-on-Film.com*. 'So with the Joker, I wanted to present him as an absolute, an agent of chaos and anarchy.' Inspiration for Nolan's take on the Joker came from the initial portrayal of the character in *Batman* #1, where he featured in two stories – 'The Joker' and 'The Joker Returns' – and was presented as the 'Harlequin of Hate', a sinister, cold-blooded and psychotic killer. It was an approach that seemed a perfect fit for the dark, realistic tone of Nolan's burgeoning universe and, much as he had in his comic book debut, the Joker of *The Dark Knight* would arrive in his complete form. 'The idea with the Joker is that if he had a back-story and if one of the stories he told you was true, somehow it would reduce the character,' explained Jonathan Nolan. 'It's more frightening because, in a sense, there is no mystery there. There is no back-story. He is exactly what he presents himself to be, which is an anarchist.'

To prepare for an iconic role that had last been tackled by the legendary screen psychopath and three-time Academy Award-winner Jack Nicholson in 1989, Heath Ledger embarked on a period of self-enforced seclusion, locking himself away in a London hotel room for a month to study the psychology of the character. To develop his approach, Ledger drew inspiration from Alan Moore's *Batman: The Killing Joke* and Grant Morrison's *Arkham Asylum: A Serious House on Serious Earth* (1989), while adding his own slant to the character based on a combination of Sex Pistols bassist Sid Vicious and Malcolm McDowell's turn as Alex DeLarge, the delinquent protagonist of Stanley Kubrick's *A Clockwork Orange* (1971).

With *The Dark Knight* officially moving into pre-production in August 2006, Christian Bale was quickly joined by a number of key players from the cast of *Batman Begins*, as Michael Caine, Gary Oldman and Morgan Freeman were all confirmed to reprise their roles as Alfred Pennyworth, James Gordon and Lucius Fox respectively. Less keen on a second outing, however, was Katie Holmes, who eventually passed on the opportunity to return as Bruce's love interest Rachel Dawes in favour of the comedy crime caper *Mad Money* (2008). Several actresses were said to be under consideration for the part, including Emily Blunt (*My Summer of Love*, 2004), Abbie Cornish (*Candy*, 2006) and Isla Fisher (*Wedding Crashers*, 2005), along with original *Batman Begins* candidates Sarah Michelle Gellar and Rachel McAdams; the role was eventually secured by Maggie Gyllenhaal (*Secretary*, 2002), who was finally announced as Holmes' replacement in March 2007.

Another character who would make a brief return to Gotham City was *Batman Begins* antagonist Dr Jonathan Crane, a.k.a. the Scarecrow, with Cillian Murphy becoming the first actor to reprise his role as a villain in the entire *Batman* theatrical film series. Meanwhile Batman would also have to contend with mob boss Sal Maroni – a long-standing *Batman* villain who was notable for being the one to scar Harvey Dent in his very first appearance in *Detective Comics* #66 in August 1942 – with Eric Roberts (*Runaway Train*, 1985) winning the part ahead of competition from James Gandolfini (*The Sopranos*, 1999–2007) and Bob Hoskins, who had also been an early candidate for the Penguin in *Batman Returns*.

Further additions to the supporting cast included new faces such as Chin Han (*3 Needles*, 2005) as mob accountant Lau, Michael Jai White (*Spawn*, 1997) as gangster Gambol, Nestor Carbonel (*Smokin' Aces*, 2006) as Mayor Anthony Garcia, Anthony Michael Hall as *Gotham Tonight* news reporter Mike Engel, William Fichtner (*Armageddon*, 1998) as the manager of the Gotham National Bank and Monique Gabriela Curnen (*Half Nelson*, 2006) and Ron Dean (*The Fugitive*) as corrupt police detectives Anna Ramirez and Michael Wuertz, while Colin McFarlane would also feature as the returning Police Commissioner Loeb. However, despite an extensive cast, there remained one crucial role left to fill.

'It became apparent as we were talking fairly early on that Harvey [Dent] was actually going to be the protagonist,' said David Goyer, referring to a character that had previously been brought to

the screen by Billy Dee Williams in *Batman* and Tommy Lee Jones in *Batman Forever*. 'The Joker doesn't change and Batman doesn't really change, but Harvey is the one that changes as a result of his interaction between the Joker and the Batman. Obviously he changes in a tragic way and that means the movie has to be a tragedy.' The tragedy that Goyer referred to was Dent's transformation into the hideously disfigured crime lord Two-Face, which – rather than occurring in a third film as originally intended – would become the driving force within the narrative of *The Dark Knight*.

In casting the all-important role of Harvey Dent, Nolan turned to an actor who first came to his attention during the auditions for the lead in his breakthrough film *Memento*. Aaron Eckhart had made his feature debut with an Independent Spirit Award-winning turn in Neil Labute's *In the Company of Men* (1997) and went on to appear in films such as *Your Friends & Neighbors* (1998) and *Any Given Sunday* (1999) before losing out on *Memento* to Guy Pearce. Nevertheless, 2000 proved to be a good year for Eckhart, with a supporting part in *Erin Brockovich* leading to roles in the likes of *The Pledge* (2001), *Possession* (2002), *Paycheck* (2003) and *The Black Dahlia* (2006). However, it was his Golden Globe-nominated performance as a smooth-talking tobacco lobbyist in *Thank You for Smoking* (2005) that convinced Nolan of Eckhart's suitability for Gotham's White Knight. While the studio expressed interest in

Matt Damon (a reported candidate for Robin in *Batman Forever*) and Mark Ruffalo (*Eternal Sunshine of the Spotless Mind*, 2004), Eckhart was confirmed in the role on 16 February 2007, just two months before shooting was set to commence.

As was becoming customary with Nolan's films, his crew for *The Dark Knight* consisted of regular collaborators such as production designer Nathan Crowley, director of photography Wally Pfister and film editor Lee Smith, each of whom had continued their association with the director on *The Prestige*. Also returning in their *Batman Begins* capacities were costume designer Lindy Hemming and composers Hans Zimmer and James Newton Howard, while the familiarity was further extended by the decision to base the production in England once more. However, rather than revisiting Shepperton Studios, Nolan chose to take the franchise back to Pinewood Studios, the celebrated production facility that had been home to Tim Burton's *Batman*, along with recent blockbusters such as *Casino Royale*, *The Da Vinci Code* (2006) and *The Bourne Ultimatum* (2007).

Just as Nathan Crowley had been responsible for the development of the Tumbler on *Batman Begins*, *The Dark Knight* would see him tasked with turning Batman's newest ride – a 'high-powered, heavily armed two-wheeled machine' known as the Batpod – into a reality. In keeping with the director's tradition of relying on practical effects, the Batpod began its life as a full-scale model built in Nolan's garage, which was then engineered into a fully functional vehicle by the BAFTA-nominated special effects supervisor Chris Corbould (*Casino Royale*). In anticipation of the possibility of accidents due to the vehicle's unique design and handling, six Batpods were constructed in total. Professional stunt rider Jean-Pierre Goy (*Tomorrow Never Dies*, 1997) proved to be the only person capable of riding the machine and spent months of dedicated training in preparation for the shoot.

While Batman's garage was getting an overhaul courtesy of Nathan Crowley, so too would his customary cape and cowl as costume designer Lindy Hemming set about creating a new Batsuit that would offer even greater mobility than her previous design. The most radical change was to the cowl, which was modelled after a motorcycle helmet, making it the first movie Batsuit to feature a separate headpiece and offering complete mobility of the neck (it would also be the first design to incorporate retractable lenses, recreating the 'white eye' look of the comic book). In addition to the Batsuit, Hemming was also responsible for creating the distinctive wardrobe of the Joker, drawing influence from notable fashion designers like Alexander McQueen and Vivienne Westwood along with musicians such as Pete Doherty, Iggy Pop and Johnny Rotten.

The task of designing the Joker's iconic 'clown' appearance fell to make-up artist John Caglione Jr (*Dick Tracy*) and prosthetics supervisor Conor

O'Sullivan (*The Last Samurai*). Inspired by a 1953 Francis Bacon painting entitled *Study of a Portrait*, Caglione worked with Ledger to create a 'lived in' look emphasizing the creases and crevices of the actor's face, while O'Sullivan and his assistant Rob Trenton (*Star Wars: Episode III – Revenge of the Sith*, 2005) were responsible for creating prosthetic scars for the character's mouth. Adopting a revolutionary new technology, the Joker make-up consisted of three pieces of stamped silicone; unlike the gruelling two-and-a-half hours required to convert Jack Nicholson into the Clown Prince of Crime, Ledger's make-up took less than an hour to apply each day. As for Two-Face, despite Nolan's preference towards practical effects, the decision was made to create his facial burns via CGI, with British visual effects company Framestore (*The Golden Compass*, 2007) using motion capture markers to digitally trace and recreate the intricacies of Aaron Eckhart's performance.

Adopting the code-name 'Rory's First Kiss', the principal photography stage of *The Dark Knight* commenced in Chicago in April 2007. As with *Batman Begins*, *The Dark Knight* continued to employ both the soundstages at Cardington Hangar and the streets of Chicago to recreate Gotham City, but this time the director intended to place a much greater emphasis on location shooting in the Windy City. However, rather than diving straight into the shoot, the first four days would see Nolan screen eight films for the cast and crew – *Heat*, *Cat People* (1942), *Citizen Kane* (1941), *King Kong* (1933), *Batman Begins*, *Black Sunday* (1977), *A Clockwork Orange* and *Stalag 17* – in order to project his influences for the upcoming film.

'The cameras are enormous and much heavier than a 35mm camera,' said Wally Pfister on the difficulties posed by Nolan's decision to realize a fifteen-year ambition by shooting over twenty minutes of *The Dark Knight* using 70mm IMAX cameras, a first for a major feature film. 'It required an entirely different approach, but like any challenge in moviemaking, you can't be so intimidated that you shy away from it.' Among the sequences shot on IMAX was the film's opening prologue, the Joker's robbery of the Gotham National Bank, which was filmed between 18 and 24 April at the Old Chicago Main Post Office Building. Other scenes that would be shot in the IMAX format included the Hong Kong escape, the armoured car chase sequence and Batman's final confrontation with the Joker.

The main portion of filming on *The Dark Knight* would take place in Chicago, running for thirteen weeks from June until September and utilizing sites such as the Richard J. Daley Center (replacing the Chicago Board of Trade Building as Wayne Enterprises), the IBM Building, Sears Tower, Illinois Center Buildings, the Navy Pier and a number of bars and restaurants across the city. South La Salle Street played host to one of the film's big set-pieces – the actual flipping of an

$185m sequel drew closer. Given the film's exceptional marketing campaign, the extensive media attention in the wake of Heath Ledger's death and extremely positive early reviews, *The Dark Knight* would arrive in cinemas amid a level of hype unprecedented in the history of the *Batman* franchise.

## RECEPTION

*The Dark Knight* received its world premiere at a star-studded IMAX screening in New York City on 14 July 2008 and went on to exceed its already lofty expectations with a stellar box-office run that saw it become one of the most successful films of all time. Released in North America on 18 July 2008, *The Dark Knight* immediately entered the record books with a midnight screening of $18.5m and would surpass both the opening day and opening weekend records set by *Spider-Man 3* (2007), finishing up with a mighty haul of $158,411,483 from its first three days on screen. *The Dark Knight* remained at the top of the cinema chart for the remainder of July and by the end of August it had become only the second film to break the $500m mark in North America – a feat it accomplished in just forty-five days, less than half the time it had taken James Cameron's *Titanic* (1997) to reach that milestone. Although it would ultimately fall short of *Titanic*'s overall box-office record, *The Dark Knight* finished its North American run with $533,345,358, almost $120m more than the entire world-wide gross of Tim Burton's *Batman*.

Crossing the Atlantic to Christopher Nolan's home country, *The Dark Knight* hit UK cinemas on Thursday 24 July and claimed first place at the box office with an opening weekend of £11,191,824, which included £2,504,511 from advance previews. The film retained this spot the following weekend, earning another £6,737,306 on its way to a final sum of £48,685,166. Overall, *The Dark Knight* would amass $468,576,467 from the international markets, giving it a grand total of $1,001,921,825 – a figure that comfortably ensured victory over nearest rival *Indiana Jones and the Kingdom of the Crystal Skull* in the race for the biggest earner of 2008. It truly was an exceptional run that positioned *The Dark Knight* as the highest-grossing comic book movie of all time (a record previously held by *Spider-Man 3* with $890.9m) and saw it become only the fourth film to generate over $1bn in box-office receipts after *Titanic*, *The Lord of the Rings: The Return of the King* (2003) and *Pirates of the Caribbean: Dead Man's Chest* (2006).

Needless to say, reaction to *The Dark Knight* from within the *Batman* fan community was overwhelmingly positive, but the film also managed to strike a chord with the wider movie-going public unlike any other comic book movie in history. As its record-breaking opening weekend drew to a close, *The Dark Knight* achieved the distinction of dethroning *The Godfather* and *The Shawshank Redemption* (1994) at the top of the IMDb Top 250, a respected ranking system generated by popular public opinion from users of the *Internet Movie Database*. Furthermore, this reaction was replicated by critics, who were full of appreciation for the way in which *The Dark Knight* stepped out from the usual 'comic book' mould to deliver an accomplished and engrossing narrative. *Variety* described *The Dark Knight* as 'an ambitious, full-bodied crime epic', while Britain's *Empire* magazine delivered a five-star review and praised the film as 'spectacular, visionary blockbuster entertainment: pretty much everything you could hope for and then some'. *The Dark Knight* would become a regular fixture come the obligatory 'Best of 2008' lists and also appeared at number 15 in *Empire*'s list of 'The 500 Greatest Movies of All Time', compiled in 2008 from a poll of 10,000 readers, 150 directors and fifty notable critics.

Central to the critical acclaim lauded upon *The Dark Knight* was universal admiration for Heath Ledger's electric performance as the Joker, which was widely cited as the defining aspect of the movie. This would lead to increasing support and speculation over the possibility of posthumous Academy Award recognition, a sentiment echoed throughout the film's cast and crew: 'Looking back, I think it's sometimes easy to forget how brave of a thing it was for Heath to do, to take the role. He just owns the part – he just is the Joker,' declared Nolan's wife and producing partner Emma Thomas in an interview with *Batman-on-*

*Film.com* in July 2008. 'I think it's an outstanding performance and would love nothing more than for Heath to be recognized like that.'

As it happened, Heath Ledger's performance was central to a run of awards success that culminated with *The Dark Knight* contending for eight Oscars at the Academy Awards, breaking the record previously held by *Dick Tracy* for most nominations for a movie based on a comic book. Ledger's posthumous success in the Best Supporting Actor field made him the first person to be honoured with an Oscar for acting in a comic book movie, while Richard King (*Master and Commander: The Far Side of the World*) added a second Academy Award to his collection for Best Sound Editing. Also nominated for their work on *The Dark Knight* were Nathan Crowley and Peter Lando (Best Art Direction); Wally Pfister (Best Cinematography); Lee Smith (Best Editing); John Caglione Jr and Conor O'Sullivan (Best Make-up); Lora Hirschberg, Gary Rizzo and Ed Novick (Best Sound); and Nick Davis, Chris Corbould, Timothy Webber and Paul J. Franklin (Best Visual Effects).

Awards recognition for *The Dark Knight* was certainly not confined to the Oscars. In all, Heath Ledger received thirty-two posthumous awards for Best Supporting Actor including the BAFTA and Golden Globe, while the Academy of Science Fiction, Fantasy & Horror bestowed five Saturn Awards – Best Action/Adventure/Thriller Film, Best Music (James Newton Howard and Hans

Zimmer), Best Special Effects (Nick Davis, Chris Corbould, Timothy Webber and Paul J. Franklin), Best Supporting Actor (Heath Ledger) and Best Writing (Christopher Nolan and Jonathan Nolan). Among its other accolades were two Critics' Choice Awards (Best Action Movie and Best Supporting Actor), a Grammy (Best Score Soundtrack Album), an MTV Movie Award (Best Villain), five People's Choice Awards (Favourite Action Movie, Favourite Cast, Favourite Movie, Favourite On-Screen Match-Up and Favourite Superhero) and two Screen Actors Guild Awards (Outstanding Performance by a Male Actor in a Supporting Role, Outstanding Performance by a Stunt Ensemble in a Motion Picture).

Having successfully reinvented the *Batman* franchise with his first foray into Gotham City, director Christopher Nolan took things to the next level with *The Dark Knight*, delivering a film that transcended the typical 'comic book' mind-set of audiences, critics and industry insiders alike and that served to legitimize the 'superhero' sub-genre. 'The wonderful thing about *The Dark Knight* is that people – *Batman* fans, comic book fans, the mainstream – are simply referring to it as "a great film" instead of "a great comic book film",' enthused executive producer Michael Uslan, the man ultimately responsible for launching Warner Bros' blockbuster film series when he first secured the rights to the character back in April 1979. 'We've come a long way and *The Dark Knight* has raised the bar for all of us … for all comic book films.'

# Miscellaneous spin-offs

## LEGENDS OF THE SUPERHEROES (1979)

Episode 1 – 'The Challenge'
Original US air date: 18 January 1979

Episode 2 – 'The Roast'
Original US air date: 25 January 1979

### CAST

Adam West (*Batman*); Burt Ward (*Robin*); Rod Haase (*The Flash*); Howard Murphy (*Green Lantern*); Bill Nuckols (*Hawkman*); Garrett Craig (*Captain Marvel*); Barbara Joyce (*The Huntress*); Danuta Rylko Soderman (*The Black Canary*); Alfie Wise (*The Atom*); Frank Gorshin (*The Riddler*); Jeff Altman (*The Weather Wizard*); Charlie Callas (*Sinestro*); Gabriel Dell (*Mordru*); Howard Morris (*Dr Theddeus Bodog Sivana*); Mickey Morton (*Solomon Grundy*); Aleisha Brevard (*Giganta*); Ruth Buzzi (*Aunt Minerva*); Brad Sanders (*Ghetto Man*); William Schallert (*Scarlet Cyclone*); Gary Owens (*Narrator*); Ed McMahon (*Host*).

### KEY CREW

Bill Carruthers, Chris Darley (*Directors*); Bill Carruthers (*Producer*); Joseph Barbara (*Executive Producer*); Joel Stein (*Associate Producer*); Mike Marmer, Peter Gallay (*Written by*); John Beal, Fred Werner (*Music*); Andy Shubert (*Editing*); Warden Neil (*Costume Design*); Lee Schaff Guardino (*Casting*); *Fred Werner* (Music).

### STORY

As the Justice League of America assemble in the Hall of Heroes to celebrate the retirement of the elderly team member Scarlet Cyclone (a.k.a. Retired Man), they receive a clue from the nefarious Legion of Doom about a plot to destroy the world by unleashing a diabolical doomsday device. With just an hour to prevent Armageddon, the heroes race against time to disarm the weapon and defeat their foes, before gathering back at the Hall of Heroes for a comedy roast hosted by the American television personality Ed McMahon.

### BRINGING BATMAN TO THE SCREEN

In 1973, the ABC network launched the long-running Saturday morning children's cartoon *Super Friends*, a loose adaptation of DC Comics' *Justice League of America* comic book produced by the celebrated animation studio Hanna-Barbera

Productions (SEE 'THE EARLY ADVENTURES OF THE ANIMATED BATMAN'). By the start of its third season in 1978, *Super Friends* had undergone a transformation, shifting from the light-hearted tone of earlier seasons for its latest incarnation, *Challenge of the Super Friends*, which saw the roster of heroes protecting the world from the Legion of Doom, a band of supervillains led by the criminal mastermind Lex Luthor. Meanwhile, having been dismissed for so long as little more than children's entertainment by the Hollywood studios, the superhero genre was enjoying a period of renewed popularity, with Warner Bros' *Wonder Woman* television series continuing to draw strong ratings and anticipation building for the arrival of Richard Donner's *Superman: The Movie* in December 1978.

With superheroes big business once again, Hanna-Barbera made the decision to develop a live-action adaptation of *Challenge of the Super Friends*, signing a deal with the NBC network to produce a two-part special entitled *Legends of the Superheroes*. Unable to secure the rights to Superman and Wonder Woman, Hanna-Barbera hoped to compensate for the absence of two of the most recognized characters by securing the services of television's original Batman and Robin, Adam West and Burt Ward. Although Burt Ward had earlier appeared alongside Yvonne Craig's Batgirl for an equal pay public service announcement in 1972, Adam West's reluctance to return as Batman meant that Dick Gautier (*Get Smart*,

1965–70) stood in as the Caped Crusader; however, West's position had softened in the intervening years and – after reuniting with Ward to voice their respective characters on the short-lived animated series *The New Adventures of Batman* in 1977 – the stars agreed to step in front of the camera once again. Joining them for the Bat-Reunion was Frank Gorshin, who also signed on to reprise his Emmy Award-winning turn as the Riddler.

Accompanying Batman and Robin for the first live-action incarnation of the Justice League was Captain Marvel, star of the earlier series *Shazam* (1974–6). The remaining members of the team would all make their live-action debuts in *Legends of the Superheroes*, which featured a roster that included the Flash, Green Lantern, Hawkman, the Black Canary and the Atom. Also making her first appearance outside panel form was the Huntress, the superheroine offspring of Bruce Wayne and Selina Kyle, who had debuted in the comic book story 'Huntress: From Each Ending … A Beginning!' by Paul Levitz, published in *DC Super-Stars* #17 (December 1977). While unknown actors were cast in the majority of the roles, a number of comic performers and celebrities were brought in to provide the 'variety' entertainment, including Ruth Buzzi (*Rowan & Martin's Laugh-In*, 1968–73), Charlie Callas (*Silent Movie*, 1976) and Howard Morris (*The Andy Griffith Show*, 1960–8), along with Ed McMahon (*The Tonight Show*), who would serve as master of ceremonies for the superhero roast. As with the majority of variety shows produced at the time, *Legends of the Superheroes* was recorded on videotape and also featured an accompanying laugh-track.

### RECEPTION

Despite the return of Adam West and Burt Ward to their signature roles, *Legends of the Superheroes* met with poor ratings when the first episode premiered on NBC on Thursday 18 January 1979, coming in as the second least-watched programme of the week. The following episode suffered the same fate as reviewers tore into the programme, criticizing its shoddy production values, overly camp tone, weak script and poor attempts at humour. It was clear that Hanna-Barbera had seriously misjudged their handling of the characters and *Legends of the Superheroes* soon became notorious among comic book fans, drawing comparisons with the universally derided *The Star Wars Holiday Special* (1978). It marked the final on-screen appearance of Adam West and Burt Ward as the Dynamic Duo (although West would later return to voice the character in animated form) and, perhaps surprisingly, it received a DVD release in 2010 as part of the Warner Archive Collection.

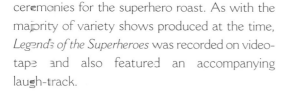

# BIRDS OF PREY (2002–3)

Premiere: 9 October 2002
Episode count: 13 (plus unaired pilot)

### CAST

Ashley Scott (*Helena Kyle/The Huntress*); Dina Meyer (*Barbara Gordon/Oracle*); Rachel Skarsten (*Dinah Redmond*); Shemar Moore (*Detective Jesse Reese*); Ian Abercrombie (*Alfred Pennyworth*); Mia Sara (*Dr Harleen Quinzel/Harley Quinn*); Shawn Christian (*Wade Brixton*); Brent Sexton (*Detective McNally*); Robert Patrick Benedict (*Gibson Kafka*); Bruce Thomas (*Batman*).

### KEY CREW

Mike Tollin, Brian Robbins, Joe Davola, Ron Koslow (*Executive Producers*); Laeta Kalogridis, Hans Tobeason, Michael Katleman (*Co-executive Producers*); Melissa Rosenberg (*Consulting Producer*); Mark Snow (*Music*).

### STORY

The streets of New Gotham are left paved with blood as the war between the Caped Crusader and the Clown Prince of Crime reaches a deadly conclusion. With his criminal empire shattered, a desperate Joker strikes out at Batman, leaving protégé Barbara Gordon paralysed and taking the life of the Dark Knight's one true love – the queen of the underworld, Catwoman. On this fateful night, a grief-stricken Bruce Wayne retires the mantle of the Bat, abandoning the city for a period of self-imposed exile, as a young Helena Kyle uncovers the truth about her parentage. Taken in by Barbara Gordon, Helena is raised to continue her father's crusade on crime as the Huntress, while the former Batgirl also reinvents herself as the Oracle in the wake of the Joker's attack. Together with the young runaway Dinah Redmond, the trio of superheroines now serve as the protectors of New Gotham — the Birds of Prey.

## BRINGING BIRDS OF PREY TO THE SCREEN

In 1999, Tollin/Robins Productions – the company behind popular Nickelodeon shows such as *All That* (1994–2005) and *Kenan & Kel* (1996–2000) – approached Warner Bros with a view to launching a television series based upon the adventures of a young Bruce Wayne (SEE 'ABORTED SPIN-OFFS'). Owing to potential conflicts with the main *Batman* movie franchise, the studio decided to shelve *Bruce Wayne* and the idea was reworked around a pre-Superman Clark Kent, resulting in the hit series *Smallville* (2001–11). As the first season of *Smallville* drew to a close, the WB Network were keen to replicate its success by adding a second superhero-based programme to their schedule, allowing Tollin/Robins the opportunity to realize their ambition of producing a television series set within the *Batman* universe, albeit one that focused on a trio of female crime-fighters.

Rather than the prequel approach of *Bruce Wayne* and *Smallville*, Tollin/Robins chose to go with an adaptation of *Birds of Prey*, the popular comic book series centring on a female superhero team led by Barbara Gordon's Oracle. To develop the pilot for *Birds of Prey*, the production company turned to Laeta Kalogridis, a screenwriter who had earned a reputation for delivering strong female characters through uncredited work on scripts such as *X-Men*, *Scream 3* (2000) and *Lara Croft: Tomb Raider*. To avoid any potential conflicts with the theatrical *Batman* revival, *Birds of Prey* would be set in a futuristic New Gotham long since forsaken by the Caped Crusader, with Oracle serving as mentor to the team of the Huntress and the Black Canary. The latter was based upon the second incarnation of the character, Dinah Laurel Lance, who made her first appearance in the comic book story 'In Each Man There Is a Demon' by Denny O'Neil, published in *Justice League of America* #75 (November 1969).

For their depiction of the Huntress, Kalogridis chose to incorporate the Bronze Age incarnation of the character, Helena Wayne, as opposed to her modern alter ego, Helena Bertinelli. While the Huntress underwent a change of surname to Helena Kyle, the decision was made to abandon the Black Canary alter ego of Dinah Lance, opting instead to portray the character as Dinah Redmond, a teenage runaway with emerging telepathic abilities. Dinah would later be revealed as the estranged daughter of the original Black Canary – now renamed Carolyn Lance – with the intention being to explore her development into a fully fledged superhero as the series progressed. The triumvirate would be aided in their quest to protect New Gotham by Bruce Wayne's faithful butler Alfred Pennyworth and the newly created police detective Jesse Reese, with the deranged psychiatrist Dr Harleen Quinzel serving as the series' primary antagonist.

Securing the lead roles for the pilot episode of *Birds of Prey* were Dina Meyer (*Starship Troopers*, 1997) as Barbara Gordon/Oracle, Ashley Scott (*Dark Angel*, 2000–2) as Helena Kyle/Huntress and Rachel Skarsten (*Little Men*, 1998–9) as Dinah Redmond. They were joined by Ian Abercrombie (*Army of Darkness*, 1992) as Alfred Pennyworth and Shemar Moore (*The Young and the Restless*, 1973–present) as Detective Jesse Reese, while Sherilyn Fenn (*Twin Peaks*) was cast as Dr Harleen Quinzel. Although the Dark Knight was to be absent from the series, he would make an appearance in flashback form during the pilot episode, with Bruce Thomas (*Thirteen Days*, 2000) donning the cape and cowl after starring as Batman the previous year in a series of six General Motors OnStar commercials alongside Michael Gough's Alfred. Joining Thomas' Batman for the flashback sequence was Maggie Baird (*Manic*, 2001) as Catwoman, with stuntman Roger Stoneburner (*Spider-Man*) providing the physical appearance of the Joker and Mark Hamill (*Star Wars: Episode IV – A New Hope*) supplying his voice, having previously lent his vocal talents to

the character in *Batman: The Animated Series* and its subsequent spin-offs (SEE 'THE DARK KNIGHT IN THE DC ANIMATED UNIVERSE').

Impressed with the pilot, the WB Network chose to commission thirteen episodes of *Birds of Prey* in May 2002, hoping to debut the show that fall. However, scheduling conflicts prevented Sherilyn Fenn from committing to the series full-time and her role was recast, with actress Mia Sara (*Ferris Bueller's Day Off*) coming in to reshoot scenes from the pilot episode as Dr Harleen Quinzel. Changes were also afoot behind the scenes as co-executive producer Laeta Kalogridis found her input restricted through creative differences with Tollin/Robins over the direction of the show. With the new television season fast approaching, Warner Bros stepped up publicity for their latest superhero-themed show, but with early reviews decidedly mixed, concerns were already being raised that *Birds of Prey* could struggle to take flight.

**RECEPTION**

*Birds of Prey* premiered on the WB Network with a special seventy-minute pilot episode on 2 October 2002 and brushed aside early criticism to deliver the network's largest audience in the 18–34 demographic for that evening with a reported 7.6m viewers. Although it quickly built a solid fan base, *Birds of Prey* was unable to maintain its early success and – with its audience dwindling by the week – Warner Bros opted against picking the show up for a full season. In November 2002 it was announced that the series had been cancelled, and despite a fan campaign to save the show *Birds of Prey* came to an end on 19 February 2003 with the broadcast of the final two episodes, which featured an appearance by the villain Clayface – portrayed by actor Kirk Baltz (*Reservoir Dogs*, 1992) – and culminated with the defeat of Harley Quinn. In July 2008, the short-lived series received a North American DVD release with a four-disc set consisting of all thirteen episodes of the series, the unaired pilot episode and the complete *Gotham Girls* animated web series.

## RETURN TO THE BATCAVE: THE MISADVENTURES OF ADAM AND BURT (2003)

**Broadcast date:** 9 March 2003 (US)
**Running time:** 90 minutes

### CAST

Adam West (*Himself*); Burt Ward (*Himself*); Jack Brewer (*Adam West/Batman*); Jason Marsden (*Burt Ward/Robin*); Lyle Waggoner (*Himself/Narrator*); Frank Gorshin (*Himself*); Julie Newmar (*Herself*); Lee Meriwether (*Waitress*); Brett Rickaby (*Frank Gorshin/The Riddler*); Julia Rose (*Julie Newmar/Catwoman*); Erin Carufel (*Yvonne Craig/Batgirl*); Bud Watson (*Cesar Romero/The Joker*); Quinn K. Redeker (*Vincent Price/Egghead*); Jim Jansen (*William Dozier*); Amy Acker (*Bonnie Lindsey*); Curtis Armstrong (*Jerry the Butler*); Stacy Kamano (*Nghara Frisbie-West*); Betty White (*Bat-Climb Cameo Woman*).

### KEY CREW

Paul A. Kaufman (*Director*); Paul A. Kaufman (*Executive Producer*); Larry Germain, Dawn Wells (*Co-executive Producers*); Jodi Ticknor (*Co-producer*); Duane Poole (*Written by*); Douglas J. Cuomo (*Music*); James Glennon (*Cinematography*); Bill Boes (*Production Design*), Greg LaVoi (*Costume Design*); Lori Openden (*Casting*).

## STORY

*Batman* stars Adam West and Burt Ward reunite for a charity benefit almost thirty-five years after the cancellation of their classic ABC television series and get to relive their crime-fighting exploits for real when the Batmobile is stolen from the event by a dastardly criminal. Working from a clue left by the perpetrator, the former Dynamic Duo set out to unravel the mystery and come to realize that the answer is hidden in their past. Reminiscing about their time on *Batman*, Adam and Burt recall the tumultuous on-set antics and wild off-camera debauchery behind the scenes of the show as they close in on the vehicle, only to find themselves lured into a deadly trap by the masterminds of the crime – former *Batman* villains Frank Gorshin and Julie Newmar.

## BRINGING BATMAN TO THE SCREEN

After the success of TV movie docudramas such *Come On, Get Happy: The Partridge Family Story* (ABC, 1999) and *Growing Up Brady* (NBC, 2000) the CBS network delivered their own 'behind-the-scenes' biopic of a classic American television show with *Surviving Gilligan's Island: The Incredibly True Story of the Longest Three Hour Tour in History* in 2001. Impressed with the creative approach taken by director Paul A. Kaufman (*Run the Wild Fields*, 2000) and writer Duane Poole (*The All New Super Friends Hour*, 1977–8), CBS commissioned the team behind *Surviving*

*Gilligan's Island* to deliver a follow-up, this time centred around William Dozier's camp pop-culture phenomenon, *Batman*.

Rather than a straightforward retelling of the creation of the series, the producers chose to incorporate elements of the ever-popular reunion movie for *Return to the Batcave*, securing the services of *Batman's* iconic lead actors – Adam West and Burt Ward – and crafting an original story around them to serve as a framing device. Despite his initial reluctance to take part in a 'reunion', Adam West was drawn towards the comedic approach of the project and also took up an opportunity to serve as executive creative consultant. Joining the Dynamic Duo in the cast were two of the series' most popular Special Guest Villains – Frank Gorshin (the Riddler) and Julie Newmar (Catwoman) – along with other familiar faces from the show's history including Lee Meriwether and Lyle Waggoner.

For the flashback sequences, production designer Bill Boes (*Scooby-Doo*) oversaw the painstaking reconstruction of a number of iconic costumes and sets, including a replica of the original Batcave. Jack Brewer (*JAG*, 1995–2005) was cast as the young Adam West, while the part of a young Burt Ward went to Jason Marsden, an actor with previous experience in the *Batman* universe, having voiced characters on *Batman: The Animated Series* and *Batman Beyond*. West and Ward would work with their counterparts to help the actors craft authentic performances, although the production found itself restricted by an inability to incorporate actual footage from the television show, owing to a dispute over rights with rival network ABC. Nevertheless, *Return to the Batcave* would include footage from Lyle Waggoner's original Batman screen-test, in addition to material from the 1966 theatrical movie.

## RECEPTION

*Return to the Batcave: The Misadventures of Adam and Burt* premiered as part of *CBS Sunday Night Movies* on 9 March 2003. The TV movie received disappointing ratings and mixed reviews, although the flashback sequences were generally praised for providing a nostalgic insight into the creation of the classic television series. *Return to the Batcave* received a North American DVD release in May 2005 and arrived in the UK the following month.

# CATWOMAN (2004)

**Release date:** 23 July 2004 (US); 13 August 2004 (UK)
**Certificate:** PG-13 (US); 12A (theatrical), 12 (DVD) (UK)
**Running time:** 104 minutes
**Budget:** $100m
**Global box office:** $82,102,379

## CAST

Halle Berry (*Patience Phillips/Catwoman*); Benjamin Bratt (*Detective Tom Lone*); Sharon Stone (*Laurel Hedare*); Lambert Wilson (*George Hedare*); Frances Conroy (*Ophelia Powers*); Alex Borstein (*Sally*); Michael Massee (*Armando*); Byron Mann (*Wesley*); Kim Smith (*Drina*); Peter Wingfield (*Dr Ivan Slavicky*).

## KEY CREW

Pitof (*Director*); Denise Di Novi, Edward L. McDonnell (*Producers*); Bruce Berman, Michael Fottrell, Robert Kirby, Michael E. Uslan, Benjamin Melniker (*Executive Producers*); Ed Jones, Marc Resteghini (*Associate Producers*); Alison Greenspan (*Co-producer*); Theresa Rebeck, John D. Brancato, Michael Ferris (*Story*); John D. Brancato, Michael Ferris, John Rogers (*Screenplay*); Bob Kane (*Characters*); Klaus Badelt (*Music*); Thierry Arbogast (*Cinematography*); Sylvie Landra (*Editing*); Bill Brzeski (*Production Design*), Angus Strathie (*Costume Design*); John Papsidera (*Casting*).

## STORY

As a timid and demure young woman trying to make her way in the city, Patience Phillips is finding out that life can sometimes be a struggle. Kept up all night by her partying neighbours and with only her friend and co-worker Sally to provide the occasional company, Patience is desperate to make an impression in her work as a graphic designer for Hedare Beauty, a cosmetics company headed up by callous CEO George Hedare and his wife, former model and 'face of the company' Laurel. However, things could soon be looking up for Patience – not only does she have the chance to present designs for the launch of a revolutionary new product, Beau-Line, but romance could also be afoot with Tom Lone, a police detective who saves her from falling when she attempts to rescue a cat, Midnight, from the ledge of her apartment.

Hoping to please her boss Patience submits her proposals for the Beau-Line launch only for them to be coldly dismissed by George. Pleading for a second chance, Patience is given until midnight to implement her changes, but when she turns up to deliver the amended designs she overhears a heated discussion between Laurel and Dr Ivan Slavicky about the ghastly side-effects of the Beau-Line cream. Patience attempts to flee and runs into a water conduit which is then flooded, casting her out into the open water where she drowns. As her lifeless body drifts upon the shore it becomes surrounded by a group of cats led by Midnight, with the animals mysteriously breathing life back into her body.

Waking the next morning without any recollection of the previous day's events, Patience sees that Midnight has returned to her apartment and traces her back to the home of Ophelia Powers, a former academic with a fondness for cats. As Patience goes to leave Ophelia hands her some catnip, causing her to experience strange sensations; as these continue to intensify, Patience gradually begins to develop feline-like reflexes, heightened senses, a craving for canned fish and an attraction to shiny objects. Things reach a head when she confronts her party-loving neighbours and, with a newfound confidence, she transforms herself into the leather-clad Catwoman. Setting off on a motorbike to 'accessorize', Catwoman interrupts a robbery at a jeweller's and confronts the crooks but is unable to resist the urge to make off with the inventory herself.

After returning the stolen jewellery, Patience visits Ophelia in search of answers to her transformation. There she uncovers the truth – that, following her murder, she was resurrected by Midnight, an Egyptian Mau cat who serves as a messenger to the goddess Bast, and is now reborn as the latest in a line of Catwomen. With fragments of her memory returning, Catwoman heads back to the factory, stumbling upon the body of Dr Slavicky. Discovered by a guard, Catwoman is falsely accused of murder and manages to escape before sneaking into the Hedare residence. Confronted by Laurel, Catwoman expresses her concerns over the Beau-Line cover-up and blames George, with the deceitful Laurel offering to help bring her husband down, revealing his location at the opera. When Catwoman confronts him, George denies all knowledge but before she can press him further the police arrive. Catwoman narrowly manages to escape apprehension by Detective Lone, who is simultaneously heading up the Catwoman case while embarking on a relationship with her alter ego.

The next day Patience receives a phone call from Laurel who promises to deliver proof of the Beau-Line cover-up. As Catwoman arrives at the Hedare residence she finds herself framed for George's murder and learns that Laurel was the one responsible for her death. Catwoman makes her escape as the police surround the house, but Detective Lone has managed to uncover her secret identity and is forced to arrest Patience. After listening to her story, the detective pays a visit to Laurel at Hedare's penthouse office and tricks her into revealing the truth, only for Laurel to shoot him in the shoulder. Fortunately, Patience has freed herself from custody by squeezing through the bars of her cell and turns up in time to save Tom's life.

In the ensuing showdown it is revealed that years of Beau-Line treatment have left Laurel with marble-like skin and she is unable to feel pain, despite the fact that Catwoman's claws manage to damage her face. As the fight draws to a conclusion Laurel slips through a broken window and is left hanging from the side of the building. Catwoman reaches out to save her but Laurel sees her ravaged reflection in the glass and chooses to let go, plummeting to her death on the streets far below. Patience is cleared of all charges, and while Tom wants to continue the relationship, he receives a letter thanking him for his help, but stating that there's no place for Catwoman in a world like his …

## BRINGING CATWOMAN TO THE SCREEN

Rumours of a solo *Catwoman* movie first emerged in the Hollywood press in the fall of 1993 when it was revealed that Pfeiffer's character was absent from the third instalment of the *Batman* series, which was gearing up for production under new director Joel Schumacher. While Burton remained nominally involved in the main *Batman* franchise as producer, the filmmaker found himself drawn to the prospect of further exploring Catwoman alongside Pfeiffer and soon became unofficially attached to the spin-off project as director. Joining Burton in the reunion were *Batman Returns* producer Denise Di Novi and scribe Daniel Waters, who then set about developing a screenplay for the prospective project. Waters handed his first draft of *Catwoman* over to Warner Bros on 16 June 1995 – the same day that *Batman Forever* opened in North American cinemas. Eschewing the fresh, 'family-friendly' approach of *Batman*

*Forever*, Waters' screenplay retained the dark tone established by Burton's earlier efforts and saw Selina Kyle suffering from amnesia after the events of *Batman Returns*; travelling to the Las Vegas-like desert city of Oasisburg, Selina encounters rampant female oppression and finds herself returning to the Catwoman persona in order to tackle a devious group of male 'superheroes'.

Despite the arrival of a screenplay, Burton – who had since collaborated with Di Novi on *The Nightmare Before Christmas*, *Cabin Boy* and *Ed Wood* – found his interest in *Catwoman* waning and opted instead to focus on other projects such as *James and the Giant Peach* (1996) and *Mars Attacks!*, along with the aborted *Superman* reboot *Superman Lives*. Following Burton's departure, Michelle Pfeiffer remained committed for a brief time until *Catwoman* entered a period of stagnation, languishing in 'development hell' as a host of writers tried their hand at the screenplay. By the time of its eventual release, *Catwoman* had passed through the hands of no fewer than twenty-eight writers, including Theresa Rebeck (*Harriet the Spy*, 1996), David Reynolds (*The Emperor's New Groove*, 2000), Harley Peyton (*Twin Peaks*), Rita Hsiao (*Toy Story 2*, 1999) and Kate Kondell (*Legally Blonde 2: Red, White and Blonde*, 2003).

Struggling to relaunch the main *Batman* franchise after the abysmal reaction towards Joel Schumacher's *Batman & Robin*, Warner Bros turned their attention back to *Catwoman* towards the end of the millennium. Working from a draft by the screenwriting duo of John Brancato and Michael Ferris (*The Game*, 1997) that had undergone additional writing by John Rogers (*Cosby*, 1996–2000), the studio eventually decided to press on with the production. In April 2001 it was reported that actress Ashley Judd – star of films such as *A Time to Kill* and *Kiss the Girls* (1997) – had signed on for the lead role. Nevertheless, it was another year before a director was secured in Pitof, a French filmmaker who had begun his career as a visual effects supervisor on the likes of *Delicatessen* (1991), *The City of Lost Children* (1995) and *Alien: Resurrection* (1997) before making his directorial debut with the well-received period mystery *Vidocq* (2001).

Just as it seemed that progress was being made on *Catwoman*, the production hit yet another snag when scheduling conflicts forced Ashley Judd to depart in favour of a Broadway adaptation of Tennessee Williams' *Cat on a Hot Tin Roof*. With the search on for a replacement, rumours circulated that *Batman Forever*'s Dr Chase Meridian, Nicole Kidman, would be offered the part. Since her appearance in the 1995 sequel Kidman had earned an Academy Award nomination for Best Actress (*Moulin Rouge!*, 2001) and was only weeks away from collecting the accolade at the second attempt for her performance as Virginia Woolf in *The Hours* (2002). However, in the run-up to the ceremony the studio announced that they had already found their Catwoman in the shape of another Oscar-winning actress with her own ties to the superhero genre.

After a number of early television parts in the late 1980s, Halle Berry enjoyed her career break-through with a supporting role as a drug addict in Spike Lee's acclaimed drama *Jungle Fever* (1991). Over the next decade Berry went on to star in a diverse range of projects such as *The Flintstones* (1994), *Bulworth* (1998) and *Swordfish* (2001), culminating with her Academy Award-winning turn as a struggling single parent in the romantic drama *Monster's Ball*. Furthermore, not only did Berry possess recent action experience as the tough NSA agent and 'Bond girl' Jinx in *Die Another Day* (2002), but she was also well known to comic book fans, having appeared as Storm in Bryan Singer's blockbuster Marvel adaptation *X-Men*, along with its soon-to-be-released sequel *X2: X-Men United*.

With Halle Berry confirmed as the fifth actress to bring Catwoman to the screen (or sixth, if you include Maggie Baird's very brief flashback appearance in the pilot episode of *Birds of Prey*) for a reported fee of $14m, the studio then set about assembling its supporting cast. To portray the villainous Laurel Hedare, Pitof turned to Sharon Stone, the former model who had first gained fame with her role as seductive sociopath Catherine Tramell in the erotic thriller *Basic Instinct* before earning her own Oscar nomination for Best Supporting Actress in Martin Scorsese's crime epic *Casino* (1995). Benjamin Bratt, best known for his

Emmy-nominated work between 1995 and 1999 as Detective Rey Curtis in the long-running police procedural *Law & Order*, signed on as the film's male lead, Detective Tom Lone, and Lambert Wilson (*The Matrix Reloaded*, 2003) was cast as Laurel's husband, George Hedare. Meanwhile the original Catwoman, Julie Newmar, declined the opportunity to appear as Ophelia Powers, with Frances Conroy (*Six Feet Under*, 2001–5) then securing the role.

As the $100m-budgeted *Catwoman* geared up for production, members of the online fan community began to voice their discontent over the direction of the film. A primary concern was the fact that a newly created character, Patience Price (later changed to Phillips), would be donning the Catsuit at the expense of Selina Kyle and that, unlike the established comic book interpretation, Patience would be a 'metahuman' possessing feline superpowers. With progress being made on Christopher Nolan's reboot of the *Batman* franchise, rumours soon began to circulate that Warner executives were re-evaluating the spin-off, but these proved unfounded when principal photography on *Catwoman* got underway in September 2003. However, the release of an early publicity image kick-started a backlash against the film that would continue right through until its release.

Just days into filming a photograph emerged depicting Halle Berry in full Catwoman attire; designed by Angus Strathie, the Academy

Award-winning costume designer behind *Moulin Rouge!*, the new-look outfit was a radical shift from previous efforts. Featuring a bra-style top, shredded leather pants, straps, chains and mask complete with oversized cat ears, the costume reveal was met with near-universal derision; Harry Knowles of *AintItCoolNews.com* – whose heavy criticism of *Batman & Robin* had led Joel Schumacher to vent his frustrations at online journalism – described the design as 'the most ridiculously awful lame-ass attempt at a Catwoman costume in history'. As fan negativity continued to swell, reports also started to emerge that all was not well behind the scenes.

Having been denied the opportunity to rework the script with *Vidocq* production designer Jean Rabasse, Pitof encountered creative differences with the studio and producer Denise De Novi, who felt that his approach was too artistic. Fearful that the growing backlash could impact on the success of their *Batman* reboot, the studio demanded changes to the script and began reworking elements of the film. Further images were released showing Berry in a more traditional biker-style outfit, but in March 2004 a rough-cut of the trailer leaked on to the internet and all but dashed the studio's hopes of generating any pre-release buzz. After similarly poor receptions to official trailers in May and June – and with just a month to go before the film's release – the studio ordered a number of reshoots in a last-gasp attempt to salvage their $100m investment.

## RECEPTION

Given the arduous development of the *Catwoman* feature and the disappointing response from the fan community towards its promotional campaign, expectations were running low when the film reached North American cinemas on 23 July 2004. *Catwoman* opened on 3,117 screens and banked $16.7m in its opening weekend, placing it third behind *The Bourne Supremacy* and *I, Robot* in the US box-office chart. In its second weekend the film slipped to sixth place and spent just three weeks in the top ten as exhibitors drastically reduced the number of screenings. By the end of its North American run *Catwoman* had grossed $40,198,710 for Warner Bros, a return that surpassed just two of their previous live-action DC Comics superhero movies – *Superman IV: The Quest for Peace* (1987) and *Steel* (1997). This dismal performance was also matched in the international markets; in the UK *Catwoman* opened in fifth place with £557,538 (including £108,288 from advance preview screenings) and reached just £1,158,075, while its total global haul of $82,102,379 meant that the spin-off failed to recoup its initial production budget.

Central to the poor box-office performance of *Catwoman* was the scathing reception given to the film by critics. In his review in the *Chicago Sun-Times*, Roger Ebert (who would later include the film among his list of 'Most Hated') tore into the lack of characterization, tired narrative and uninspiring action sequences, while in a similarly ferocious piece *Variety* accused Warner Bros of plummeting 'to the dimmest recesses of popcorn inanity'. Britain's *Empire* magazine gave *Catwoman* one star and suggested 'this is only worth seeing if you can handle shallow characters and dull, plastic action scenes for the sake of unintentional laughs'. While Harry Knowles of *AintItCoolNews.com* described *Catwoman* as 'a stodgy, yowly, no fun to play with neutered, overfed house tabby', he did concede that 'this isn't a disaster of a film, this isn't the worst movie ever. This isn't even close … unfortunately the film has just enough good moments to reach that impossible height in filmmaking that we call … mediocrity.'

Despite its critical and commercial failure, *Catwoman* did manage to enjoy a trace of success on the awards circuit. Jayne Dancose and Norma Hill-Patton shared Best Make-up Artist for a Feature Film at the Canadian Network of Make-up Artists Awards, while Zoe Bell was nominated for Best High Work at the World Stunt Awards and Halle Berry lost out to Hilary Duff (*A Cinderella Story*, 2004) for Favourite Movie Actress at the Kids' Choice Awards. Predictably, it was also a favourite of the Golden Raspberry Awards, collecting seven nominations in total and receiving 'recognition' in the categories of Worst Picture, Worst Screenplay, Worst Director and Worst Actress. In attending the ceremony, Halle Berry became one of only a handful of recipients to collect a 'Razzie' in person, thanking Warner Bros in her acceptance speech 'for putting me in this piece of shit, God-awful movie'.

While rumours persisted throughout the production of *Catwoman* that the Caped Crusader could make a cameo appearance in the spin-off, as it turned out the only connection to the main *Batman* franchise proved to be an image of Michelle Pfeiffer's Catwoman, visible briefly during a scene between Berry and Frances Conroy's Ophelia Powers. In hindsight it was certainly a wise decision for Warner Bros to keep the two properties distinct, with the studio desperate to reclaim credibility for the Caped Crusader after the complete failure of *Batman & Robin* – a feat they would achieve the following year with the release of Christopher Nolan's *Batman Begins*.

Val Kilmer accepted the role of Batman in the Joel Schumacher film *Batman Forever* without even reading the screenplay, receiving a reported fee of $7m for his services.

As far as Warner Bros were concerned, there was but one creative mandate for the 1997 film *Batman & Robin*, starring George Clooney as Batman, Alicia Silverstone as Batgirl and Chris O'Donnell as Robin, which was best exemplified by the film's promotional tagline of 'More Heroes … More Villains … More Action …'

When Heath Ledger took on the role of
the Joker for the 2008 film *The Dark
Knight* he embarked on a period of
self-enforced seclusion, locking himself
away in a London hotel room for a month
to study the psychology of the character.

Central to the critical acclaim for *The Dark Knight* was universal admiration for Heath Ledger's electric performance as the Joker, which was widely cited as the defining aspect of the movie. 'Looking back, I think it's sometimes easy to forget how brave of a thing it was for Heath to do, to take the role,' declared producer Emma Thomas. 'He just owns the part – he just is the Joker.'

Gary Oldman as Lieutenant James Gordon introduces Christian Bale's Batman to Aaron Eckhart's Harvey Dent for the first time in a seminal moment for the 2008 film *The Dark Knight*.

# Aborted spin-offs

## BRUCE WAYNE

In the summer of 1999, with Warner Bros' feature film department struggling to reignite the *Batman* franchise in the wake of the catastrophic reception given to *Batman & Robin*, the studio's television division decided to move forward with a project based upon the formative years of the Caped Crusader. Entitled *Bruce Wayne*, the proposed series was the brainchild of screenwriter Tim McCanlies (*The Iron Giant*, 1999), who devised a concept centring on the teenage billionaire and socialite as he secretly hones his skills and develops an understanding of the criminal mind in preparation for his eventual crusade against crime.

Meeting with Tollin/Robbins Productions, McCanlies was commissioned to write a pilot script for *Bruce Wayne*, with Warner Bros Television subsequently finalizing a deal to secure the broadcast rights for the WB Television Network. Completed in November 1999, the resulting script was narrated by Alfred Pennyworth and saw a headstrong Bruce Wayne returning to Gotham City just days before his eighteenth birthday to discover a city rife with crime and corruption. Intending to sign his family business over

to board member Charles Palantine, Bruce comes to suspect that WayneCorp may be instrumental in the city's decline and – with his own life coming under threat – he forges an alliance with Detective James Gordon; choosing to remain in Gotham, Bruce gains control of WayneCorp and takes the first steps towards his destiny as the Dark Knight.

McCanlies' teleplay also incorporated a number of supporting characters from the rich history of the *Batman* universe in addition to Alfred and Detective Gordon, including best friend and law student Harvey Dent, WayneCorp intern Lucius Fox, mysterious partygoer Selina Kyle, budding reporter Vicki Vale and a juvenile Barbara Gordon, all of whom were intended to become recurring cast members. Envisioning the show as running for five or six seasons, McCanlies produced a show bible and planned to introduce a host of additional characters as the series progressed, such as the temperamental comedian Jack Napier (the future Joker), medical student Harleen Quinzel, psychology professor Dr Jonathan Crane, con-man Edward Nygma, mobsters Carmine Falcone, Rupert Thorne and

Oswald Cobblepot, and a 'strange' farm boy from Smallville, Kansas, called Clark Kent.

By the turn of the millennium word began to spread that the WB Network was prepping a series based upon the adventures of a young Bruce Wayne, but this was quickly followed by reports of an internal struggle between Warner Bros' television and movie divisions. Determined to revive the lucrative film series, the studio was exploring the possibility of reinterpreting the Dark Knight's origins with a feature adaptation of Frank Miller's *Batman: Year One*, for which they would secure the services of director Darren Aronofsky in 2000. Amid casting rumours linking up-and-coming actors Shawn Ashmore (*X-Men*) and Trevor Fehrman (*Odd Man Out*, 1999–2000) to the title role in *Bruce Wayne*, Warner Bros wanted to avoid any potential conflict and chose to put the series on hold in favour of moving forward with their theatrical ambitions.

The decision to explore Bruce's journey to the Dark Knight as a feature film was reinforced by the box-office success of Bryan Singer's *X-Men* in the summer of 2000, which rejuvenated the superhero genre and effectively brought about an end to *Bruce Wayne*. Development on the series officially came to a halt in mid-2000, with Tollin/Robbins Productions then reworking the initial concept around another popular DC Comics character later in the year, hiring the team of Alfred Gough and Miles Millar (*The Strip*, 1999–2000) to produce a pilot episode for *Young Clark Kent*. After undergoing a change of name to *Smallville*, the show premiered on the WB Network on 16 October 2001 and was an instant success, giving the network its highest ever debut with 8.4 million viewers.

Despite fervent speculation from fans about the possibility of a guest appearance in *Smallville*, the character of Bruce Wayne remained absent from the series, which ran for a total of ter seasons before finally drawing to a close in May 2011. At the height of its popularity, Alfred Gough and Miles Millar approached Warner Bros about resurrecting *Bruce Wayne* as a companion show to *Smallville*, but the idea was nixed by the studio as development got underway on *Batman Begins*. Tollin/Robins did achieve their goal of producing a *Batman*-related television show with the short-lived spin-off *Birds of Prey* in 2002, and in October 2008 Warner Bros also announced plans for a new *Smallville*-type series centred around a pre-Robin Dick 'DJ' Grayson entitled *The Graysons*, only to call a halt to the pilot before a script was written.

## BATMAN VS SUPERMAN

Although Warner Bros were finding it difficult to relaunch the Dark Knight after *Batman & Robin*, the struggle was nothing compared to that of their other major DC property, *Superman*. Having ushered in the modern superhero film in 1978 with Richard Donner's *Superman: The Movie*, the Man of Steel had been absent from the screen since his own franchise-killer, *Superman IV: The Quest for Peace*, which the studio co-produced with Cannon Films back in 1987. The failure of *Superman IV* brought an end to a proposed fifth instalment in the Christopher Reeve series, with *Batman* producer Jon Peters subsequently coming on board in the early 1990s and commissioning a number of scripts based upon DC Comics' *The Death and Return of Superman* story arc (October 1992–October 1993).

Passing through the hands of writers such as Jonathan Lemkin (*Lethal Weapon 4*, 1998), Gregory Poirier (*Rosewood*, 1997), Kevin Smith (*Clerks*, 1994), Wesley Strick, Dan Gilroy (*Freejack*, 1992) and William Wisher Jr (*Judge Dredd*, 1995), a new *Superman* movie did get as far as pre-production in 1997, with Tim Burton set to direct Academy Award-winner Nicolas Cage (*Leaving Las Vegas*, 1995) as the Last Son of Krypton in *Superman Lives*. The eventual collapse of that project meant that Warner Bros entered the twenty-first century with their two biggest superhero properties in exile from the screen and – rather than trying to continue the previous series – the studio then made the decision to start afresh with new origin stories for both characters. In February 2002, J.J. Abrams (*Alias*, 2001–6) was hired to pen a screenplay for director McG (*Charlie's Angels*, 2000) entitled *Superman: Flyby*, while Darren Aronofsky and Frank Miller continued to develop their adaptation of *Batman: Year One*. However, much like *Year One*, *Superman: Flyby*

would fail to get off the ground and both projects were put on indefinite hold in July 2002 when Warner Bros announced that the two superheroes were to come face to face on the big screen for the very first time.

In August 2001, *Se7en* screenwriter Andrew Kevin Walker pitched an idea for *Batman vs Superman*, with German-born filmmaker Wolfgang Petersen (*The Perfect Storm*, 2000) attached as director. Intrigued by the potential to kick-start both franchises at once, Warner Bros gave Walker the go-ahead to develop a script, which then underwent a rewrite courtesy of *Batman Forever* and *Batman & Robin* scribe Akiva Goldsman. Set in the same continuity as the previous movies, the script for *Batman vs Superman* began with a down-on-his-luck Clark Kent set to finalize his divorce from Lois Lane as close friend Bruce Wayne prepares to enter into married life with fiancée Elizabeth Miller. Having given up the mantle of the Bat after the deaths of Dick Grayson, Alfred Pennyworth and Commissioner Gordon, Bruce is forced to come out of retirement when a resurrected Joker kills Elizabeth. When he vows to take the life of his arch-nemesis in revenge, Superman attempts to prevent Batman from crossing the line and the two come into conflict, only to discover that Lex Luthor has orchestrated a scheme to turn the superheroes against one another.

Officially confirmed on 8 July 2002, the idea was to fast-track *Batman vs Superman* through development, shooting the film the following February for a release in the summer of 2004. Discussing the 'World's Finest' cross-over shortly after it was given the green light, Wolfgang Petersen stated that he was looking for young actors in the 'Matt Damon-mould' for his two leads. Reports quickly emerged of a shortlist that included Christian Bale, Colin Farrell (*Tigerland*, 2000) and James Franco (*Spider-Man*) for the Dark Knight and Josh Hartnett, Jude Law, Brandon Routh (*Undressed*, 1999–2002) and Paul Walker (*The Fast and the Furious*, 2001) for the Man of Steel. It was alleged that both Christian Bale and Josh Hartnett declined offers to join the cast and, barely a month after the film had been announced, the project was left in limbo as Wolfgang Petersen vacated the director's chair to helm the historical epic *Troy* (2004).

The final nail in the coffin for *Batman vs Superman* came in September 2002 when Warner Bros' Executive Vice President of Worldwide Motion Picture Production Lorenzo di Bonaventura resigned from the studio amid talk of creative differences with President and Chief Operating Officer Alan Horn. Di Bonaventura had been a strong supporter of *Batman vs Superman*, whereas Horn favoured the idea of relaunching the characters individually; Horn immediately resurrected *Superman: Flyby* under director Brett Ratner (*Rush Hour*, 1998) and in January 2003 Christopher Nolan signed on to develop a new *Batman* movie, resulting in the 2005 reboot *Batman Begins* star-

ring Christian Bale. Although *Superman: Flyby* eventually fell apart, Bryan Singer eventually brought the Man of Steel back to the screen in 2006 with *Superman Returns*, a quasi-sequel to the earlier Christopher Reeve movies starring Brandon Routh. Despite a favourable reception from critics, Warner Bros were disappointed by the financial returns on their $209m investment and in 2010 the studio announced plans to reboot the *Superman* franchise, securing the services of producer Christopher Nolan, screenwriter David S. Goyer, director Zack Snyder (*Watchmen*, 2009) and former Dark Knight candidate Henry Cavill for *Man of Steel* (2013).

## JUSTICE LEAGUE: MORTAL

After relaunching their two major superhero franchises with Christopher Nolan's *Batman Begins* and Bryan Singer's *Superman Returns*, Warner Bros were busy developing sequels to both films – along with a proposed *Wonder Woman* feature from writer-director Joss Whedon – when the decision was made to take their stable of DC Comics characters down a similar path to that of rival publisher Marvel. Establishing their own independent film production division in 2005, Marvel Studios had announced plans to produce a slate of solo movies in *Iron Man*, *The Incredible Hulk*, *Thor* (2011) and *Captain America* (2011), building towards their star-studded superhero cross-over *The Avengers* (2012). Having enjoyed little success outside Batman and Superman with their DC properties, Warner Bros executives were drawn towards the prospect of using a superhero team-up as a platform to launch their lesser-known characters, and with the Justice League of America they already possessed an ensemble more than capable of matching up to the Avengers.

Tracing its origins back to the Bronze Age's first superhero team, the Justice Society of America, the Justice League made their Silver Age debut in the comic book story 'Justice League of America' by Gardner Fox, published in *The Brave and the Bold* #28 (March 1960). Featuring an original line-up of Batman, Superman, Wonder Woman, the Flash, Green Lantern, Aquaman and Martian Manhunter, *Justice League of America* quickly became one of DC's biggest selling titles and its success went on to influence Marvel Comics, who introduced their own team of superheroes with the release of *Fantastic Four* #1, kick-starting a revival in fortunes for the comic book industry. A version of the Justice League first appeared on screen in the animated series *The Superman/Aquaman Hour of Adventure* (1967–8), while the following decade saw the team serving as the inspiration for the long-running Saturday morning cartoon series *Super Friends* (SEE 'THE EARLY ADVENTURES OF THE ANIMATED BATMAN'). The producers of *Super Friends*, Hanna-Barbera, would also develop a live-action incarnation of the cartoon in 1979 entitled *Legends of the Superheroes*, although rights issues prevented Superman

and Wonder Woman from joining the roster for the two-part variety show special.

In 1997 a live-action pilot was produced for a *Justice League of America* television series, which omitted Batman, Superman and Wonder Woman from its line-up and was ultimately rejected by the CBS network. The ensemble did arrive on the small screen four years later when *Batman: The Animated Series* co-creator Bruce W. Timm launched *Justice League* as the latest entry in the popular DC Animated Universe (SEE 'THE DARK KNIGHT IN THE DC ANIMATED UNIVERSE'), and in January 2007 a version of the team appeared on *Smallville* in the sixth-season episode *Justice*. The following month, Warner Bros decided to move forward with their plans to bring the superheroes together for a cinematic adventure, hiring the screenwriting duo of Keiran and Michelle Mulroney to start work on a script for a *Justice League* feature.

The announcement of a *Justice League* movie was met with a mixed response by the fan community, raising questions as to how the studio intended to incorporate the film alongside their current projects, specifically Christopher Nolan's *The Dark Knight*, which was about to commence principal photography for release the following summer. Speculation increased in June when *Variety* reported that both Batman and Superman were present in the Mulroneys' script, leaving fans wondering whether Christian Bale and Brandon Routh were set to bring their respective characters together on screen. However, Bale expressed his uneasiness over the project and by the time that George Miller (*Mad Max*, 1979) came on board as director in September, it seemed increasingly likely that another actor would don the cape and cowl for a new interpretation of the Caped Crusader.

Following Miller's arrival, reports emerged that Warner Bros were considering the possibility of producing *Justice League* using performance capture technology, an increasingly popular form of digital animation that had been pioneered by Robert Zemeckis' ImageMovers studio on the likes of *The Polar Express* (2004) and *Beowulf* (2007). Alleged script details soon leaked to the internet, suggesting that the Mulroneys' script – entitled *Justice League: Mortal* – drew heavily from the comic book continuity, adopting a plot that centred around a spy satellite constructed by Batman in order to keep track of his fellow League members and provide him with details of their weaknesses. Falling into the hands of the corrupt businessman Maxwell Lord, the satellite would be used to turn Superman against his allies before a final showdown between the Justice League of America and Lord's army of cyborgs. The script also tied into the continuity of *Batman Begins* and featured the inclusion Ra's al Ghul's daughter, Talia, a character first introduced in the comic book story 'Into the Den of the Death-Dealers!' by Denny O'Neil, published in *Detective Comics* #411 (May 1971).

Fast-tracking *Justice League: Mortal* through pre-production to avoid the impending Writers Guild of America strike, Warner Bros intended to commence principal photography in Australia in February 2008, hoping to fill a void in their schedule for the summer of 2009. In casting his team of superheroes, Miller auditioned over forty possible contenders, searching for actors that he felt could grow into their roles over a series of movies. While no deals were ever officially announced, several sources confirmed that Miller had found his line-up and details began to emerge as to who would fill out the roster of the Justice League in the $220m-budgeted production.

Securing the role of the Dark Knight was Armie Hammer, an up-and-coming actor whose resumé included appearances in shows such as *Arrested Development* (2003–6), *Veronica Mars* (2004–7) and *Desperate Housewives* (2004–12), and he was to be joined by a cast that included D.J. Cotrona (*Skin*, 2003–4) as Clark Kent/Superman, Megan Gale (*Stealth*, 2005) as Princess Diana of Themyscira/Wonder Woman Adam Brody (*The O.C.*, 2003–7) as Barry Allen/The Flash, Anton Yelchin (*Hearts in Atlantis*, 2001) as Wally West/The Flash, Hugh Keays-Byrne (*Mad Max*) as J'onn J'onzz/Martian Manhunter, Santiago Cabrera (*Heroes*, 2006–10) as Arthur Curry/Aquaman and Common (*American Gangster*, 2007) as John Stewart/Green Lantern. Zoe Kazan (*Fracture*, 2007) was also set to feature as Barry Allen's wife Iris, and Jay Baruchel (*Knocked*

*Up*, 2007) and Teresa Palmer (*December Boys*, 2007) were chosen to portray the villainous pairing of Maxwell Lord and Talia al Ghul.

The first signs that *Justice League: Mortal* was running into trouble came in January 2008, when Warner Bros revealed that they were temporarily putting the project on hold. The studio had hoped to secure tax-break incentives from the Australian government but failed to qualify for the 40 per cent rebate on expenditure offered to domestic productions, while the ongoing Writers Guild of America strike prevented script concerns from being addressed. It was rumoured that Christopher Nolan expressed displeasure over the decision to tie *Justice League* into his own *Batman* continuity and George Miller's casting choices were also poorly received, with the studio subsequently allowing the options on the actors to expire. It came as a surprise, then, when the project was revived just six weeks later only for the studio to pull the plug once again, placing the big-budget superhero team-up on indefinite hiatus.

Although George Miller remained insistent that *Justice League: Mortal* would come to fruition, Warner Bros decided to change their strategy in the wake of *The Dark Knight*'s blockbuster success. In August 2008, studio president Jeff Robinov announced a shift towards solo outings for their DC characters, stating that development was already underway on a number of potential adaptations including *The Flash*, *Green Arrow*, *Green Lantern* and *Wonder Woman*, along with a sequel to *The Dark Knight* and reboot of *Superman*. With progress on *Justice League: Mortal* grinding to a halt, Miller eventually departed to direct a sequel to his Academy Award-winning animated hit *Happy Feet* (2006). Meanwhile Warner Bros were eventually successful in bringing one member of the Justice League to the screen with the arrival of *Green Lantern* in the summer of 2011, although the film disappointed at the box office and received decidedly mixed reviews.

Despite the collapse of *Justice League: Mortal*, talk of a DC Comics superhero team-up persisted, especially when it was revealed that the studio had appointed Christopher Nolan as producer of their *Superman* reboot, *Man of Steel* in 2010. Nolan soon played down speculation, stating that he saw the worlds inhabited by both heroes as entirely distinct from one another, and the idea of bringing the Justice League together on screen seemed to have died down until March 2011 when Jeff Robinov reiterated the studio's desire to move forward with development on *The Flash* and *Wonder Woman*, building to a potential *Justice League* feature in 2013 (SEE 'BATMAN OF THE FUTURE').

# ANIMATED BATMAN

# The early adventures of the animated Batman (1960s–80s)

Following the cancellation of ABC's live-action *Batman* television series in 1968, rival network CBS sought to capitalize on the character's popularity with younger viewers by adding the Caped Crusader to their Saturday morning cartoon schedule. CBS had first dipped their toes into the world of animated superheroes two years previously, commissioning Norm Prescott and Lou Scheimer's Filmation Associates to develop a series of animated shorts entitled *The New Adventures of Superman* (1966–70) and *The Adventures of Superboy* (1966–9), which were then packaged together as a single thirty-minute show. After a successful first year, the block was expanded to incorporate new *Aquaman* shorts and renamed *The Superman/Aquaman Hour of Adventure*, but the 1968/1969 season would see Superman teamed with his World's Finest partner as CBS secured the rights to Filmation's latest offering, *The Adventures of Batman*.

Lending his vocal talents to the first animated incarnation of the Caped Crusader was Olan Soule, a veteran character actor who had earlier featured as a newscaster in the first season *Batman* episode 'The Pharaoh's in a Rut'. Soule also provided the voice of Alfred Pennyworth, and he was joined by radio personality Casey Kasem (*The Famous Adventures of Mr Magoo*, 1964–5) as the Boy Wonder, along with Jane Webb (*Journey to the Center of the Earth*, 1967–9) as Batgirl and Catwoman, and Larry Storch (*F Troop*, 1965–7) as the Joker. Another integral member of the cast was Ted Knight (*The New Loretta Young Show*, 1962–3), who served as narrator on each of Filmation's superhero cartoons and voiced a number of characters in *The Adventures of Batman*, including Commissioner Gordon, the Penguin, the Mad Hatter, Mr Freeze and the Scarecrow.

Premiering on 14 September 1968 as part of *The Batman/Superman Hour*, the *Batman* portion of the show featured three six-minute segments, consisting of a two-part story separated by a single self-contained tale each week. The series ran for seventeen episodes before drawing to a close in January 1969, with the thirty-four stories then repackaged as a separate thirty-minute show and broadcast later in the year under the new title of *Batman with Robin the Boy Wonder*. In 1985 Warner Home Video released five episodes of *The Adventures of Batman* on VHS as part of their Super Powers Collection, and while the series is yet to arrive on DVD, all seventeen episodes were made available for digital download in 2008.

Although *The Adventures of Batman* had come to a swift end, Olan Soule and Casey Kasem continued to voice the characters for a series of Filmation-produced educational shorts which were broadcast as part of *Sesame Street* between 1969 and 1971. However, the voice actors soon made the jump to a rival studio as the rights to DC Comics' stable of superheroes were acquired by William Hanna and Joseph Barbera, the acclaimed animation team behind classic cartoons such as *The Flintstones* (1960–6), *The Yogi Bear Show* (1961–2), *Top Cat* (1961–2), *The Jetsons* (1962–3) and *Scooby-Doo, Where Are You?* (1969–70). The Dynamic Duo made their first animated appearances under Hanna-Barbera Productions on CBS, guest starring in two episodes of *The New Scooby-Doo Movies* entitled 'The Dynamic Scooby-Doo Affair' and 'The Caped Crusader Caper', which saw Casey Kasem moonlighting as the Boy Wonder in addition to his signature role of Shaggy Rogers. The

two episodes were collected together and released on DVD under the title of *Scooby-Doo Meets Batman* in 2002.

After debuting Batman and Robin in *The New Scooby-Doo Movies* in 1972, Hanna-Barbera began to develop a new series that would bring together their roster of DC superheroes while returning the Dynamic Duo to their original home on the ABC network. Entitled *Super Friends*, the series was a loose adaptation of the *Justice League of America* comic book and centred on a core team of Batman, Robin, Superman, Aquaman and Wonder Woman. Aimed squarely at the younger viewer, *Super Friends* incorporated the same campy tone as the live-action *Batman* series and also featured a trio of newly created 'Junior Super Friends' side-kicks – teenagers Wendy Harris and Marvin White, along with their costumed canine, Wonder Dog. Olan Soule and Casey Kasem were joined in the cast by commercials voiceover 'king' Danny Dark as Superman, Norman Alden (*The Sword in the Stone*, 1963) as Aquaman and Shannon Farnon (*Love Hate Love*, 1971) as Wonder Woman, while Ted Knight continued to serve as narrator.

Premiering on ABC on 8 September 1973, the first season of *Super Friends* ran until 30 August 1974 and consisted of sixteen hour-long episodes that were repeated several times throughout the year. Despite the fact that *Super Friends* proved a hit with its target audience, ABC chose not to renew the series for their 1974/1975 schedule, but the success of the live-action pilot *The New Original Wonder Woman* (1975) and subsequent *Wonder Woman* series forced a rethink from the network. In February 1976, the original episodes of *Super Friends* returned to screens as a mid-season replacement and continued to air in a half-hour format until September 1977, at which point a new batch of fifteen episodes were broadcast under the title of *The All-New Super Friends Hour*. Bill Woodson (*Escape from the Planet of the Apes*, 1971) took over narration duties from Ted Knight and the 'Junior Super Friends' were replaced in the line-up by another three original characters – superheroes in training Zan and Janya, a.k.a. the Wonder Twins, and their pet space-monkey, Gleek.

During reruns of the original *Super Friends* episodes, the Caped Crusader returned to CBS with the launch of Filmation's *The New Adventures of Batman* in February 1977. Serving as a direct sequel to the earlier Filmation series, *The New Adventures of Batman* retained the majority of the character designs from its predecessor but, with Olan Soule and Casey Kasem under contract to Hanna-Barbera, the task of voicing the Dynamic Duo fell to the very two actors who had spent the best part of a decade living in the shadows of their costumed counterparts. Although Burt Ward had earlier reprised the role of the Boy Wonder for a public service announcement in 1972, *The New Adventures of Batman* marked Adam West's first return as the Caped Crusader. The pair were joined in the cast by Melendy Britt (*The Lawyer*, 1970) as Batgirl and Catwoman, along with Filmation co-founder Lou Scheimer as Bat-Mite – the magical sidekick who made his first appearance in the comic book story 'Batman Meets Bat-Mite' by Bill Finger, published in *Detective Comics* #267 (May 1959) – while Lennie Weinrib (*H.R. Pufnstuf*, 1969–70) voiced Commissioner Gordon and the various villains of the Rogues Gallery. Filmation produced sixteen episodes in total and they were repackaged several times, receiving subsequent airings as part of *The Batman/Tarzan Adventure Hour* (1977–8), *Tarzan and the Super 7* (1978–80) and *Batman and the Super 7* (1980–1). In 2007, Warner Home Video released *The New Batman Adventures* on DVD under their 'DC Comics Classic Collection' banner.

With *The All-New Super Friends Hour* continuing to deliver strong ratings for ABC, the show underwent a dramatic revamp for its third season, splitting into two distinct half-hour segments under the new title *Challenge of the Super Friends*. The first segment continued in the same vein as the previous season, while the second section took a more serious approach, dropping comic relief characters such as the Wonder Twins and introducing a new criminal collective known as the Legion of Doom. Led by Lex Luthor, the Legion consisted of the supervillains Bizarro, Black Manta, Brainiac, Captain Cold, Cheetah, Giganta, Gorilla Grodd, the Riddler, the

Scarecrow, Sinestro, Solomon Grundy and the Toyman. To combat this threat, the original *Super Friends* roster was also expanded to include the Flash, Green Lantern and Hawkman, along with the newly created heroes Black Vulcan, Apache Chief and Samurai, each of whom were designed to increase the ethnic diversity of the team. Consisting of sixteen hour-long episodes, *Challenge of the Super Friends* ran from 9 September 1978 until 15 September 1979, during which time Hanna-Barbera also produced the two-part live-action NBC special *Legends of the Superheroes*, which featured the on-screen return of Adam West and Burt Ward.

*Super Friends* underwent yet another change of moniker to *The World's Greatest Superfriends* for the 1979/1980 season, with Hanna-Barbera reverting to the roster of *The All-New Super Friends Hour* for eight new hour-long episodes, which were broadcast alongside reruns of earlier instalments (at the time of writing, *The World's Greatest Superfriends* are the only episodes yet to receive a DVD release from Warner Home Video). For the next two years, Hanna-Barbera ceased production of new episodes in favour of seven-minute shorts, three of which were broadcast each week alongside a half-hour rerun under the original title of *Super Friends*. Forty-two shorts were broadcast before *Super Friends* entered weekday syndication across the United States in 1983, with ABC then making the decision to pull the series from

its Saturday morning schedule for the 1983/1984 season. During this time, an additional twenty-four shorts were created and sold to international markets; referred to as 'the lost episodes', three of these were broadcast in the US in 1984 and the rest eventually received an airing on the USA Network in 1995.

Despite the cancellation of *Super Friends*, the syndicated episodes continued to prove popular and in 1984 Kenner Products launched a highly successful 'Super Powers Collection' toy line, leading to a flood of merchandizing and promotional tie-ins. As part of the 'Super Powers' push, Hanna-Barbera produced eight new thirty-minute episodes of *Super Friends*, with the show returning to ABC's Saturday morning programming block for the 1984/1985 season under the title of *Super Friends: The Legendary Super Powers Show*. This revival saw Olan Soule vacate the role of the Caped Crusader in favour of ABC's original Batman, Adam West, while the series also marked the animated debut of its primary antagonist, the god-like tyrant Darkseid. West continued to voice the character for what ultimately proved to be the final season of *Super Friends*, with ABC calling time on the series after just eight instalments of the latest incarnation, *The Super Powers Team: Galactic Guardians*.

Among the tales produced by Hanna-Barbera for the final run of *Super Friends* was an episode entitled 'The Fear', which had initially been intended as a pilot for a new animated

*Batman* series. Considerably darker in tone than the majority of the *Super Friends* episodes, 'The Fear' was particularly notable for detailing Batman's origins for the very first time outside the comic book and was written by Alan Burnett (*Challenge of the GoBots*, 1984–5), an up-and-coming writer-producer who would come to play an increasingly important role in the animated adventures of the Caped Crusader (SEE 'THE DARK KNIGHT IN THE DC ANIMATED UNIVERSE'). This final run of episodes also included the first and only appearance of the Penguin, along with Batman's arch-nemesis the Joker, who had originally been intended as a member of the Legion of Doom, only for Hanna-Barbera to encounter rights issues with competitors Filmation over the inclusion of the character.

Having been a regular fixture of the Saturday morning television schedule for the best part of twelve years, *Super Friends* came to an end with the broadcast of 'The Death of Superman' on 6 November 1985, marking the penultimate outing for Adam West as the Caped Crusader (in 1997, he would lend his voice to the character for an episode of *Animaniacs* entitled 'Boo Wonder'). With a lack of new material forthcoming, the syndicated broadcasts of *Super Friends* continued to attract decent viewing figures, but it was almost seven years before the Caped Crusader returned for more cartoon exploits as Warner Bros Animation produced a

new series that revolutionized children's animation and went on to earn a reputation as one of the greatest superhero adaptations ever to grace the screen.

# The Dark Knight in the DC Animated Universe

## BATMAN: THE ANIMATED SERIES (1992–5)

Premiere: 5 September 1992 (US)
Episode count: 85

### VOICE CAST

Kevin Conroy (*Bruce Wayne/Batman*); Efrem Zimbalist Jr (*Alfred Pennyworth*); Bob Hastings (*Commissioner James Gordon*); Loren Lester (*Dick Grayson/Robin*); Robert Costanzo (*Detective Harvey Bullock*); Ingrid Oliu, Liane Schirmer (*Officer Renee Montoya*); Melissa Gilbert (*Barbara Gordon/Batgirl*); Mari Devon (*Summer Gleeson*); Lloyd Bochner (*Mayor Hamilton Hill*); Mark Hamill (*The Joker*); Adrienne Barbeau (*Catwoman*); Richard Moll (*Harvey Dent/Two-Face*); Arleen Sorkin (*Harley Quinn*); John Vernon (*Rupert Thorne*).

### KEY CREW

Alan Burnett, Paul Dini, Eric Radomski, Bruce W. Timm (*Producers*); Jean MacCurdy, Tom Ruegger (*Executive Producers*); Bob Kane (*Characters*); Andrea Romano (*Casting/Voice Director*); Danny Elfman (*Theme*); Shirley Walker (*Supervising Composer*).

### STORY

Orphaned at the hands of a robber as a child, the young Bruce Wayne swore an oath to devote his life and his fortune to fighting crime and corruption in the sprawling, industrial cesspit of Gotham City. Aided by his trusted friend and butler, Alfred Pennyworth, and former protégé Dick Grayson, Bruce assumes the mantle of the Bat, using his brilliant detective skills, high-tech gadgetry and expert combat skills to watch over the city and strike fear into the hearts of Gotham's criminals as the legendary grim avenger of the night, Batman.

### BRINGING BATMAN TO THE SCREEN

By the time that the long-running Saturday morning cartoon series *Super Friends* drew to a close in 1985, the Caped Crusader had spent almost two decades living in the shadow of the 1960s *Batman* television series. However, in the summer of 1989, mainstream audiences finally embraced a new interpretation of the character as director Tim Burton took the Dark Knight back to his noir-infused roots with the release of *Batman*. Having generated over $1bn in combined box-office and merchandizing revenue, Batman was big business once again and, as Warner Bros pressed ahead with plans for a theatrical sequel, their fledging animation division set out to bring the Dark Knight back to the small screen.

Coinciding with the release of *Batman* was a drive by Warner Bros Animation to venture beyond their *Looney Tunes* stable of characters, hiring former Hanna-Barbera and Marvel executive Jean MacCurdy to spearhead an expansion into general television production. During the 1980s, MacCurdy had served as executive in charge of production on a number of popular cartoons including *The Smurfs* (1981–9), *Challenge of the GoBots* and *Muppet Babies* (1984–91), along with the final two *Super Friends* incarnations – *Super Friends: The Legendary Super Powers Show* and *The Super Powers Team: Galactic Guardians*. One of MacCurdy's first acts at Warner Bros was to bring in her former Hanna-Barbera producer Tom Ruegger (*A Pup Named Scooby-Doo*, 1988–91), before partnering up with Steven Spielberg's Amblin Entertainment to launch their debut offering, the multi-award-winning *Tiny Toon Adventures* (1990–5). Among the crew of *Tiny Toons* were two aspiring animators, Bruce W. Timm and Eric Radomski, who together would supply the creative vision for what was to become known as *Batman: The Animated Series*.

Beginning his career as a layout artist at Filmation Associates on the likes of *He-Man and the Masters of the Universe* (1983–5) and *She-Ra:*

*Princess of Power* (1985–7), Bruce Timm went on to build his CV as a character designer on titles such as *G.I. Joe: A Real American Hero* (1983–6), *Mighty Mouse, the New Adventures* (1987–8) and *The Real Ghostbusters* (1986–91) before arriving at Warner Bros Animation in 1989 to serve as a model and background designer on *Tiny Toons*. There he was joined by Eric Radomski, another background artist who started out as a cel painter on the Disney short *Winnie the Pooh and a Day for Eeyore* (1983) and honed his skills on a number of commercials and network specials throughout the remainder of the decade. When it was announced that Warner Bros were to produce a new *Batman* series for the Fox network, both artists pitched their designs individually, with Timm presenting a number of character drawings and Radomski supplying background samples of Gotham City.

Impressed by the look of both sets of designs, the studio brought the individual talents of Bruce Timm and Eric Radomski together to produce a short promo reel. This collaboration saw the two animators create a distinctive visual style, incorporating the 'otherworldly timelessness' of Tim Burton's feature with a 1940s-inspired period setting and an Art Deco design aesthetic. To replicate Burton's brooding vision of Gotham City, Radomski pioneered a technique that broke with industry conventions, creating atmospheric backgrounds by painting light colours against black paper in a process dubbed 'Dark Deco'. 'I never thought that [Warner Bros] would go that far in a cartoon,' reflected Radomski in an interview with *Animation World Magazine* in 2000. 'They attached to this look immediately, and that was exciting for me. I thought, "Well, at the very best I'm going to get to paint or set the style for the show."'

Complimenting this innovative Dark Deco approach were the distinctive character designs of Bruce Timm, which simultaneously evoked the classic imagery of Fleischer Studios/Famous Studios' theatrical *Superman* (1941–3) shorts while blending smooth curves and sharp straights to present a highly stylized, angular approach. 'We came up with a fairly successful formula for how to design the characters for animation,' explained Timm in an interview with Emru Townsend of *The Critical Eye* in 1999. 'It's like Alex Toth's [*Space Ghost*, 1966–8] designs for Hanna-Barbera in the 60s and the really, really strongly graphic design that the Disney artists did on *Sleeping Beauty* [1959], that's kind of the quote-unquote "*Batman* style".'

After impressing executives Jean MacCurdy and Tom Ruegger with their short promotional reel in the early part of 1991, Bruce Timm and Eric Radomski were handed the task of creating sixty-five episodes of *Batman: The Animated Series* in a producing capacity – a role neither man had previously fulfilled. As Radomski concentrated on the organizational aspects of developing the show, Timm set about outlining his take on the Dark Knight by producing a series writer's bible. Assisting him in this task was the writer and filmmaker

Mitch Brian (*Night Screams*, 1988), along with another member of the *Tiny Toons* family, Paul Dini. Launching his career as a freelance writer in the late 1970s, Dini penned episodes of cult cartoons such as *Dungeons & Dragons* (1983–5), *He-Man and the Masters of the Universe*, *G.I. Joe* and *The Transformers* (1984–8) and went on to embark on a four-year stint at Lucasfilm. During this time he helped to develop the animated *Star Wars* series *Droids* (1985–6) and *Ewoks* (1985–6) before leaving for Warner Bros Animation, where he was employed as a story editor on *Tiny Toons*. Initially, Dini continued to fulfil these duties while contributing to the development of *Batman* on a part-time basis, but he would soon make the switch full time, a decision that saw him go on to become an integral member of the creative team.

Given Timm and Radomski's lack of experience, Jean MacCurdy decided to add a third member to the producing team, approaching a writer-producer who had earlier attempted to launch a darker take on the Caped Crusader in the mid-1980s. Serving as a story editor on *Super Friends: The Legendary Super Powers Show*, Alan Burnett delivered a pilot script for a new animated *Batman* series, which was ultimately rejected by Hanna-Barbera as being too adult for Saturday morning television. The teleplay was produced as an episode of *The Super Powers Team: Galactic Guardians* entitled 'The Fear', with Burnett then going on to work on shows such as *The Smurfs* and *DuckTales* (1987–90) before accepting

MacCurdy's offer to finally realize his ambition of bringing an animated Dark Knight to the screen.

'We didn't want it to be just action/adventure,' said Eric Radomski on the creative vision for *Batman: The Animated Series*. '[We wanted to] really get some heart and soul into this thing, instead of just doing another merchandizable episodic series. We wanted them to be dramatic mini-features.' To accomplish this, the producers intended to cut down on excessive dialogue and placed a much greater emphasis on visual storytelling, delivering a mature sophisticated show far removed from the light-hearted campiness of the Caped Crusader's previous animated outings. Although the radical new direction encountered some early resistance from within the studio, this soon ceased when the producers delivered their very first episode, 'On Leather Wings', which was written by Mitch Brian and directed by Kevin Altieri (*C.O.P.S.*, 1988–9). It immediately met with resounding approval from enthused executives.

'[*Batman*] was groundbreaking in a lot of ways. It was, of course, darker than any animated series at the time – both story-wise and visually,' stated series director Dick Sebast (*Challenge of the Super Friends*) in an interview with *WorldsFinestOnline.com* in 2006. 'But perhaps its greatest achievement was that it abandoned conventional cartoon voice-acting in favour of more realistic performances.' Central to this was the work of casting and voice director Andrea Romano (*The Super Powers Team: Galactic Guardians*), who

broke from convention to have the actors read their lines together, similar to the recording of a radio play, allowing for a much greater performance than was typically present in Saturday morning cartoon programming.

Working alongside the producers, Romano also secured a respected cast that was led by Kevin Conroy (*Tour of Duty*, 1987–90) as the Dark Knight and his billionaire alter ego Bruce Wayne. A classically trained stage actor and former soap opera star, Conroy's prior screen credits included brief stints on *Another World* (1964–99), *Search for Tomorrow* (1951–86) and *Dynasty* (1981–6); although he had previously supplied voiceover work for commercials, *Batman* would be his first foray into the world of animation.

Joining Conroy in the cast for *Batman: The Animated Series* was Clive Revill (*Star Wars: Episode V – The Empire Strikes Back*) as Alfred Pennyworth, with the producers choosing to recast the role after the first three episodes, settling instead on the Golden Globe-winning screen veteran Efrem Zimbalist Jr (*Home Before Dark*, 1958). The voice of Commissioner Gordon was supplied by Bob Hastings – who had earlier lent his vocal talents to a young Clark Kent in *The Adventures of Superboy* and also made a guest appearance in the 1967 *Batman* episode 'Penguin Sets a Trend' – while other allies of the Dark Knight included Loren Lester (*Defenders of the Earth*, 1986–7) as Dick Grayson/Robin, Brock Peters (*To Kill a Mockingbird*, 1962) as Lucius Fox

## SUPERMAN: THE ANIMATED SERIES (1996–2000)

Premiere: 6 September 1996 (US)
Episode count: 54

### VOICE CAST

Tim Daly (*Clark Kent/Superman*); Dana Delany (*Lois Lane*); David Kaufman (*Jimmy Olsen*); Clancy Brown (*Lex Luthor*); Lauren Tom (*Angela Chen*); George Dzundza (*Perry White*); Corey Burton (*Brainiac*); Michael Ironside (*Darkseid*); Mike Farrell (*Jonathan Kent*); Shelley Fabares (*Martha Kent*).

### KEY CREW

Alan Burnett, Paul Dini, Bruce W. Timm (*Producers*); Jean MacCurdy (*Executive Producer*); Haven Alexander (*Associate Producer*); Jerry Siegel, Joe Shuster (*Characters*); Andrea Romano (*Voice Director*); Leslie Lamers, Andrea Romano (*Casting*); Shirley Walker (*Theme*); Kristopher Carter, Lolita Ritmanis, Michael McCuistion (*Music*).

### STORY

Rocketed into space just moments before the destruction of his home world Krypton, the baby Kal-El crash-lands on Earth where he is discovered by Jonathan and Martha Kent and raised as their adoptive son, Clark Kent. As he reaches maturity, Clark develops superhuman abilities, and after learning of his true origins he decides to use his powers for good. Moving to Metropolis to serve as a reporter for *The Daily Planet*, Clark assumes the identity of Superman to combat a terrorist threat and soon forges a reputation as the greatest of all superheroes, battling sinister villains and using his powers to protect humanity as the Man of Steel.

### BRINGING SUPERMAN TO THE SCREEN

With Fox calling time on *Batman: The Animated Series* in 1995, Warner Bros moved quickly to secure the creative team behind the Emmy Award-winning show to deliver a similar take on the Man of Steel that would serve as a flagship title for the Kids' WB programming block of their recently launched television network, The WB. Despite the departure of *Batman* co-creator Eric Radomski, the remaining members of the producing team – Bruce Timm, Alan Burnett and Paul Dini – were joined by their established cohort of artists, animators, writers and directors as work got underway on the next instalment of the DC Animated Universe, *Superman: The Animated Series*.

'I knew immediately what to do with Batman, whereas with Superman I wasn't quite sure what to do with him,' explained Bruce Timm. 'He doesn't make as much sense in the modern world as he did when he was first created.' Retaining the same mature approach as with its predecessor, the producers opted to update the visual style with a crisp, simplified look, which also coincided with a shift from the 'timeless' 1940s-infused setting of *Batman* to a vibrant retro-futuristic Metropolis, partly to avoid comparisons with Fleischer Studios' seminal *Superman* shorts. Joining the voice cast for *Superman: The Animated Series* were Tim Daly (*Wings*, 1990–7) as Clark Kent/Superman, Clancy Brown (*Highlander*, 1986) as the villainous Lex Luthor and *Batman: Mask of the Phantasm's* Dana Delany as Lois Lane.

## RECEPTION

*Superman: The Animated Series* premiered on The WB on 6 September 1996 with the broadcast of a three-part episode entitled 'The Last Son of Krypton' and the show ran for three seasons before drawing to a close, with fifty-six episodes produced in total. Much like the initial batch of *Batman* episodes, *Superman* ran without an on-screen title but was eventually christened *The New Superman Adventures* to coincide with the launch of the 'revamped' companion series *The New Batman Adventures* in September 1997, with both shows subsequently airing together under the moniker of *The New Batman/Superman Adventures*.

Although *Superman: The Animated Series* never quite managed to generate the level of acclaim afforded to *Batman*, it was very well received by fans and has come to be regarded as one of the finest screen adaptations of the Man of Steel. Having received a Daytime Emmy Award nomination in the field of Outstanding Special Class – Animated Program in 1997, *Superman* went one step better the next year when it collected the accolade for the three-part story 'World's Finest'. This also marked the first guest appearance of the Dark Knight, as Bruce Wayne travels to Metropolis in search of the Joker and joins forces with the Man of Steel to take on Lex Luthor and the Clown Prince of Crime. The episodes, which saw Kevin Conroy and Mark Hamill reprising their roles from *Batman*, were later edited together and released in 1998 as the direct-to-video feature *The Batman/Superman Movie: World's Finest*, a tactic that had been employed two years earlier with *Superman: The Last Son of Krypton*.

In addition to the three-part 'World's Finest', the series contained two further Batman-themed crossover episodes – 'Knight Time' and 'The Demon Reborn'. Meanwhile, the duo also brought further industry recognition to the creative team, with *The Batman/Superman Adventures* claiming an Annie Award for Outstanding Achievement in an Animated Daytime Television Program in 1998 and adding a second Daytime Emmy Award the following year for Outstanding Achievement in Sound Mixing – Special Class.

Finishing its run of original episodes in February 2000, *Superman: The Animated Series* was later released across three DVD volumes as part of Warner Home Video's DC Comics Classic Collection, while 2006 saw the voice cast return for the straight-to-video feature *Superman: Braniac Attacks,* although this is not considered to be a part of the DC Animated Universe canon.

# THE NEW BATMAN ADVENTURES (1997–9)

**Premiere:** 13 September 1997 (US)
**Episode count:** 24

## VOICE CAST

Kevin Conroy (*Bruce Wayne/Batman*); Mathew Valencia (*Tim Drake/Robin*); Tara Strong (*Barbara Gordon/Batgirl*); Efrem Zimbalist Jr (*Alfred Pennyworth*); Bob Hastings (*Commissioner James Gordon*); Loren Lester (*Dick Grayson/Nightwing*); Robert Costanzo (*Detective Harvey Bullock*); Liane Schirmer (*Detective Renee Montoya*); Mark Hamill (*The Joker*); Adrienne Barbeau (*Catwoman*); Richard Moll (*Two-Face*); Arleen Sorkin (*Harley Quinn*).

## KEY CREW

Alan Burnett, Paul Dini, Bruce W. Timm (*Producers*); Jean MacCurdy (*Executive Producer*); Haven Alexander (*Associate Producer*); Bob Kane (*Characters*); Andrea Romano (*Casting/Voice Director*); Shirley Walker (*Theme*); Shirley Walker (*Supervising Composer*).

## STORY

As Batman's war against the criminals of Gotham City rages on, former protégé Dick Grayson steps out of the shadow of the Dark Knight to embark on his own path as the costumed crime-fighter Nightwing. Meanwhile, the Caped Crusader forges new alliances, taking the teenage street orphan Tim Drake under his wing and training him as the next Robin. The new look Dynamic Duo join forces with Barbara Gordon's Batgirl and together they continue the fight for justice.

## BRINGING BATMAN TO THE SCREEN

While *Batman: The Animated Series* had come to an end in 1995, Fox continued to earn strong ratings broadcasting reruns of the critically acclaimed show as part of their Fox Kids programming block the following season. However, with Fox's contract set to expire in 1997, Warner Bros were keen to bring the Caped Crusader over to their own network, where he would eventually join his 'World's Finest' partner, Superman, as part of an expanding DC Animated Universe. Produced under the working title of *Batman: Gotham Knights*, the latest series would serve as a continuation of the earlier show and eventually adopted the official moniker of *The New Batman Adventures*.

'When they came back at us and said that the WB wanted to do new episodes of *Batman*, at first I wasn't even really interested, because we'd done so many of them,' said *Batman: The Animated Series* co-creator Bruce Timm, who was joined by fellow producers Alan Burnett and Paul Dini for a second spell in Gotham City. 'So while I was just thinking about it at home one night, I just said, "If I could do *Batman* again, what would I do different?" And I just started sketching

Batman again, and … that's when I came up with that really radically angular, flat design, and I thought, "Wow, that's pretty neat".' After redesigning the Batman and Joker models to bring them in line with the art style of *Superman: The Animated Series*, Timm worked with *Superman* art director Glen Murakami to redefine the colourful cast of supporting characters, presenting an updated visual take on the Caped Crusader that came to be referred to by fans as the 'Revamp'.

In addition to an artistic overhaul, the 'New Look' *Batman* saw a much greater emphasis placed upon the exploits of the Dark Knight's allies, with an expanded roster of crime-fighters that included screen debuts for Nightwing and Tim Drake's Robin (his character merged with that of Jason Todd, the second Boy Wonder), along with a more prominent role for Barbara Gordon's Batgirl, who had made just four appearances in the original series. The majority of the original voice actors returned to reprise their roles, although Melissa Gilbert was replaced as Barbara Gordon by Tara Strong (*Beetlejuice*, 1989–91) and Mel Winkler (*All the Right Moves*, 1983) took over from Brock Peters as Lucius Fox, while Mathew Valencia (*Lawnmower Man 2: Beyond Cyberspace*, 1996) also joined the cast as the voice of Tim Drake.

## RECEPTION

After a two-year absence, the Caped Crusader resumed his animated exploits on 13 September 1997, with the revamped series running alongside

In terms of casting for *Batman Beyond*, Kevin Conroy extended his tenure as Bruce Wayne and he was joined by Will Friedle (*Boy Meets World*, 1993–2000) as the voice of his on-screen successor, Terry McGinnis. Barbara Gordon was voiced by Stockard Channing (*Six Degrees of Separation*, 1993), with Angie Harmon (*Baywatch Nights*, 1995–7) taking over for the final season. The series also attracted a host of notable guest stars including the likes of Rachel Leigh Cook (*She's All That*, 1999), Seth Green (*Buffy the Vampire Slayer*), George Lazenby (*On Her Majesty's Secret Service*, 1969) William H. Macy (*Fargo*) and Michael Rosenbaum (*Smallville*). Despite the focus on new villains, several of the Caped Crusader's former adversaries also made their return, with David Warner and Michael Ansara reprising their roles as Ra's al Ghul and Mr Freeze and Olivia Hussey (*Romeo & Juliet*, 1968) replacing Helen Slater (*Supergirl*, 1984) as Talia.

## RECEPTION

Premiering on the WB Network on 10 January 1999, *Batman Beyond* brushed aside early scepticism towards its premise to quickly develop a loyal and dedicated fan-base. While it had been designed to appeal to younger viewers, the series – which was broadcast as *Batman of the Future* in certain international markets – retained the same dark tone as its predecessors and soon earned a reputation for rich, complex storytelling and characterization. *Batman Beyond* also continued the DC Animated Universe's run of awards success, receiving three Annie Awards (Outstanding Individual Achievement for Storyboarding in an Animated Television Production, Outstanding Individual Achievement for Directing in an Animated Television Production, and Outstanding Achievement in a Daytime Animated Television Production) and two Daytime Emmys (Outstanding Achievement in Music Direction and Composition and Outstanding Special Class Animated Program).

Given the popularity of *Batman Beyond*, Warner Bros initiated plans to develop a live-action feature film adaptation in 2000, hiring Alan Burnett and Paul Dini to craft a screenplay for director Boaz Yakin. This project was eventually discarded in favour of the aborted *Batman: Year One* adaptation, but *Batman Beyond* did spawn the direct-to-video feature *Batman Beyond: Return of the Joker* and the first two episodes were also edited together and released on home-video as *Batman Beyond: The Movie*. The entire series was later made available on DVD as part of the DC Comics Classic Collection, while the character of Terry McGinnis finally extended beyond the small screen in 2010 when he made the transition to panel form, debuting in mainstream DC Comics continuity with an appearance in 'Time and the Batman' by Grant Morrison, published in *Batman* #700 (August 2010).

By the start of the third and final season of *Batman Beyond* in September 2000, big changes were afoot within the DC Animated Universe. A brand new series, *Static Shock*, was about to launch on Kids' WB! and development was well underway on the *Batman Beyond* spin-off *The Zeta Project*. Meanwhile, Bruce Timm was also turning his attention towards a new project, testing the water with a two-part *Batman Beyond* episode entitled 'The Call', which featured a group of superheroes called the Justice League Unlimited.

## BATMAN BEYOND: RETURN OF THE JOKER (2000)

**Release date:** 12 December 2000 (US)
**Certificate:** Not rated (original cut), PG-13 (director's cut) (US); 12 (UK)
**Running time:** 74 minutes (original cut), 77 minutes (director's cut)

### VOICE CAST

Will Friedle (*Terry McGinnis/Batman*); Kevin Conroy (*Bruce Wayne/Batman*); Mark Hamill (*The Joker, Jordan Price*); Angie Harmon (*Commissioner Barbara Gordon*); Dean Stockwell (*Tim Drake*); Teri Garr (*Mart McGinnis*); Arleen Sorkin (*Dr Harleen Quinzel/Harley Quinn*); Tara Strong (*Young Barbara Gordon/Robin*); Mathew Valencia (*Young Tim Drake/Robin*); Melissa Joan Hart (*Delia Dennis/Deidre Dennis/Dee Dee*); Michael Rosenbaum (*Stewart Carter Winthrop III/Ghoul*), Don Harvey (*Charles Buntz/Chucko*); Henry Rollins (*Benjamin Knox/Bonk*); Frank Welker (*Woof the Hyena-Man/Ace*).

### KEY CREW

Curt Geda (*Director*); Alan Burnett, Paul Dini, Glen Murakami, Bruce W. Timm (*Producers*); Michael E. Uslan, Benjamin Melniker, Jean MacCurdy (*Executive Producers*); Shaun McLaughlin (*Associate Producer*); Paul Dini, Bruce W. Timm, Glen Murakami (*Story*); Paul Dini (*Screenplay*);

Bob Kane (*Characters*); Andrea Romano (*Voice Director*); Leslie Lamers (*Casting*); Kristopher Carter (*Music*); Joe Gall (*Editing*).

## STORY

Despite Bruce Wayne's insistence that he witnessed the death of the Joker many years ago, all signs point to the re-emergence of his arch-enemy as the Clown Prince of Crime appears in Neo-Gotham, assuming control of the Jokerz street gang and embarking on a spate of robberies. As Terry McGinnis attends a nightclub with his girlfriend Dana, the Joker ambushes Bruce Wayne in the Batcave, subjecting him to a brutal attack before leaving the former Caped Crusader for dead. Terry eventually returns to find an injured Bruce, and after taking his mentor to the hospital he demands that Commissioner Barbara Gordon reveals the truth behind the Joker's apparent death. Recalling her final days as Batgirl, Barbara explains how the Joker and Harley Quinn kidnapped Tim Drake, brainwashing him into becoming a miniature version of the maniacal clown. Rescued by Batman, the Boy Wonder then shot the Joker, who was buried beneath Arkham as part of a cover-up while Tim underwent therapy to return him to his normal state.

Upon learning of Tim's past, Terry immediately suspects that he is responsible for the recent crimes but finds little evidence when, as Batman, he confronts the former Boy Wonder.

Eventually, Terry tracks the impostor to an abandoned factory and discovers the shocking truth as he witnesses Tim transform into the Joker before his very eyes. Using stolen genetics technology, the Joker had secretly implanted a chip inside Tim's brain, allowing him to transfer his consciousness into the boy, where he has lain dormant ever since. After getting the better of Batman, the Clown Prince of Crime prepares to crush the crime-fighter, only for Terry to destroy the microchip using the Joker's electric hand buzzer, freeing Tim of the fiend once and for all. Recovering in hospital, Tim receives a visit from Barbara and they are soon joined by Bruce; as the trio of legendary crime-fighters reunite for the first time in forty years, Terry dons the Batsuit and takes to the skies of Neo-Gotham as the Tomorrow Knight …

## BRINGING BATMAN TO THE SCREEN

Approached by Warner Bros to develop a direct-to-video feature based upon their latest series, producers Alan Burnett, Paul Dini and Bruce Timm crafted a story far removed from the network's 'kid-friendly' ethos for *Batman Beyond*, using its futuristic setting to bring closure to the bitter war between the Dark Knight and the Clown Prince of Crime with a dark psychological tale entitled *Batman Beyond: Return of the Joker*. Hoping to produce the movie concurrently with the second season of *Batman Beyond*, series director Curt Geda (*Superman: The Last Son of Krypton*) was tasked with helming the project, while the regular voice cast were joined by Mark Hamill, Arleen Sorkin, Tara Strong and Mathew Valencia, all of whom returned as their respective characters from *The New Batman Adventures*. Further additions to the cast included Dean Stockwell (*Quantum Leap*, 1989–93) as the adult Tim Drake and Melissa Joan Hart (*Clarissa Explains It All*, 1991–4) as Harley Quinn's granddaughters, the Dee Dee Twins.

Despite being free of the limitations imposed by Broadcast Standards and Practices, the creative team found themselves at odds with the studio, who requested several changes to Paul Dini's screenplay in order to make the content more acceptable for younger viewers. After the screenplay had been toned down, the film was storyboarded and sent for animation, only for executives to then highlight additional concerns, which were amplified once the final edit was delivered. To satisfy the studio, a host of cuts were made to the feature, trimming much of the on-screen violence and making considerable changes to the dialogue. Blood and weapons such as knives were digitally removed, along with the majority of the scenes depicting the Joker's brainwashing and torture of Tim Drake, while the villain's first death was also altered to depict the Clown Prince of Crime stumbling into electrical wires rather than being shot by the Boy Wonder.

## RECEPTION

Released in its edited form on 12 December 2000 *Batman Beyond: Return of the Joker* met with a warm reception from critics and audiences and received an Annie Award for Outstanding Achievement in an Animated Home Video Production. However, Warner Bros came under pressure to deliver the uncut version of the film after bootlegs of the original began to circulate among the fan community. The studio finally relented and *Batman Beyond: Return of the Joker (The Original Uncut Version)* eventually arrived on DVD in April 2002, becoming the first animated *Batman* film to receive a PG-13 certificate from the Motion Picture Association of America and quickly establishing a reputation as a firm fan favourite.

## GOTHAM GIRLS (2000—2)

Premiere: 27 July 2000 (online)
Episode count: 30

### VOICE CAST

Tara Strong (*Barbara Gordon/Batgirl*); Adrienne Barbeau (*Selina Kyle/Catwoman, Detective Renee Montoya*); Diane Pershing (*Dr Pamela Isley/Poison Ivy*); Arleen Sorkin (*Dr Harleen Quinzel/Harley Quinn*); Jennifer Hale (*Caroline Greenaway, Dora Smithy*); Stacie Randall (*Zatanna Zatara*).

### KEY CREW

Jeremy Rosenberg, Ben Stein (*Producers*).

### STORY

Having fought to protect Gotham City from the likes of Catwoman, Harley Quinn and Poison Ivy, Batgirl is forced to question her loyalties when Commissioner Gordon enforces a new 'Get Tough on Costumed Villains' policy. Finding herself a fugitive of the law, Batgirl uncovers a diabolical scheme to crack down on supervillains, led by Dora Smithy, the sister of Mr Freeze's wife Nora Fries.

### BRINGING GOTHAM GIRLS TO THE SCREEN

A co-production between Warner Bros Animation and Noodlesoup Productions, *Gotham Girls* was a loose spin-off from the DC Animated Universe that focused on the female population of Gotham City and saw Tara Strong, Adrienne Barbeau, Diane Pershing and Arleen Sorkin reprising their roles from *The New Batman Adventures*. Catering very much to the younger viewer, the Flash-animated series adopted a humorous approach to its storytelling, with each episode lasting between two and five minutes and featuring the inclusion of mini-games, puzzles and interactive decision-making elements. While the first two seasons consisted of self-contained episodes, the final season presented a single half-hour narrative that tied into the events of *Batman & Mr Freeze: SubZero*. Although Batman never featured within the series himself, the male population of Gotham City wasn't overlooked entirely as Bob Hastings returned to voice Commissioner Gordon for four episodes.

### RECEPTION

Debuting online on the now-defunct *Gotham Girls.com* on 27 July 2000, the web series ran for a total of thirty episodes over three seasons. The complete series was included as a special feature on the DVD box-set of *Birds of Prey*.

# STATIC SHOCK (2000—4)

Premiere: 23 September 2000 (US)
Episode count: 52

## VOICE CAST

Phil LaMarr (*Virgil Ovid Hawkins/Static*); Jason Marsden (*Richie Osgood Foley/Gear*); Kevin Michael Richardson (*Robert Hawkins*); Michele Morgan (*Sharon Hawkins*); Crystal Scales (*Daisy Watkins*); Danica McKellar (*Frieda Goren*).

## KEY CREW

Alan Burnett (*Supervising Producer*); Denys Cowan, Swinton O. Scott III, Scott Jeralds (*Producers*); Sander Schwartz (*Executive Producer*); J.C. Cheng, Kathy Page, Shaun McLaughlin (*Associate Producers*); Dwayne McDuffie (*Character*); Andrea Romano (*Voice Director*); Andrea Romano, Leslie Lamers (*Casting*); Lil' Romeo (*Static Shock Theme*); Richard Wolf (*Music*).

## STORY

Teenager Virgil Hawkins was like any other typical high-school student until he developed electromagnetic abilities after being exposed to a mutagenic gas during an event known as the 'Big Bang'. Choosing to use his newfound powers for good, Virgil transforms himself into the electrically charged superhero Static. With the help of his best friend Richie, Static takes to the streets of Dakota City in order to tackle the growing number of mutated 'bang babies' and make a positive impact on his community.

## BRINGING STATIC SHOCK TO THE SCREEN

With *Batman Beyond*'s youthful hero Terry McGinnis proving popular with audiences on Kids' WB!, Warner Bros decided to produce a new series set within the DC Animated Universe that centred on another teenage superhero, Static. Making his first appearance in the comic book story 'Burning Sensation' by Dwayne McDuffie and Robert L. Washington III, published in *Static* #1 (June 1993), the electrically charged African-American teenager became one of the key figures of Milestone Comics – a DC imprint specializing in minority heroes – and his television debut in *Static Shock* pre-dated his integration into mainstream DC continuity by more than eight years. Kevin Conroy's Batman would make several guest appearances alongside the young hero, featuring in the episodes 'The Big Leagues', 'Hard as Nails', 'A League of Their Own' and 'Fallen Hero', the latter of which also included Will Friedle as the Tomorrow Knight.

## RECEPTION

Premiering as part of the Saturday morning Kids' WB! block, *Static Shock* ran for four seasons, with fifty-two episodes produced in total. Confronting issues such as bullying, peer pressure and gang culture, the show earned Dwayne McDuffie and Alan Burnett a Humanitas Prize in the Children's Animation Category in 2003, and the following year *Static Shock* enjoyed further award success, winning a Daytime Emmy for Outstanding Achievement in Music Direction and Composition. Although *Static Shock* delivered strong ratings and continued to grow in popularity throughout its run, the show failed to secure the necessary merchandizing tie-ins to ensure profitability and Warner Bros opted against producing a fifth season. At the time of writing, only the first six episodes have been released on DVD as part of Warner Home Video's DC Comics Kids' Collection, with the entire first season available digitally on demand.

# THE ZETA PROJECT (2001–2)

**Premiere:** 27 January 2001 (US)
**Episode count:** 26

## VOICE CAST

Diedrich Bader (*Zeta*); Julie Nathanson (*Rosalie Rowan*); Kurtwood Smith (*Agent James Bennet*); Michael Rosenbaum (*Agent West*); Lauren Tom (*Agent Lee*).

## KEY CREW

Liz Holzman (*Supervising Producer*); Robert Goodman, Alan Burnett (*Producers*); Jean MacCurdy (*Executive Producer*); Haven Alexander, Kathryn Page (*Associate Producer*); Andrea Romano (*Voice Director*); Leslie Lamers (*Casting Director*); Lolita Ritmanis (*Theme*); Shirley Walker (*Supervising Composer*); Michael McCuistion (*Music*).

## STORY

A robotic assassin built by the National Security Agency, Infiltration Unit Zeta becomes a fugitive of the US government after developing an understanding of the value of human life and refusing to kill. Aided by a young runaway named Rosalie Rowan, Zeta goes on the run across America, hoping to locate his enigmatic creator and secure his freedom.

## BRINGING THE ZETA PROJECT TO THE SCREEN

Created by DC Animated Universe staff writer Robert Goodman (*The Real Adventures of Johnny Quest*, 1996–7), the rogue military assassin Infiltration Unit Zeta made his first appearance in the Season Two *Batman Beyond* episode 'Zeta', which was originally intended to end with the synthoid's death. However, spotting potential for a spin-off based around the character, 'Zee' was given a reprieve as Warner Bros Animation charged Goodman with developing a new series to run alongside *Batman Beyond* and *Static Shock* as part of their Saturday morning Kids' WB! programming block. Although Gary Cole (*Midnight Caller*, 1988–91) had supplied Zeta's voice in *Batman Beyond*, he was replaced by his *Office Space* (1999) co-star Diedrich Bader, with the character also enjoying a visual overhaul in preparation for his starring role in *The Zeta Project*.

## RECEPTION

Catering firmly for a junior target audience, *The Zeta Project* received a mixed reaction when it premiered on 27 January 2001, with a number of fans deterred by the show's 'family-friendly' storytelling and bright colour palette. The series underwent a number of changes for its second season in an attempt to appease fans, but after placing the show in hiatus several times, Warner Bros finally elected to cancel *The Zeta Project* and it came to an end in August 2002 after just twenty-six episodes.

Bruce Wayne and his successor Terry McGinnis made a solitary appearance in *The Zeta Project*, with Kevin Conroy and Will Friedle voicing their respective characters in the first season episode 'Shadows'; this was broadcast alongside the penultimate *Batman Beyond* episode 'Countdown', which saw Zeta return to Neo-Gotham as part of a cross-over between the two sister shows. Since *The Zeta Project* came to an end, Warner Home Video have released the first season on DVD, with the remaining fourteen episodes unavailable at the time of writing.

## JUSTICE LEAGUE (2001–4)

Premiere: 17 November 2001 (US)
Episode count: 52

### VOICE CAST

Kevin Conroy (*Bruce Wayne/Batman*); George Newbern (*Clark Kent/Superman*); Susan Eisenberg (*Princess Diana of Themyscira/Wonder Woman*); Michael Rosenbaum (*Wally West/The Flash*); Phil LaMarr (*John Stewart/Green Lantern*); Carl Lumbly (*J'onn J'onzz/Martian Manhunter*); Maria Canals (*Shayera Hol/Hawkgirl*).

### KEY CREW

Rich Fogel, Glen Murakami, Bruce W. Timm, James Tucker (*Producers*); Sander Schwartz (*Executive Producer*); Shaun McLaughlin (*Line Producer*); Andrea Romano (*Voice Director*); Leslie Lamers, Andrea Romano (*Casting*); Lolita Ritmanis (*Theme*).

### STORY

When alien forces threaten Earth, the planet's greatest superheroes join together to repel the invasion, leading to the formation of the Justice League. Putting aside their personal differences, heroes such as Superman, Batman, Wonder Woman, Green Lantern, the Flash, Hawkgirl and Martian Manhunter agree to work together, protecting humanity from global catastrophes and extra-terrestrial peril.

## BRINGING JUSTICE LEAGUE TO THE SCREEN

Throughout much of the 1990s, speculation had been rife as to whether Bruce Timm and his creative team would eventually turn their attention towards bringing the DC Animated Universe together with a new take on the legendary team of superheroes, the Justice League of America. Although early consideration had been given to introducing the Justice League in *Superman: The Animated Series*, Timm remained hesitant to commit to an independent series, citing concerns over the difficulties in staging action sequences with such a large cast of characters, along with the challenge of balancing them in terms of story.

Buoyed by the popularity of Grant Morrison's 'back-to-basics' Justice League comic book title *JLA*, Timm eventually bowed to the pressure and, with *Batman Beyond* drawing to a close, plans were put into motion for a new series that would bring the stable of DC superheroes back together in animated form for the first time since *Super Friends*. With the WB Network looking to incorporate more youthful characters into their Kids' WB! programming block, Timm approached Cartoon Network with a view to hosting the new Justice League cartoon and his offer was immediately accepted. While Paul Dini continued his involvement with the latest series in a writing capacity, *Justice League* would see Bruce Timm and Glen Murakami joined by two newcomers to the producing team in James Tucker (*Animaniacs*) and Rich Fogel (*Super Friends: The Legendary Super Powers Show*), both of whom possessed extensive experience within the previous instalments of the DC Animated Universe.

In terms of the cast for *Justice League*, Kevin Conroy returned to extend his spell as the voice of the Dark Knight, with George Newbern (*Father of the Bride*, 1991) replacing Tim Daly from *Superman: The Animated Series* as the Man of Steel and Susan Eisenberg (*Jackie Chan Adventures*, 2000–5) securing the role of Wonder Woman. For the remaining members of the team, the producers recruited DC Animated Universe regulars Michael Rosenbaum as the Flash, Phil LaMarr (*Pulp Fiction*) as the Green Lantern, Carl Lumbly (*Men of Honour*, 2000) as the Martian Manhunter and Maria Canals (*America's Sweethearts*, 2001) as Hawkgirl. A number of familiar faces from Batman's earlier adventures would also return for guest appearances in *Justice League*, including the likes of Alfred Pennyworth (Efrem Zimbalist Jr), Clayface (Ron Perlman), Harley Quinn (Arleen Sorkin) and the Joker (Mark Hamill).

## RECEPTION

Premiering on Cartoon Network on 17 November 2001 with the broadcast of the three-part opener 'Secret Origins', *Justice League* went on to enjoy a similar level of popularity as its predecessors, earning further acclaim for Bruce Timm and his team from both fans and critics alike. Lolita Ritmanis was honoured with a Primetime Emmy Award nomination for Outstanding Main Title Theme Music in 2002, with Rich Fogel, John Ridley (*Undercover Brother*, 2002) and Dwayne McDuffie contesting a Writers Guild of America TV Award for Best Animation for 'Starcrossed', the three-part Season Two finale. Several of the multi-part stories were collected together and issued on DVD under the titles of *Secret Origins* (2002), *Justice on Trial* (2002), *Paradise Lost* (2003) and *Starcrossed – The Movie* (2004), while both seasons have subsequently been issued on DVD and Blu-ray as part of Warner Home Video's DC Comics Classic Collection.

Although *Justice League* came to an end after just two seasons in May 2004, the legendary team of DC superheroes would soon be back – and in greater numbers – as Cartoon Network announced an immediate follow-up, *Justice League Unlimited*.

## BATMAN: MYSTERY OF THE BATWOMAN (2003)

**Release date:** 21 October 2003 (US)
**Certificate:** PG (US); 12 (UK)
**Running time:** 74 minutes

### VOICE CAST

Kevin Conroy (*Bruce Wayne/Batman*); Kimberly Brooks (*Kathleen 'Kathy' Duquesne*); Kelly Ripa (*Dr Roxanne 'Rocky' Ballantine*); Elisa Gabrielli (*Detective Sonia Alcana*); Kyra Sedgwick (*Batwoman*); David Ogden Stiers (*The Penguin*); Kevin Michael Richardson (*Carlton Duquesne*); Eli Marienthal (*Tim Drake/Robin*); Efrem Zimbalist Jr (*Alfred Pennyworth*); Tara Strong (*Barbara Gordon*); Bob Hastings (*Commissioner Jim Gordon*); Robert Costanzo (*Detective Harvey Bullock*); John Vernon (*Rupert Thorne*); Hector Elizondo (*Bane*).

### KEY CREW

Curt Geda (*Director*); Alan Burnett (*Supervising Producer*); Curt Geda, Margaret M. Dean (*Producers*); Michael E. Uslan, Benjamin Melniker, Sander Schwartz (*Executive Producers*); Kathryn Page (*Associate Producer*); Alan Burnett (*Story*); Michael Reaves (*Written by*); Bob Kane (*Characters*); Jennifer Graves, Tim Maltby (*Sequence Directors*); Andrea Romano (*Casting/Voice Director*); Lolita Ritmanis (*Music*); Margaret Hou (*Editing*).

### STORY

A new hero takes to the streets of Gotham City – an enigmatic female crime-fighter going by the name of Batwoman. Striking with ruthless efficiency against the illegal arms-dealing set-up of the Penguin and Rupert Thorne, Batwoman quickly becomes the talk of the town but her dangerous techniques and disregard for human life raise concerns with the Caped Crusader. As Batman attempts to uncover her motives – and her true identity – the Penguin and Rupert Thorne turn to their hired muscle, Carlton Duquesne, to take the mysterious vigilante down. Despite Duquesne's best efforts, the mobsters' plans are dealt a severe blow when Batwoman destroys their weapons manufacturing plant, forcing them to take their operation off-shore and call in the services of an outside expert – the formidable South American mercenary Bane.

Through his investigation, the Caped Crusader highlights three potential Batwoman suspects, each of whom have their own motive for the attacks – GCPD Detective Soria Alcana, Wayne Tech employee Dr Roxanne 'Rocky' Ballantine and Kathy Duquesne, the daughter of mobster Carlton Duquesne and Bruce Wayne's newest love interest. The Dark Knight Detective eventually deduces that all three women have been working together, but not before Kathy is taken captive by Bane after sneaking aboard the villains' cruise-liner dressed as Batwoman. The Caped Crusader launches a rescue mission, saving

Kathy before squaring against Bane as the Penguin and Thorne attempt to flee in a speedboat. The gangsters come under attack from Rocky and Sonia in their Batwoman suits and are soon rounded up by the police, while Batman manages to escape Bane's clutches as the cruise-liner crashes into a bridge. Later, with Carlton Duquesne agreeing to testify against his fellow crooks, Kathy drives off into the sunset, accompanied by Bruce Wayne.

## BRINGING BATMAN TO THE SCREEN

'Warner Bros Animation decided to do one last direct-to-video about Batman. They gave it to Alan Burnett, who was my producer on *Batman: The Animated Series*, and he hired me to write it,' recalled screenwriter Michael Reaves, detailing the origins of *Batman: Mystery of the Batwoman* in an interview with James Harvey of *Worlds FinestOnline.com* in 2008. Unlike *Mask of the Phantasm* and *SubZero*, the latest movie would adopt the 'New Look' character models of *The New Batman Adventures*, albeit with a noticeably brighter style of animation. 'It was a conscious decision to lighten this one up a bit,' explained Reaves. 'We felt that, over the years, we'd put Bats through a fair bit of angst and suffering, and since this would be our farewell to the *Animated Series* universe, why not let him get the girl for once?'

The girl in question proved to be the original character of Kathy Duquesne, but the mobster's daughter was also joined by two other newly created female leads in Dr Roxanne Ballantine and Detective Sonia Alcana; together they would serve as the DC Animated Universe incarnation of Batwoman, the female crime-fighter who made her debut under the alter ego of Kathy Kane in the comic book story 'The Batwoman' by Edmond Hamilton, published in *Detective Comics* #233 (July 1956). Having never featured in *The New Batman Adventures*, the character Rupert Thorne underwent a makeover from his original appearance to bring the crime boss in line with the streamlined art style of the later series, while the Batsuit was also revamped slightly, incorporating similar highlights to those of the Dark Knight's *Justice League* design.

As with *Batman Beyond: Return of the Joker*, the task of directing *Mystery of the Batwoman* fell to Curt Geda, who first began his association with the Caped Crusader as a storyboard artist on *Batman: The Animated Series*. Also reprising their roles from the original 1992 series were Kevin Conroy, Bob Hastings, Robert Costanzo, John Vernon and Efrem Zimbalist Jr, with *The New Batman Adventures*' Tara Strong returning as the voice of Batgirl. Hector Elizondo (*Chicago Hope*, 1994–2000) and David Ogden Stiers (*M*A*S*H*, 1972–83) stepped in for their only outings as Bane and the Penguin respectively, while Eli Marienthal (*American Pie*, 1999) continued in the role of Robin, having voiced the Boy Wonder in an episode of *Static Shock*. Cast as the trio of female vigilantes were Kimberly Brooks (*Dexter's Laboratory*, 1996–2003) as Kathy, Kelly Ripa (*All My Children*, 1970–present) as Rocky and Elisa Gabrielli (*Gargoyles*, 1994–7) as Sonia, with Kyra Sedgwick (*Secondhand Lions*, 2003) supplying the voice of Batwoman and Kevin Michael Richardson (*Lilo & Stitch*, 2002) featuring as Kathy's father, Carlton Duquesne.

## RECEPTION

*Batman: Mystery of the Batwoman* was released direct-to-video on 21 October 2003, and reviews were generally favourable, although it failed to generate the same kind of acclaim afforded to earlier animated *Batman* features. A number of fans expressed displeasure over the lighter tone of the feature compared to prior outings – especially director Curt Geda's previous effort, *Batman Beyond: Return of the Joker* – whereas others praised the film as a return to the character-driven stories of the original *Batman* episodes. Accompanying the DVD release of *Batman: Mystery of the Batwoman* was a silent six-minute short entitled *Chase Me*, which featured the Dark Knight pursuing Catwoman across Gotham and was directed by Curt Geda from a script by Alan Burnett and Paul Dini.

# JUSTICE LEAGUE UNLIMITED (2004–6)

Premiere: 31 July 2004 (US)
Episode count: 39

## VOICE CAST

Kevin Conroy (*Bruce Wayne/Batman*); George Newbern (*Clark Kent/Superman*); Susan Eisenberg (*Princess Diana of Themyscira/Wonder Woman*); Michael Rosenbaum (*Wally West/The Flash*); Phil LaMarr (*John Stewart/Green Lantern*); Carl Lumbly (*J'onn J'onzz/Martian Manhunter*); Maria Canals (*Shayera Hol/Hawkgirl*).

## KEY CREW

Dwayne McDuffie, Bruce W. Timm, James Tucker (*Producers*); Sander Schwartz (*Executive Producer*); Shaun McLaughlin (*Line Producer*); Andrea Romano (*Casting/Voice Director*) Michael McCuistion (*Theme*).

## STORY

The founding members of the Justice League are joined by an expanding roster of heroes including Captain Atom, Green Arrow and Supergirl as they continue the fight to protect humanity, while a new threat emerges as a legion of supervillains band together to form a secret society.

## BRINGING JUSTICE LEAGUE TO THE SCREEN

As production drew to a close on the second season of *Justice League*, the DC Animated Universe was facing an uncertain future. Producer Glen Murakami had left the creative team to concentrate on Cartoon Network's latest animated superhero series *Teen Titans* (SEE 'MISCELLANEOUS ANIMATED SERIES'), while Warner Bros Animation were also readying the Dark Knight's return to the WB Network for a brand new interpretation entitled *The Batman* (SEE 'THE FURTHER ANIMATED ADVENTURES OF THE CAPED CRUSADER'). However, in February 2004, Cartoon Network announced that DC's team of superheroes would return for a follow-up series, with *Justice League* head writer Dwayne McDuffie joining producers Bruce Timm and James Tucker for the rebranded *Justice League Unlimited*.

Accompanying the change in title was an updated opening sequence and new theme tune, along with a greatly expanded roster of superheroes, many of whom were yet to appear outside of the comic books. Despite the influx of characters, the producers would run into difficulties due to a policy introduced by Warner Bros in the wake of their expanding stable of superhero media properties. Known as the Bat-Embargo, this effectively limited the use of certain characters outside *The Batman* and *Batman Begins*, meaning that popular villains such as the Joker, Harley Quinn, the Penguin, Two-Face and the Scarecrow were off-limits

to *Justice League Unlimited*. The creative team also encountered further restrictions with regard to their new alliance of supervillains – an updated version of *Challenge of the Super Friends*' Legion of Doom – whom they were unable to refer to by that particular name at the insistence of DC Comics.

## RECEPTION

*Justice League Unlimited* premiered on Saturday 31 July 2004 as part of Cartoon Network's Toonami programming block and went on to run for thirty-nine episodes over three seasons. Like its predecessor, the series was nominated for a Primetime Emmy, with Michael McCuistion contesting the award for Outstanding Main Title Theme Music in 2005. That same year saw the broadcast of the Season Two finale 'Epilogue', which also served as the series finale to *Batman Beyond* and was originally intended to provide closure to the entire DC Animated Universe. As it happened, Cartoon Network renewed *Justice League Unlimited* for one final batch of episodes, with the curtain falling on the 'Timmverse' on 13 May 2006, almost fourteen years after *Batman: The Animated Series* had first reinvented children's animated programming.

Following the conclusion of the show, the entire run of *Justice League Unlimited* was collected together across two volumes of Warner Home Video's DC Comics Classic Collection, with the first twenty-six episodes released on

DVD and Blu-ray as *Justice League Unlimited: Season One* and the remaining thirteen as *Justice League Unlimited: Season Two.* Meanwhile, much of the creative talent behind the DC Animated Universe remained integral to the ongoing adventures of the Caped Crusader and his superhero colleagues, with Warner Bros launching a number of television projects, along with a series of direct-to-video features (SEE 'DC UNIVERSE ANIMATED ORIGINAL MOVIES'). 'I doubt that we'll be formally, "officially" doing another movie or TV series set in the [DC Animated Universe] – but I suppose anything's possible,' explained Bruce Timm in response to intense fan interest towards a revival of the popular canon. 'Instead of saying "the DC Animated Universe is dead", maybe we can just say it's in a state of suspended animation until further notice.'

# THE FURTHER ANIMATED ADVENTURES OF THE CAPED CRUSADER

## THE BATMAN (2004–8)

**Premiere:** 11 September 2004 (US)
**Episode count:** 65

### VOICE CAST

Rino Romano (*Bruce Wayne/The Batman*); Alistair Duncan (*Alfred Pennyworth*); Evan Sabara (*Dick Grayson/Robin*); Danielle Judovits (*Barbara Gordon/Batgirl*); Ming-Na (*Detective Ellen Yin*); Mitch Pileggi (*Commissioner James Gordon*); Adam West (*Mayor Grange*).

### KEY CREW

Duane Capizzi, Michael Goguen (*Supervising Producers*); Glen Murakami, Jeff Matsuda, Linda M. Steiner (*Producers*); Alan Burnett, Sander Schwartz (*Executive Producers*); Kimberley Smith (*Associate/Line Producer*); Ginny McSwain, Andrea Romano (*Voice Directors*); Bob Kane (*Characters*); Michael Hack, Ginny McSwain, Andrea Romano (*Casting*); The Edge (*Theme*); Thomas Chase Jones (*Music*).

### STORY

Striking from a secret Batcave with an incredible arsenal of high-tech gadgets, the young billionaire bachelor Bruce Wayne brings justice to the streets and dark alleys of Gotham City as its greatest protector, the Batman. As the legend of the Caped Crusader grows, dangerous new enemies emerge to threaten the city and other costumed crime-fighters soon look to join his crusade, including Batgirl, Robin and the Justice League of America.

### BRINGING THE BATMAN TO THE SCREEN

With *Teen Titans* and *Justice League Unlimited* airing on Cartoon Network, 2004 saw the Caped Crusader return to the WB Network for a new series from Warner Bros Animation entitled *The Batman*. 'Unlike *Batman: The Animated Series*, we had the opportunity to unfold an epic saga which charts Batman's course from vigilante, to working covertly with members of Gotham P.D., to being publicly accepted as Gotham's hero and responding to the Bat-Signal, to gaining new alliances and beyond,' explained supervising producer Duane Capizzi (*Jackie Chan Adventures*) in an interview with *WorldsFinestOnline.com* in 2005. 'So, we could "re-tell" Batman's history in a sequential order, more or less paralleling the years of *Batman* mythology, and hopefully find interesting ways to introduce a new audience to classic scenarios.'

As part of this retelling, Capizzi's *Jackie Chan Adventures* colleague Jeff Matsuda (*Gary the Rat*, 2003) served as chief character designer for *The Batman*, adopting an anime-influenced visual style and reimagining many of the classic villains from the Caped Crusader's Rogues Gallery in an effort to differentiate from the acclaimed *Batman: The Animated Series*. The decision was also made to go with a younger incarnation of Batman, with Rino Romano (*Spider-Man Unlimited*, 1999–2001) cast as the voice of the 26-year-old Bruce Wayne, who begins the series in his third year of crime-fighting as the Dark Knight. Joining Romano in the regular voice cast for *The Batman* was Alistair Duncan (*The Hound of the Baskervilles*, 1988) as Alfred Pennyworth, while later seasons would also see the introduction of further allies, including Mitch Pileggi (*The X-Files*) as Commissioner Gordon, Danielle Judovits (*Naruto*, 2002–7) as Barbara Gordon/Batgirl and Evan Sabara (*The Polar Express*) as Dick Grayson/Robin.

Although *The Batman* was set in its own continuity, the crew consisted of several veterans of the DC Animated Universe, such as Alan Burnett, Glen Murakami and Andrea Romano. Furthermore, the voice cast incorporated a number of actors with prior experience in Gotham City, most notably Adam West, who featured as the voice of Mayor Grange for the first four seasons. West was joined by fellow *Batman* star Frank Gorshin, who swapped his Emmy Award-winning turn as the Riddler to voice the character of Professor Hugo Strange until the actor's death in 2005. Other familiar names included Will Friedle as Gearhead, Phil LaMarr as Maxie Zues, Ron Perlman as Bane and Killer Croc and Kevin Michael Richardson as the Joker, while Kevin Conroy and Mark Hamill featured as John Grayson and Tony Zucco respectively in the fourth-season Robin-origin episode, 'A Matter of Family'. Despite bearing no connection to the DC Animated Universe, the fifth and final season of *The Batman* saw the introduction of the Justice League, with George Newbern reprising his role as Superman from the Cartoon Network series and Clancy Brown returning as Lex Luthor, a character he had voiced since his introduction in *Superman: The Animated Series*.

## RECEPTION

*The Batman* received its premiere on 11 September 2004 as part of the Kids' WB! programming block of the WB Network. While it proved popular with audiences, the reaction from fans and critics was decidedly mixed, with many condemning the show for its cartoonish, toyetic approach. However, it soon amassed a loyal following of devoted fans and also enjoyed considerable success on the awards circuit, receiving three Annie Award nominations and contesting for a grand total of fourteen Daytime Emmy Awards. From those fourteen nominations *The Batman* was victorious on six occasions, receiving accolades for Outstanding Achievement in Sound Editing – Live Action and Animation in four consecutive years (2005–8), along with two awards for Outstanding Special Class Animated Program (2006 and 2007) and the award for Outstanding Achievement in Sound Mixing – Live Action and Animation (2008). *The Batman* came to an end in 2008 after running for five seasons, all of which have since been released on DVD by Warner Home Video as part of their DC Comics Kids' Collection.

## THE BATMAN VS DRACULA: THE ANIMATED MOVIE (2005)

**Release date:** 18 October 2005 (US)
**Certificate:** Not rated
**Running time:** 83 minutes

### VOICE CAST

Rino Romano (*Bruce Wayne/The Batman*); Peter Stormare (*Dracula*); Tara Strong (*Vicki Vale*); Tom Kenny (*Oswald Cobblepot/The Penguin*); Kevin Michael Richardson (*The Joker*); Alistair Duncan (*Alfred Pennyworth*).

### KEY CREW

Michael Goguen (*Director*); Duane Capizzi, Michael Goguen (*Supervising Producers*); Jeff Matsuda, Linda M. Steiner (*Producers*); Benjamin Melniker, Michael Uslan, Sander Schwartz, Alan Burnett (*Executive Producers*); Kimberly Smith (*Associate Producer*); Duane Capizzi (*Written by*); Bob Kane, Bram Stoker (*Characters*); Seung Eun Kim, Sam Liu, Brandon Vietti (*Sequence Directors*); Ginny McSwain (*Casting/Voice Director*); Thomas Chase Jones (*Music*).

### STORY

Hoping to uncover a stash of stolen money buried within Gotham Cemetery, the Penguin inadvertently awakens the fabled vampire, Count Dracula, whose remains had been brought to

Gotham many years before. Posing as the Eastern European aristocrat Dr Alucard, the Count hatches a plan to create an army of bloodthirsty vampires in Gotham, reigning over the city as their king. As a spate of disappearances grip the city, Bruce Wayne attends a party with Vicki Vale where he meets with Dr Alucard and quickly deduces the fiendish truth behind his identity. After capturing an infected Joker and taking him to the Batcave, the Batman takes a blood sample and uses this to develop a cure for vampirism. Meanwhile, the Prince of Darkness captures Vicki, intending to use her body to reincarnate his former bride, Carmilla. The Batman tracks Dracula to the catacombs beneath Gotham Cemetery, using the antidote to cure his victims and freeing Vicki before the ceremony can be completed. Unable to best the Count in combat, the Dark Knight lures his adversary through the catacombs to the Batcave, where he uses a prototype solar-energy device from Wayne Industries to blast Dracula with rays of sunlight, turning the legendary vampire to ash and finally bringing an end to his accursed spell over the people of Gotham.

## BRINGING THE BATMAN TO THE SCREEN

To coincide with the DVD release of *Batman Begins* in October 2005, Warner Bros Animation developed a feature-length direct-to-video movie based upon their latest animated series *The Batman*. Unlike the television series, which was aimed at a pre-teen audience, the movie adopted a much darker tone as the Caped Crusader fought to save Gotham from Count Dracula, the classic archetypal vampire created by Bram Stoker for his 1897 Gothic horror novel, *Dracula*. The feature marked the Count's first official screen appearance in the Batman universe, although the character had appeared in two unauthorized movies during the 1960s – *Batman Dracula* (1964), which was produced and directed by the artist Andy Warhol, and *Batman Fights Dracula* (1967), a Filipino release directed by Leocy M. Diaz (*Durango*, 1967).

Drawing upon elements of the graphic novel *Batman & Dracula: Red Rain* by Doug Moench and Kelley Jones, which was published in 1991 under DC's alternate reality 'Elseworlds' imprint, the screenplay for *The Batman vs Dracula* was written by Duane Capizzi, with producing colleague Michael Goguen (*Men in Black: The Series*, 1997–2001) handling directing duties. Voice actors such as Rino Romano, Kevin Michael Richardson, Alistair Duncan and Tom Kenny (*SpongeBob SquarePants*, 1999–present) all reprised their roles from the series, while Peter Stormare (*Fargo*) was cast as Dracula. Tara Strong also made the jump from the DC Animated Universe to supply the voice of Vicki Vale, with the character depicted as a television reporter for her first ever animated appearance.

## RECEPTION

*The Batman vs Dracula: The Animated Movie* was released on DVD on 18 October 2005 and subsequently received its first television broadcast on Cartoon Network's Toonami programming block four days later. The film was nominated for an Annie Award for Best Home Entertainment Production and reviews were generally positive, with particular praise reserved for its dark, mature storytelling and solid animation. Bill Ramey of *Batman-on-Film.com* suggested that, 'If you group all of the animated *Batman* movies together, this is one of the better ones', although – as with the series itself – a percentage of fans felt that it paled in comparison next to the acclaimed offerings of the DC Animated Universe.

# BATMAN: THE BRAVE AND THE BOLD (2008–11)

**Premiere:** 14 November 2008 (US)
**Episode count:** 65

## VOICE CAST

Diedrich Bader (*Bruce Wayne/Batman*); John DiMaggio (*Aquaman*); James Arnold Taylor (*Green Arrow, Guy Gardner*); Will Friedle (*Blue Beetle*); Corey Burton (*Red Tornado*); Tom Kenny (*Plastic Man*).

## KEY CREW

Michael Jelenic, James Tucker, Linda M. Steiner (*Producers*); Sam Register (*Executive Producer*); Amy McKenna (*Line Producer*); Bob Kane (*Characters*); Andrea Romano (*Casting/Voice Director*); Andy Sturmer (*Theme*); Michael McCuistion, Lolita Ritmanis, Kristopher Carter (*Music*).

## STORY

As Batman continues his never-ending quest to bring justice to the hoodlums of Gotham City, the Caped Crusader finds himself teaming up with fellow members of the superhero community such as Aquaman, Blue Beetle, the Green Arrow and Plastic Man to fight crime and battle supervillains across the globe and beyond.

## BRINGING BATMAN TO THE SCREEN

With *The Batman* drawing to a close in 2008 after five seasons, Warner Bros Animation and Cartoon Network were keen to present a new take on the Caped Crusader, with Executive Vice President, Creative Affairs, Sam Register turning to a creative team headed up by James Tucker, an experienced producer of popular DC animated shows such as *Justice League, Justice League Unlimited* and *Legion of Super Heroes* (2006–8). Joining Tucker in the endeavour was Michael Jelenic, story editor on *The Batman* and *Legion of Super Heroes*, along with Linda Steiner, a producer whose credits included *Justice League, The Batman, Legion of Super Heroes, Teen Titans* and *Krypto the Superdog* (SEE 'MISCELLANEOUS ANIMATED SERIES').

'If Sam [Register] had presented it to me as just continuing what had already been done so well before, then I would have probably said "not interested",' explained James Tucker in an interview with Matt MacNabb of *LegionsofGotham.org* in 2008. 'To me, Batman is a character we all know so well, and there's so much available of him in the media that we really had to show him in a different light than he's been seen since the 80s at least.' This view was shared by Michael Jelenic, who was drawn towards the prospect of exploring a fresh interpretation of Bob Kane's Dark Knight Detective, telling *LegionsofGotham.org* that: 'I think whenever you work with Batman your instinct is to play up the darker elements of his mythos, but since both James Tucker and I had already done darker incarnations of the character, it gave us the freedom to try something different.'

To differentiate from the Caped Crusader's previous animated adventures, the new show took its inspiration from the award-winning comic book series *The Brave and the Bold*, which had originally launched as an anthology title in August 1955. Prompted by the success of the *Batman* television series, *The Brave and the Bold* underwent a change from Issue #67 (September 1966), taking the form of a 'team-up' series that saw Batman venturing out of his typical Gotham City setting to join forces with various superheroes from the DC universe. The first run of *The Brave and the Bold* came to an end with Issue #200 in July 1983 and it was later relaunched without the Dark Knight for two six-issue mini-series during the 1990s, before a third volume began publication in 2007, this time featuring a rotating roster of character team-ups.

'My temptation with Batman was always to go towards the darker side and I had to fight against that urge,' revealed casting and voice director Andrea Romano, who continued her long-running association with the Caped Crusader for the latest series, *Batman: The Brave and the Bold*. 'With this incarnation, we pushed for the lighter edge. I'm not making *Batman: The Animated Series*, so there's slightly more colour to it, it's just a brighter series overall.' To voice the

Capec Crusader, Romano turned to Diedrich Bader, an actor whose previous credits included the title role in *The Zeta Project*, along with appearances in *Batman Beyond* and *The Batman*. Joining Bader in the regular cast were experienced voice actors Corey Burton, Will Friedle, Tom Kenny John DiMaggio (*Futurama*, 1999–present) and James Arnold Taylor (*Star Wars: The Clone Wars*, 2008–present). The regular cast members would all take on multiple roles throughout the series and they were joined by a host of guest stars with previous experience of the *Batman* universe, including the likes of Jeff Bennett, Clancy Brown, Kevin Conroy, Dana Delany, Mark Hamill, Loren Lester Jason Marsden, Richard Moll, Ron Perlman, Paul Reubens, Kevin Michael Richardson, Tara Strong and Adam West.

## RECEPTION

*Batman: The Brave and the Bold* premiered on Cartoon Network in North America on 14 November 2008. Although it was aimed firmly at young children, the show soon earned acclaim for its creative and refreshing approach, along with its inclusion of 'lesser known' characters from the rich history of the DC universe. In 2010, Kristopher Carter, Michael McCuistion, Lolita Ritmanis, Michael Jelenic and James Tucker were nominated for a Primetime Emmy Award for Outstanding Music Composition for a Series (Original Dramatic Score) for the episode 'Mayhem of the Music Meister'. That same year

at the San Diego Comic-Con International, it was announced that the series would come to an end after three seasons, with the final episodes broadcast in the UK in August 2011. Warner Home Video released the first twenty-six episodes of *Batman: The Brave and the Bold* across six DVD volumes, each containing between four and five episodes, while the entire first season was subsequently made available as the two-disc sets *Batman: The Brave and the Bold – Season One, Part One* and *Season One, Part Two*. This was followed by *Season Two, Part One* in August 2011, with the remaining episodes unavailable on home video at the time of writing.

# DC Universe Animated Original Movies

## JUSTICE LEAGUE: THE NEW FRONTIER (2008)

**Release date:** 26 February 2008 (US)
**Certificate:** PG-13 (US)
**Running time:** 75 minutes

### VOICE CAST

Jeremy Sisto (*Bruce Wayne/Batman*); David Boreanaz (*Hal Jordan/Green Lantern*); Miguel Ferrer (*J'onn J'onzz/Martian Manhunter*); Neil Patrick Harris (*Barry Allen/The Flash*); John Heard (*Kyle 'Ace' Morgan*), Lucy Lawless (*Princess Diana of Themyscira/Wonder Woman*); Kyle MacLachlan (*Clark Kent/Superman*); Kyra Sedgwick (*Lois Lane*); Shane Haboucha (*Dick Grayson/Robin*); Lex Land (*Rick Flagg*); Phil Morris (*King Faraday*); Corey Burton (*Abin Sur*); Alan Ritchson (*Arthur Curry/Aquaman*).

### KEY CREW

Dave Bullock (*Director*); Stan Berkowitz, Darwyn Cooke, Bruce W. Timm (*Producers*); Gregory Noveck, Sander Schwartz (*Executive Producers*); Michael Goguen (*Supervising Producer*); Kimberly Smith (*Line Producer*); Stan Berkowitz (*Written by*); Darwyn Cooke (*Graphic Novel/Additional Material*); Andrea Romano (*Voice Director*); Andrea Romano, Barbara Wright (*Casting*); Kevin Manthei (*Music*); Elen Orson (*Editing*).

### STORY

In the 1950s, Cold War paranoia and government distrust in superheroes has led to the disbandment of the Justice Society. Although Superman and Wonder Woman remain aligned with the United States government, other crime-fighters such as Batman and the Flash are forced to operate as vigilantes, working under the radar to protect humanity. Investigating a kidnapping attributed to a cult, Batman joins forces with Gotham City police detective John Jones – whom the Dark Knight soon discovers to be the Martian Manhunter J'onn J'onzz – and together they uncover the impending arrival of a powerful entity known as the Centre. The being finally launches its assault on Earth, taking the form of a primordial island and quickly defeating Superman as it attacks the Florida coast. In order to stop the Centre, the world's superheroes – including the newest member of the Green Lantern Corps, test pilot Hal Jordan – come together for a joint offensive with the military, and through their combined efforts they are successful in defeating the creature. As Earth celebrates the great victory, public opinion towards superheroes shifts dramatically, paving the way for the formation of a new team of heroes … the Justice League.

## BRINGING JUSTICE LEAGUE TO THE SCREEN

In 2007, DC Comics' Senior Vice President, Creative Affairs Gregory Noveck (*Jeremiah*, 2002–4) launched a new series of direct-to-video features under the banner of DC Universe Animated Original Movies with the release of *Superman/Doomsday*, an animated adaptation of the acclaimed story arc *The Death and Return of Superman*, which had run in DC Comics throughout 1992 and 1993. Produced in conjunction with Warner Bros Animation and Warner Premiere, *Superman/Doomsday* featured the creative involvement of experienced DC animation alumni such as Bruce Timm and Sander Schwartz (*Loonatics Unleashed*, 2005–7) and was a huge success, shifting over 680,000 copies in North America alone. Meanwhile work was already well underway on the next instalment, an ambitious adaptation of *DC: The New Frontier*, a Shuster Award-winning limited series by Darwyn Cooke (*Men in Black: The Series*) that was published between 2003 and 2004 and looked to bridge the gap between DC's Golden Age and Silver Age superheroes.

Although the original comic book story was a sprawling tale that spanned the entire DC universe, the decision was made to narrow the focus for the feature, concentrating instead on the characters of Batman, the Flash, the Green Lantern, J'onn J'onzz, Superman and Wonder Woman. With their extensive experience in the DC Animated Universe, Dave Bullock (*Star Wars: The Clone Wars*) was tasked with directing the movie while Stan Berkowitz (*Spider-Man*, 1994–8) developed a screenplay with assistance from producer Darwyn Cooke, who acted as a creative consultant both for the story and the visuals. Supplying the voice of the Dark Knight for *Justice League: The New Frontier* was Jeremy Sisto (*Six Feet Under*), while other cast members included Kyle MacLaughlin (*Twin Peaks*) as Superman, David Boreanaz as the Green Lantern, Lucy Lawless (*Xena: Warrior Princess*, 1995–2001) as Wonder Woman, Miguel Ferrer (*RoboCop*, 1987) as J'onn J'onzz, Neil Patrick Harris (*Doogie Howser, M.D.*, 1989–93) as the Flash and Shane Haboucha (*Desperation*, 2006) as Robin the Boy Wonder.

## RECEPTION

*Justice League: The New Frontier* arrived on DVD in North America on 26 February 2008 and received its first television airing on Cartoon Network that October. The movie was nominated for a Primetime Emmy Award for Outstanding Animated Program (For Programming One Hour or

More) and also contested the Annie Award for Best Animated Home Entertainment Production. Fans and critics responded positively to the feature, praising it for its mature storytelling and high-quality voice acting. Nevertheless, it failed to replicate the success of *Superman/Doomsday* and went on to sell just over 300,000 copies in the US, earning $5,233,834 in gross sales.

## BATMAN: GOTHAM KNIGHT (2008)

**Release date:** 8 July 2008 (US); 14 July 2008 (UK)
**Certificate:** PG-13 (US); 15 (UK)
**Running time:** 75 minutes

### VOICE CAST

Kevin Conroy (*Bruce Wayne/Batman*); Corey Burton (*The Scarecrow, The Russian, Ronald Marshall*); Jim Meskimen (*Lieutenant James Gordon, Deadshot*); Ana Ortiz (*Detective Anna Ramirez*); Rob Paulsen (*Sal Maroni, Mole Man*); Jason Marsden (*Thomas Wayne*); Andrea Romano (*Martha Wayne*); Will Friedle (*Anton*); Kevin Michael Richardson (*Lucius Fox, Avery*); David McCallum (*Alfred Pennyworth*).

### KEY CREW

Yasuhiro Aoki, Futoshi Higashide, Toshiyuki Kubooka, Morioka Hiroshi, Jong-Sik Nam, Shojuro Nishimi (*Directors*); Toshi Hiruma (*Producer*); Benjamin Melniker, Michael E. Uslan, Emma Thomas, Bruce W. Timm (*Executive Producers*); Kimberly Smith (*Line Producer*); Jordan Goldberg (*Story*); Josh Olson, Greg Rucka, Brian Azzarello, Alan Burnett, David S. Goyer (*Screenplay*); Bob Kane (*Characters*); Andrea Romano (*Casting/Voice Director*); Christopher Drake, Robert Kral, Kevin Manthei (*Music*); Joe Gall (*Editing*).

## STORY TITLES

(1) Have I Got a Story for You; (2) Crossfire; (3) Field Test; (4) In Darkness Dwells; (5) Working Through Pain; (6) Deadshot.

## STORY

After defending the city from the League of Shadows, Bruce Wayne maintains his role as Gotham's protector, learning from experience to refine his skills and tactics while strengthening his partnership with Lieutenant James Gordon of the Major Crimes Unit. As children swap fantastic stories of the Dark Knight's legendary exploits, a gang war erupts between rival mobsters Sal Maroni and the Russian, with Batman coming to the aid of police detectives Allen and Ramirez as they become caught in the crossfire. Later, the Scarecrow unleashes his fear toxin in a cathedral, leading to a riot in which a cardinal is abducted by the disfigured murderer Waylon Jones, a.k.a. Killer Croc. Venturing into the sewers to investigate, the Dark Knight is bitten by Killer Croc and becomes infected with the toxin. Freeing the Cardinal from the Scarecrow, Batman is shot in the stomach and draws upon his training to control the pain as he makes his way through the sewer to rendezvous with his trusted butler Alfred. Meanwhile the assassin Deadshot arrives in Gotham City, aiming to carry out a hit on Lieutenant Gordon. Batman manages to disrupt the assassination attempt and discovers that he is the true target; confronting Deadshot on top of a speeding train, the Dark Knight manages to subdue the hitman, turning him over to the police before returning to Wayne Manor to treat his injuries. As he debates the effectiveness of his crusade with Alfred, Bruce looks up to see the Bat-Signal illuminating the sky once more.

## BRINGING BATMAN TO THE SCREEN

Having appeared as part of the ensemble in *Justice League: The New Frontier*, the Caped Crusader took centre-stage for the third entry in Warner Bros' series of DC Universe Animated Original Movies, *Batman: Gotham Knight*. Whereas the previous two instalments had been adaptations of comic book stories, *Gotham Knight* was a collection of six original tales set in the universe created by Christopher Nolan with his 2005 reboot, *Batman Begins*. 'When we decided to make this film, we wanted to get the best Japanese animators and the best *Batman* writers we could,' explained Gregory Noveck. 'The idea was to bring in some of these really well known Japanese animators, people who might have always wanted to work on *Batman* and never had the opportunity, and just let them have at it.'

Handling scripting duties for *Gotham Knight* was an impressive line-up of talent, with experienced *Batman* scribes Brian Azzarello, Alan Burnett, David S. Goyer and Greg Rucka joined by Josh Olson (*A History of Violence*, 2005) and Jordan Goldberg, associate producer on *The Dark*

*Knight*. In order to present *Gotham Knight* with authentic anime visuals far removed from any of the Caped Crusader's prior cartoon incarnations, animation duties were farmed out to the acclaimed Japanese studios Bee Train (*Noir*, 2001), Madhouse (*Ninja Scroll*, 1993), Production I.G. (*Ghost in the Shell: Stand Alone Complex*, 2002–3) and Studio 4°C (*The Animatrix*, 2003). 'What they did really exceeded anything beyond what I'd imagined,' said Noveck. 'They gave Batman so many new, different looks, and still kept him recognizable as Batman, and that's what we wanted.'

'I think the film works as a standalone in the *Batman* mythos as a unique – actually, six very unique – visions of Batman,' explained executive producer Bruce Timm in an interview with Simon Brew of *DenofGeek.com* in 2008. 'But it was also designed to give *Batman* fans a little something extra, to fill in some blanks that fall within the *Batman Begins* and *The Dark Knight* version of the character.' Serving as a bridge between the two films, *Gotham Knight* explored the emerging partnership of Batman and Jim Gordon as they attempt to clean up the Narrows following the events of *Batman Begins*, as well as introducing the characters of crime lord Sal Maroni and police detective Anna Ramirez into the 'Nolanverse' prior to their live-action debuts. Meanwhile, two years after the conclusion of *Justice League*, fan favourite Kevin Conroy reprised his signature role as the voice of Batman, joining a voice cast that included DC animated regulars such as Will Friedle, Jason Marsden, Kevin Michael Richardson and Corey Burton (*The Transformers*).

## RECEPTION

As anticipation built for the theatrical arrival of *The Dark Knight*, Warner Premiere released *Batman: Gotham Knight* on DVD and Blu-ray on 8 July, advertising it as the first animated *Batman* movie to be rated PG-13, despite the fact that the uncut edition of *Batman Beyond: Return of the Joker* had earlier received the classification back in 2002. North American sales of *Gotham Knight* exceeded those of *Justice League: The New Frontier*, with the third instalment of the DC Universe Animated Original Movies shifting over 395,000 copies for a US gross of $8,061,199. It was met favourably by fans and critics, with *WorldsFinestOnline.com* describing *Gotham Knight* as 'something new and entirely fresh for the Dark Knight', while Glen Ferris of Britain's *Empire* magazine bestowed a four-star review, describing the feature as 'a must-see for all Caped Crusader completists'. *Batman: Gotham Knight* was honoured with Best Sound Editing – Direct to Video by the Motion Picture Sound Editors at the 2009 Golden Reel Awards and also contested the Annie Awards for Best Animated Home Entertainment Production and Best Music in an Animated Feature Production.

# SUPERMAN/BATMAN: PUBLIC ENEMIES (2009)

**Release date:** 29 September 2009 (US); 19 July 2010 (UK)
**Certificate:** PG-13 (US); 12 (UK)
**Running time:** 67 minutes

## VOICE CAST

Kevin Conroy (*Bruce Wayne/Batman*); Tim Daly (*Clark Kent/Superman*); Clancy Brown (*Lex Luthor*); Xander Berkley (*Nathaniel Christopher Adam/Captain Atom*); Corey Burton (*Captain Marvel*); Ricardo Chavira (*Clifford Zmeck/Major Force*); Allison Mack (*Karen Starr/Power Girl*); John C. McGinley (*John Corben/Metallo*); CCH Pounder (*Amanda Waller*); LeVar Burton (*Jefferson Pierce/Black Lightning*); Rachael MacFarlane (*Eve Eden/Nightshade*); Alan Oppenheimer (*Alfred Pennyworth*); Brian George (*Gorilla Grodd*); Calvin Tran (*Hiro Okamura/Toyman*); Andrea Romano (*Dr Doris Zuel/Giganta*); Bruce W. Timm (*Mongul*).

## KEY CREW

Sam Liu (*Director*); Michael Goguen, Bobbie Page (*Producers*); Michael E. Uslan, Benjamin Melniker, Sam Register, Bruce W. Timm (*Executive Producers*); Alan Burnett (*Co-producer*); Stan Berkowitz (*Written by*); Bob Kane, Joe Shuster, Jerry Siegel, C.C. Beck (*Characters*); Jeph Loeb, Ed McGuinness (*Comic Book*); Andrea Romano (*Casting/Voice Director*); Christopher Drake (*Music*); Margaret Hou (*Editing*).

## STORY

Amid an economic depression, Lex Luthor is elected President of the United States of America and – despite the distrust of Batman and Superman – the criminal mastermind quickly begins to rebuild the country while assembling his own team of superheroes headed up by Captain Atom. When the government discover that a Kryptonite meteor is heading on a collision course with Earth, Luthor arranges to meet with Superman in Gotham City, having secretly hired Metallo to attack the Man of Steel. After battling with Superman and Batman, Metallo is killed by an unknown assailant and Luthor immediately frames Superman for the crime. Luthor's team of superheroes engage Batman and Superman in combat, during which time it is revealed that the superhero Major Force was responsible for Metallo's death. Amanda Waller also discovers that Luthor has been driven insane by Kryptonite steroids and plans to allow the meteor to strike Earth, hoping to rule over the survivors. Waller provides Batman and Superman with data on the meteor and the two heroes head to Tokyo, seeking help from their Japanese ally Toyman. Meanwhile, Waller attempts to have Luthor arrested but he manages to evade capture and dons a power suit before setting off in pursuit of Superman and Batman. The Toyman develops a rocket to destroy the meteor, which Batman volunteers to pilot; as the Caped Crusader heads into space, Luthor arrives in Tokyo and battles with Superman. Believing Batman to have sacrificed himself to stop the meteor, Superman overpowers Luthor and defeats his enemy before flying into space to see that Batman has survived thanks to an escape craft built inside the rocket. Luthor is arrested by Captain Atom and his team and – with Superman cleared of the murder charge – the Man of Steel reunites with Lois Lane as Batman returns to Gotham City.

## BRINGING THE WORLD'S FINEST TO THE SCREEN

After producing the animated features *Wonder Woman* and *Green Lantern: First Flight*, Warner Premiere completed a hat-trick of releases in 2009 with the sixth entry in their direct-to-video movie series, bringing their two biggest superhero properties together for *Superman/Batman: Public Enemies*. Whereas the Caped Crusader's previous outing, *Gotham Knight*, had presented a collection of original tales, for their latest offering the filmmakers returned to the rich history of DC's comic book continuity, adapting the first six-issue story arc from their *World's Finest Comics* update, *Superman/Batman*, which had launched under writer Jeph Loeb and illustrator Ed McGuiness in August 2003.

As with prior entries under the DC Universe Animated Original Movies banner, the creative team behind *Superman/Batman: Public Enemies* were well versed in the animated history of the eponymous heroes. Director Sam Liu (*Hulk vs*, 2009) had helmed a number of episodes of *The Batman* and also served as a sequence director on the feature spin-off *The Batman vs Dracula*, while scriptwriter Stan Berkowitz possessed extensive experience within the DC Animated Universe, having begun his involvement as a story editor on *Superman: The Animated Series* back in 1996. This association with the DC Animated Universe would also extend to the voice cast with Kevin Conroy, Tim Daly and Clancy Brown reprising their roles as Batman, Superman and Lex Luthor respectively; joining them in the supporting cast were other DC veterans such as Xander Berkley (*24*, 2001–10), Corey Burton and Alan Oppenheimer (*Superman*, 1988), in addition to casting and voice director Andrea Romano and executive producer Bruce Timm.

## RECEPTION

Released on DVD and Blu-ray in North America on 29 September 2009, *Batman/Superman: Public Enemies* went on to become the second most successful of Warner Premiere's DC Universe Animated Original Movies line, selling almost 538,000 units and grossing $8,076,149. Zack Demeter of *WorldsFinestOnline.com* gave *Public Enemies* a 'highly recommended' rating, praising the film for its 'superb voice cast, excellent character designs and simple, easily progressed story'.

Meanwhile, despite warning *Batman* fans that 'this is Superman's film first and foremost with the Dark Knight playing second fiddle to the Man of Steel', Bill Ramey of *Batman-on-Film.com* wrote that *Superman/Batman: Public Enemies* is yet another solid effort from the folks behind the DCU animated flicks'.

## JUSTICE LEAGUE: CRISIS ON TWO EARTHS (2010)

**Release date:** 23 February 2010 (US)
**Certificate:** PG-13 (US)
**Running time:** 75 minutes

### VOICE CAST

William Baldwin (*Bruce Wayne/Batman*); Mark Harmon (*Clark Kent/Superman*); Chris Noth (*Lex Luthor*); Gine Torres (*Superwoman*); James Woods (*Owlman*); Jonathan Adams (*J'onn J'onzz/Martian Manhunter*); Brian Bloom (*Ultraman*); Bruce Davison (*President Slade Wilson*); Josh Keaton (*Wally West/The Flash, Aquaman*); Vanessa Marshall (*Princess Diana of Themyscira/Wonder Woman*); Nolan North (*Hal Jordan/Green Lantern*); Richard Green (*Jimmy Olsen*).

### KEY CREW

Sam Liu, Lauren Montgomery (*Co-directors*); Bobbie Page (*Producer*); Sam Register, Bruce W. Timm (*Executive Producers*); Alan Burnett (*Co-producer*); Dwayne McDuffie (*Written by*); Andrea Romano (*Voice Director*); Maria Estrada (*Casting*); James L. Venable (*Music*); Margaret Hou (*Editing*).

### STORY

In an alternate universe, a heroic Lex Luthor attempts to steal an unknown device from the Crime Syndicate of America, a team of supervillains that includes the likes of Ultraman, Superwoman, Owlman, Power Ring, Johnny Quick and J'edd J'arkus, all of whom possess virtually identical powers to their counterparts in the Justice League. To escape his enemies, Luthor travels through other-world dimensions to the Earth of the Justice League, handing himself over to the authorities and requesting help from the legendary team of superheroes. Despite Batman's concerns that the League are spreading themselves too thinly, the heroes travel to Luthor's Earth where they discover that the Crime Syndicate are holding the planet to ransom. They soon uncover a much greater threat, as Owlman plans to destroy the original Earth-Prime using a weapon known as the Quantum Eigenstate Device, causing a chain reaction that will destroy all of the parallel Earths in the multiverse. Owlman's scheme is eventually foiled by the Caped Crusader, who sends his evil counterpart to an uninhabited world; meanwhile the rest of the Justice League defeat the Crime Syndicate, liberating Luthor's Earth and ensuring the safety of the entire universe.

## BRINGING JUSTICE LEAGUE TO THE SCREEN

For the seventh of their direct-to-video series, Warner Bros turned to an earlier story from Bruce Timm and Dwayne McDuffie that was originally planned as a DC Animated Universe feature back in 2004. Entitled *World's Collide*, the film was intended to serve as a bridge between *Justice League* and *Justice League Unlimited* and reached as far as the casting and storyboard stages before the studio's home video department placed the project on hold. Although Timm remained hopeful that *World's Finest* would come to fruition, the conclusion of *Justice League Unlimited* seemed to put an end to the prospect until a new opportunity presented itself with the DC Universe Animated Original Movies line.

Employing elements of the Crime Syndicate's first comic book appearance in 'Crisis on Earth-Three!/The Most Dangerous Earth of All!' by Gardner Fox, published in *Justice League of America* #29–30 (August–September 1964), along with Grant Morrison's graphic novel *JLA: Earth 2* (2000), writer Dwayne McDuffie reworked his original script to remove references to the DC Animated Universe, setting *Justice League: Crisis on Two Earths* in its own continuity. To further emphasize *Crisis on Two Earths* as a stand-alone movie, Andrea Romano assembled an all-new voice cast that included *Batman Forever* candidate William Baldwin as Batman, along with Mark Harmon (*NCIS: Naval Criminal Investigative Service*, 2003–present) as Superman and Vanessa Marshall (*The Spectacular Spider-Man*, 2008–9) as Wonder Woman. Other talent to feature included the likes of Bruce Davison (*X-Men*) as President Slade Wilson and James Woods as the Dark Knight's Crime Syndicate counterpart, Owlman.

## RECEPTION

Released in North America on 23 February 2010, *Justice League: Crisis on Two Earths* continued to earn acclaim from fans and critics, although it failed to match the sales of the Caped Crusader's previous two outings in the direct-to-video series. However, the feature did manage to outperform *Justice League: The New Frontier*, with sales in excess of 355,000 units generating $5,254,322 in revenue. Sadly, *Justice League: Crisis on Two Earths* proved to be Dwayne McDuffie's penultimate contribution to the *Batman* universe, with the award-winning writer and producer passing away on 21 February 2011 after suffering complications from heart surgery, aged just 49. The following day saw the release of *All Star Superman* (2011), the tenth instalment of Warner Premiere's DC Universe Animated Original Movies and the second to be penned by McDuffie, while he had also completed scripting duties on *Justice League: Doom*, an adaptation of the comic book story *JLA: Tower of Babel* set to arrive in 2012.

# BATMAN: UNDER THE RED HOOD (2010)

**Release date:** 27 July 2010 (US); 4 October 2010 (UK)
**Certificate:** PG-13 (US); 12 (UK)
**Running time:** 75 minutes

## VOICE CAST

Bruce Greenwood (*Bruce Wayne/Batman*); Jensen Ackles (*Jason Todd/The Red Hood*); John Di Maggio (*The Joker*); Neil Patrick Harris (*Nightwing*); Jason Isaacs (*Ra's al Ghul*); Wade Williams (*Black Mask*); Gary Cole (*Commissioner James Gordon, Bobo*), Kelly Hu (*Ms Li*); Vincent Martella (*Young Jason Todd/Robin*); Jim Piddock (*Alfred Pennyworth*), Phil LaMarr (*Rick*); Kevin Michael Richardson (*Tyler Bramford*); Dwight Schultz (*Freddie*); Bruce W. Timm (*The Riddler*).

## KEY CREW

Brandon Vietti (*Director*); Bobbie Page, Bruce W. Timm (*Producers*); Michael E. Uslan, Benjamin Melniker, Sam Register (*Executive Producers*); Alan Burnett (*Co-producer*); Judd Winick (*Written by*); Bob Kane (*Characters*); Andrea Romano (*Casting/Voice Director*); Christopher Drake (*Music*); Margaret Hou (*Editing*).

## STORY

In a warehouse in Sarajevo, the Joker brutally attacks the second Robin, Jason Todd, beating the

Boy Wonder senseless with a crowbar. Batman arrives on a motorcycle but is too late to save Jason's life as an explosion tears through the building. Five years later, a new vigilante arrives on the streets of Gotham, using the Joker's old alias of the Red Hood to assume control of the city's drug trade. Batman and Nightwing encounter the Red Hood and give chase, with the vigilante leading Batman to the Ace Chemical Factory – the sight of his confrontation with the original Red Hood, which gave birth to the Joker – but the newcomer manages to escape after rigging the factory with explosives. The crime-fighters pay a visit to the Joker in Arkham Asylum hoping to gather information on his successor, but the Joker denies all involvement and taunts the Dark Knight over Jason's death. The duo get a second chance to capture the Red Hood after a failed hit on Black Mask, but the mysterious vigilante proves more than equal to their efforts and evades justice once again. Batman returns to the Batcave to watch a recording of the latest pursuit, during which he notices that the Red Hood referred to him as 'Bruce'.

After collecting a blood sample from the Red Hood, the Caped Crusader is shocked to discover that he is a perfect match for Jason Todd and exhumes his grave, finding a latex dummy in place of his body. Searching for answers, Batman visits Ra's al Ghul where he learns that Ra's used the magical healing properties of the Lazarus Pit to revive Jason, only for him to disappear. Back in Gotham, a desperate Black Mask breaks the Joker out of Arkham, hiring the homicidal maniac to kill the Red Hood. However, the Red Hood soon captures the Joker, demanding that Batman meet them in Crime Alley. The Caped Crusader arrives and confronts Jason, who is furious that Batman never avenged him by killing the Joker. Batman admits that he wanted to but could not break his code of honour, and following a brief tussle between the two Jason detonates a bomb. While Batman manages to find the Joker alive in the rubble, his former partner is nowhere to be found. Later, in the Batcave, Alfred asks if he should remove Jason's memorial and Batman declines, stating that nothing has changed between the two.

## BRINGING BATMAN TO THE SCREEN

For the Caped Crusader's second solo adventure in the DC Universe Animated Original Movies collection, Warner Bros chose to adapt one of the most controversial comic book story arcs in *Batman* history, *Under the Hood*. Written by Judd Winick and running in *Batman* #635–41 and #645–50 between February 2005 and March 2006, the storyline saw the return of Jason Todd, the second Robin, who had apparently met his demise in the four-issue story arc *A Death in the Family* by Jim Starlin, published in *Batman* #426–9 (December 1988–January 1989). This classic tale gained mainstream press attention when DC

Comics placed the fate of Dick Grayson's successor in the hands of Batman fans, who voted 5,343 to 5,271 in favour of Jason's death, only for Winick to revive the character fifteen years later under the Joker's previous alias, the Red Hood.

Having directed numerous episodes of *The Batman* and *Batman: The Brave and the Bold* – along with the first DC Universe Animated Original Movie, *Superman/Doomsday* – Brandon Vietti (*Legion of Super Heroes*) took charge of the project, with writer Judd Winick adapting his own story for the screen. Bruce Greenwood (*Star Trek*, 2009) became the fourth actor to voice the Dark Knight in the series of direct-to-video features; he was joined by a strong supporting cast for *Batman: Under the Red Hood* that included Jensen Ackles (*Supernatural*, 2005–present) as Jason Todd/the Red Hood, John DiMaggio as the Joker, Neil Patrick Harris as Dick Grayson/Nightwing, Jason Isaacs (*Harry Potter and the Chamber of Secrets*, 2002) as Ra's al Ghul, Gary Cole as Commissioner Gordon and Wade Williams (*Prison Break*, 2005–9) as Black Mask.

## RECEPTION

*Batman: Under the Red Hood* was released in North America on 27 July 2010 and went on to earn $5,736,455 in gross sales, becoming only the third feature in the series to shift over 500,000 copies. It was also met with an enthusiastic response from fans and critics; in his review, James Harvey of *WorldsFinestOnline.com* described *Under the Red Hood* as 'the most mature DC Universe Animated Original Movie title yet, and the best Batman-focussed animated feature since *Batman Beyond: Return of the Joker*', while Bill Ramey of *Batman-on-Film.com* suggested the film to be 'better than both *SubZero* and *Batman Beyond: Return of the Joker*, and right up there with – and might even surpass – the classic *Mask of the Phantasm*.' At the time of writing, *Batman: Under the Red Hood* remains the highest-rated animated *Batman* feature on the film review aggregator site *RottenTomatoes.com*, holding a 100 per cent 'fresh' rating.

## SUPERMAN/BATMAN: APOCALYPSE (2010)

**Release date:** 28 September 2010
**Certificate:** PG-13 (US); 12 (UK)
**Running time:** 78 minutes

### VOICE CAST

Kevin Conroy (*Bruce Wayne/Batman*); Tim Daly (*Clark Kent/Superman*); Andre Braugher (*Darkseid*); Susan Eisenberg (*Princess Diana of Themyscira/Wonder Woman*); Summer Glau (*Kara Zor-El/Supergirl*); Julianne Grossman (*Big Barda*); Edward Asner (*Granny Goodness*); Rachel Quaintance (*Lyla*); Andrea Romano (*Stompa, Vicki Vale*); Salli Saffioti (*Gilotina*).

### KEY CREW

Lauren Montgomery (*Director*); Lauren Montgomery, Bobbie Page, Bruce W. Timm (*Producers*); Michael E. Uslan, Benjamin Melniker, Sam Register (*Executive Producers*); Alan Burnett (*Co-producer*); Tab Murphy (*Written by*); Bob Kane, Joe Shuster, Jerry Siegel, Jack Kirby, William M. Marston (*Characters*); Jeph Loeb, Michael Turner (*Graphic Novel*); Andrea Romano (*Voice Director*); Maria Estrada (*Casting*); John Paesano (*Music*); Margaret Hou (*Editing*).

### STORY

In the months following the impeachment of Lex Luthor, a spaceship crash lands in Gotham City carrying a young girl with Kryptonian-like powers. Batman manages to subdue her using a shard of Kryptonite and with the help of Superman they discover she is Kara Zor-El, the biological cousin of the Man of Steel. As Kal-El (Superman) attempts to integrate her into society, a concerned Batman notifies Wonder Woman and Lyla and together they convince Superman to take Kara to Themyscira where she can learn to control her powers.

Meanwhile, on the planet Apokolips, the villainous Darkseid sends his minions to capture Kara, hoping she can replace Big Barda as the leader of the Female Furies. Themyscira comes under attack from an army of Doomsday clones, who are eventually defeated by Superman's heat-vision; however, they are unable to prevent Kara's abduction and Lyla is also killed during the confrontation.

Enlisting Big Barda as their guide, the heroes head to Apokolips where Superman comes under attack from a brainwashed Kara. Wonder Woman and Barda fight with the Female Furies while Batman discovers a room full of Hell Spores, the source of Apokolips' fire pits. The Caped Crusader threatens to use the Hell Spores to destroy Apokolips unless Darkseid relents and frees Kara. Darkseid agrees and the heroes return to Earth, but the Dark Lord ambushes Superman and blasts him into space. As Kara battles with Darkseid, Superman returns and attacks his foe, allowing Kara to use Darkseid's Mother Box to create a

Boom Tube, teleporting the New God into the far reaches of space. With the threat of Darkseid averted, Kara vows to remain on Earth and use her powers to fight crime and protect humanity under the alias of Supergirl.

## BRINGING THE WORLD'S FINEST TO THE SCREEN

Following strong sales for *Superman/Batman: Public Enemies*, development began on a follow-up that would become the first – and to date, only – direct sequel in the DC Universe Original Animated Movies collection. Directed by Lauren Montgomery (*Wonder Woman*, 2009) and written by Tab Murphy (*Brother Bear*, 2003), the feature was an adaptation of the story arc *The Supergirl from Krypton* by Jeph Loeb, published in *Superman/Batman* #8–13 (May–October 2004). Along with the returning Kevin Conroy and Tim Daly, Susan Eisenberg reprised her role from *Justice League* and *Justice League Unlimited* as Wonder Woman. Andre Braugher (*The Mist*, 2007) was cast as Darkseid and Summer Glau (*Firefly*, 2002) lent her voice to Kara Zor-El, the most familiar version of Supergirl who had originally debuted in the comic book story 'The Supergirl from Krypton!' by Otto Binder, published in Action Comics #252 (May 1959).

## RECEPTION

*Superman/Batman: Apocalypse* was released on DVD and Blu-ray on 28 September 2010, but it received a mixed reception compared to previous DC Universe Animated Original Movies. In his review on *Batman-on-Film.com*, Bill Ramey wrote that '*Superman/Batman: Apocalypse* is not up to par with any of [Warner Premiere's] previous endeavours' and suggested that '*Batman* fans might want to skip this one altogether', while a number of commentators felt that the film suffered from awkward pacing and character designs, along with a lack of focus on its titular heroes. Nevertheless, the film performed better than *Justice League: The New Frontier* and *Justice League: Crisis on Two Earths*, selling over 360,000 copies in North America and generating $5,974,799 in gross sales.

roster of superheroes with a new comedy adventure show from Warner Bros Animation, *Krypto the Superdog*. Intended for the younger viewer, the series focused on the adventures of Superman's eponymous canine companion, who had first debuted in the Superboy story 'The Superdog from Krypton!' by Otto Binder, published in *Adventure Comics* #210 (March 1955). While the production counted DC Animated Universe alumni such as Alan Burnett and Paul Dini among its creative team, *Krypto the Superdog* was a stand-alone project that took place entirely in its own continuity. Although the Caped Crusader never made an appearance himself, the canine crime-fighter Ace the Bat-hound was a prominent supporting character, combating enemies such as Bud and Lou (the Joker's Hyenas), Artie, Griff and Waddles (the Penguin's birds) and Isis (Catwoman's pet cat).

## RECEPTION

*Krypto the Superdog* premiered in March 2005 on Cartoon Network and ran thirty-nine episodes, each containing two eleven-minute stories. Coming to an end after just two seasons, the series continued to receive regular reruns in a number of countries, with Warner Home Video also releasing ten episodes across two compilation DVDs – *Krypto the Superdog Vol. 1: Cosmic Canine* and *Krypto the Superdog Vol. 2: Super Pets Unleashed*.

# YOUNG JUSTICE (2010–PRESENT)

**Premiere:** 7 January 2011 (US)
**Episode count:** Ongoing

## VOICE CAST

Jesse McCartney (*Dick Grayson/Robin*); Nolan North (*Conner Kent/Superboy, Clark Kent/Superman*); Khary Payton (*Kaldur'Ahm/Aqualad*); Jason Spisak (*Wally West/Kid Flash*); Danica McKellar (*M'gann M'orzz/Miss Martian*); Stephanie Lemelin (*Artemis*); Bruce Greenwood (*Bruce Wayne/Batman*).

## KEY CREW

Brandon Vietti, Greg Weisman (*Producers*); Sam Register (*Executive Producer*); Jamie Thomason (*Casting/Voice Director*); Michael McCuistion, Lolita Ritmanis, Kristopher Carter (*Music*).

## STORY

Teenage superheroes Robin, Superboy, Artemis, Kid Flash, Miss Martian and Aqualad look to step out of the shadows of their older counterparts in the Justice League, embarking on a series of covert missions as the special operations team Young Justice under the mentorship of the Caped Crusader.

## BRINGING YOUNG JUSTICE TO THE SCREEN

Following the conclusion of *Teen Titans* and *The Batman*, Warner Bros Animation Executive Vice

President, Creative Affairs, Sam Register proposed a new teen-orientated superhero show similar to *Young Justice*, the comic book series launched by writer Todd DeZago and artist Todd Nauck in June 1998. Rather than presenting a straightforward adaptation of the comic, producers Brandon Vietti (*Batman: Under the Red Hood*) and Greg Weisman (*The Spectacular Spider-Man*) drew upon elements of *Young Justice* and *Teen Titans* to craft an original concept set in its own continuity and focusing on a 'covert' offshoot of the Justice League made up of superhero protégés and side-kicks. Working from a pool of more than fifty young DC superheroes, Vietti and Weisman selected Robin, Superboy, Aqualad, Kid Flash, Miss Martian and Artemis as their core line-up, with their Justice League counterparts – Batman, Superman, Aquaman, the Flash, Martian Manhunter and the Green Arrow – all serving as major supporting characters.

Batman's role in *Young Justice* was described by the producers as that of the team's Jim Phelps, referring to the mission controller of the television series *Mission: Impossible* (1966–73). Other characters to make regular appearances included the Black Canary, Captain Marvel and the Red Tornado. Having voiced the Dark Knight in the DC Universe Animated Original Movie *Batman: Under the Red Hood*, Bruce Greenwood continued in the role of the Caped Crusader, joining regular cast members such as Jesse McCartney (*Alvin and the Chipmunks*, 2007) as Robin and

Nolan North (*Justice League: Crisis on Two Earths*) as both Superboy and Superman. A number of Notable Guest Stars would also feature throughout the series, including Rob Lowe (*The West Wing*, 1999–2006), Danny Trejo (*Machete*, 2010) and Arnold Vosloo (*G.I. Joe: The Rise of Cobra*, 2009), alongside veteran DC animation voice actors like Jeff Bennett, Miguel Ferrer, Phil LaMarr, Vanessa Marshall, Kevin Michael Richardson and Tara Strong.

## RECEPTION

After ordering a first season of twenty-six episodes, Cartoon Network premiered *Young Justice* on 26 November 2010 with the broadcast of the two-part pilot 'Independence Day'. A further seven episodes were aired between January and March 2011 before the network placed the series on temporary hiatus. In July 2011, Warner Home Video released the first four episodes of the series to DVD as *Young Justice: Season One – Volume One* and it was confirmed that the series would resume on Cartoon Network from September 2011. Producer Greg Weisman also revealed that the show had been picked up for a second season, consisting of a ten-part mini-series entitled *Young Justice: Invasion*.

# BATMAN OF THE FUTURE

Since Lewis Wilson made history in 1943 as the first actor to bring the Dark Knight Detective to life, the costumed crime-fighter has gone on to spawn eight theatrical features with combined global box-office receipts in excess of $2.6bn, along with a hit live-action television show and numerous award-winning animated series and direct-to-video releases. Following the staggering success of *The Dark Knight* in 2008, *Batman* remains one of the most popular franchises of all-time and – almost seventy years after the character's first screen appearance – the Caped Crusader is showing little sign of slowing down, with Warner Bros developing several projects to take the legendary crime-fighter into 2012 and beyond.

As you read this, Christopher Nolan will have likely completed his *Batman* trilogy with the release of the hotly anticipated final instalment, *The Dark Knight Rises*. After tantalizing audiences with *The Dark Knight*, Nolan initially left fans guessing over the future of the series as he went on to direct the mind-bending thriller *Inception* (2010), assembling a cast that included Leonardo DiCaprio, Joseph Gordon-Levitt (*3rd Rock from the Sun*, 1996–2001), Ellen Page (*Juno*, 2007), Tom Hardy (*Bronson*, 2008) and Academy Award-winner Marion Cotillard (*La Vie en Rose*, 2007) alongside Gotham City veterans Michael Caine, Cillian Murphy and Ken Watanabe. However, on 9 February 2010, it was announced that Warner Bros had tasked Nolan with producing their *Superman* reboot *Man of Steel*, which would also be accompanied by the third and final instalment of his *Batman* tale in the summer of 2012.

Based on a story by Nolan and David S. Goyer and scripted by Jonathan Nolan, *The Dark Knight Rises* moved into pre-production in late 2010, with the filmmaker surrounding himself with regular collaborators such as production designer Nathan Crowley, cinematographer Wally Pfister, costume designer Lindy Hemming, film editor Lee Smith and composer Hans Zimmer. Along with returning actors Christian Bale (Bruce Wayne/Batman), Michael Caine (Alfred Pennyworth), Gary Oldman (Commissioner Gordon), Morgan Freeman (Lucius Fox) and Nestor Carbonell (Mayor Anthony Garcia), Nolan also secured the services of *Inception* star Tom Hardy as the villainous Bane, while Anne Hathaway (*The Devil Wears Prada*, 2006) was announced as Selina Kyle/Catwoman. Furthering the *Inception* reunion were the appointments of Joseph Gordon-Levitt and Marion Cotillard as the mysterious characters John Blake and Miranda Tate, with the latter assumed to be Talia al Ghul.

Other cast members revealed during the run-up to the filming of *The Dark Knight Rises* included

Matthew Modine (*Full Metal Jacket*) as Nixon, Alon Abutbul (*Body of Lies*, 2008) as a 'mad scientist', Juno Temple (*Atonement*, 2007) as a 'street-smart Gotham girl' and Josh Pence (*The Social Network*, 2010) as a young Ra's al Ghul, while it was also reported that Liam Neeson and Cillian Murphy would reprise their roles from *Batman Begins* for brief cameo appearances. Principal photography got underway on the $250m sequel on 6 May 2011 at Mehrangarh Fort in Jodhpur, India, kicking off a shoot that saw Pittsburgh, Pennsylvania, doubling as Gotham City, with other locations including Bucharest, Glasgow, London and Nottingham, along with studio work at Warner Bros' Burbank lot in Los Angeles, California. Filming on *The Dark Knight Rises* was scheduled to wrap in November 2011, ahead of the film's theatrical release on 20 July 2012.

Outside of the theatrical series, rumours persist that Warner Bros are keen to develop a new live-action adaptation of the Caped Crusader for the small screen, but at the time of writing these remain unsubstantiated. As for his cartoon counterpart, the character is set to continue as a supporting player in *Young Justice*, although plans for a new animated series from producer James Tucker (*Batman: The Brave and the Bold*) appeared to have fallen by the wayside by June 2010. Nevertheless, reports soon emerged that Glen Murakami (*Batman Beyond*) was working on a CG-animated show to serve as a companion piece to Bruce Timm's *Green Lantern: The Animated Series* (2011), and in October 2011 it was confirmed that the new series – entitled *Beware the Batman* – would debut as part of Cartoon Network's 'DC Nation' programming block in 2013. Meanwhile, at the 2011 San Diego Comic-Con International, Bruce Timm also revealed that Batman will feature heavily in Warner Premiere's upcoming DC Universe Animated Original Movies line-up; along with the previously announced *Justice League: Doom*, the producer confirmed a two-part adaptation of Frank Miller's seminal tale, *Batman: The Dark Knight Returns*, which he promised would 'be very, very faithful to the comic'.

Despite Christopher Nolan's epic *Batman* saga drawing to a close with the release of *The Dark Knight Rises*, Warner Bros Pictures President of Production Jeff Robinov has already reaffirmed the studio's commitment towards a *Justice League* movie, which they plan to use as a springboard to launch solo outings for heroes such as the Flash and Wonder Woman. As for the Dark Knight, Robinov also revealed that the character will remain central to their superhero feature film line-up, with Christopher Nolan and his wife and producing partner Emma Thomas likely to stay on as producers for the Warner Bros series, guiding the cinematic future of a 'reinvented' Batman.

Having managed to retain his popularity for almost three-quarters of a century, there appears to be no end in sight for the Dark Knight and his war on the criminal element of Gotham City.

# References

## BATMAN (1966–8)

'ABC had bought the concept without …' William Dozier quoted in 'Batty over *Batman*?' by Dwight Whitney, *TV Guide*, March 1966

'They actually signed me the first day …' Adam West, quoted in 'An Exclusive Interview with Adam West' by Matt MacNabb, *Legionsof Gotham.org*, 2004

'When I tried out for the part …' Burt Ward, quoted in 'Burt Ward – A *Slice of SciFi* Interview' by Mark Ellitz, *SliceofSciFi.com*, 27 April 2011

'As a kid, I read the comic books …' Adam West, quoted in 'An Exclusive Interview with Adam West' by Matt MacNabb, *LegionsofGotham.org*, 2004

'With each script and new situation …' Adam West, quoted in 'The *Den of Geek* Interview: Adam West' by Martin Anderson, *DenofGeek.com*, 26 June 2008

## BATMAN (1989)

'I want[ed] to make the definitive …' Michael Uslan, quoted in 'An Interview with Michael Uslan' by Bill Ramey, *Batman-on-Film.com*, 8 November 2005

'Taking someone like Michael and …' Tim Burton, quoted in '*Batman* in Production' by Alan Jones, *Cinefantastique*, November 1989

'I wanted Michael from the start …' Tim Burton, quoted in 'Tim Burton: The Man Behind *Batman*' by David Elliot, *San Diego Union-Tribune*, 25 June 1989

'Tim said in order to make this work …' Michael Uslan, quoted in 'An Interview with Michael Uslan' by Bill Ramey, *Batman-on-Film.com*, 8 November 2005

'Since no city was ever created …' Anton Furst, quoted in *Batman: The Official Book of the Movie* by John Marriott, New York: Bantam Books, 1989

'Gotham City is basically New York …' Tim Burton, quoted in 'Batman in Production' by Alan Jones, Cinefantastique, November 1989

'We decided in the very early stages …' Anton Furst, quoted in 'Anton Furst – Production Designer' by Esther Eley, Film Review, August 1989

'I envisaged Gotham the way …' Bob Kane, quoted in 'Dark Knight in the City of Dreams' by Iain Johnstone, Empire magazine, August 1989

'We didn't want to put [the Batmobile] …' Anton Furst, quoted in 'Dark Knight in the City of Dreams' by Iain Johnstone, Empire magazine

'He was very angry and screaming …' Peter Guber, quoted in 'How Hollywood Had the Last Laugh' by Tom Shone, Daily Telegraph, 28 September 2004

'It was a rough thing but Tim …' Danny Elfman, quoted in 'Danny Elfman Recalls Batman Score Stand-Off' by Kara Warner, MTV.com, 29 September 2010

'A masterpiece of sinister comic acting …' in 'Batman', Variety, June 1989

'Less movie than corporate behemoth …' David Handelman, quoted in The Films of Tim Burton: Animating Live Action in Contemporary Hollywood, edited by Alison McMahan, New York: Continuum, 2005

## BATMAN RETURNS (1992)

'I would just keep looking at [Batman] …' Tim Burton, quoted in 'Dark Knight Director' by Marc Shapiro, in Tim Burton Interviews, edited by Kristian Fraga, Jackson, MS: University Press of Mississippi, 1992

'Tim had the attitude of "I dare you …"' Daniel Waters, quoted in 'Daniel Waters on Batman Returns' by Marc Shapiro, Horrorzone, August 1992

'I got paid for almost being Robin …' Marlon Wayans, quoted in 'Wayans' World' by Nathan Rabin, AVClub.com, 25 February 1998

'Batman Returns is not really a sequel to Batman …' Tim Burton, quoted in Batman Returns: The Official Movie Book by Michael Singer, London: Hamlyn, 1992

'It's about oppression … it made sense …' Bo Welch, quoted in 'Design on Decay' by Henry Sheehan, St Louis Post, July 1992

'The more money that's spent on a movie …' Tim Burton, quoted in 'Tim Burton Talks Batman' by Bill Ramey, Batman-on-Film.com, April 2008

'Burton continues to capture the essence of …'

Philip Thomas, quoted in *'Batman Returns'*, *Empire* magazine

*'The second* Batman *was – in my estimation …'* Michael Uslan quoted in 'An Interview with Michael Uslan' by Bill Ramey, *Batman-on-Film.com*, 8 November 2005

## BATMAN FOREVER (1995)

*'After the first two movies I went in to talk …'* Tim Burton, quoted in 'Tim Burton in Amsterdam' by Edgar Kruize, *Zeenz.nl*, 10 April 2008

*'I said to Warner that I wouldn't do a* Batman *…'* Joel Schumacher, quoted in 'Interview: Joel Schumacher' by Nathan Rabin, *AVClub.com*, 2 April 2003

*'I wanted to play Two-Face …'* Billy Dee Williams, quoted in 'Billy Dee Williams Reflects on His Fanboys Legacy' by Clayton Neuman, *FilmCritic.com*, 2 February 2009

*'They put me in the third one …'* Marlon Wayans, quoted in 'Wayans' World' by Nathan Rabin, *AVClub.com*, 25 February 1998

*'Schumacher's spin of the black-suited vigilante …'* Ian Nathan, quoted in *'Batman Forever'*, *Empire* magazine

*'Succeeds on some basic levels while …'* Brian Lowry, quoted in *'Batman Forever'*, *Variety*, 13 June 1995

*'Batman Forever, no question about it …'* Michael Uslan quoted in 'An Interview with Michael Uslan' by Bill Ramey, *Batman-on-Film.com*, 8 November 2005

## BATMAN & ROBIN (1997)

*'With* Batman & Robin, *everybody got …'* Joel Schumacher, quoted in 'Interview: Joel Schumacher' by Nathan Rabin, *AVClub.com*, 2 April 2003

*'He sort of quit, we sort of fired him …'* Joel Schumacher, quoted in 'Psycho Kilmer' by Rebecca Ascher-Walsh, *Entertainment Weekly*, 31 May 1995

*'George wanted a new Batsuit …'* Joel Schumacher, quoted in 'Holy Happy Set!' by Benjamin Svetkey, *Entertainment Weekly*, 12 July 1996

*'It just felt like everything got a little soft …'* Chris O'Donnell, quoted in *Shadows of the Bat: The Cinematic Saga of the Dark Knight*, Warner Home Video

*'No matter how bad you have heard …'* Harry Knowles, quoted in *'Batman & Robin* Review', *AintItCool.com*, June 1997

'*Camp end to dreadful era for Schumacher* ...' Neil Jeffries, quoted in '*Batman and Robin*', *Empire* magazine, June 1997

## BATMAN ON HIATUS (1997–2003)

'*I believe I actually killed [the* Batman *franchise]* ...' George Clooney, quoted in 'I Killed Batman' by Gill Pringle, *Sunday Mirror*, 19 October 1997

'*During an unrelated pitch at Warner Bros* ...' Lee Shapiro, quoted in 'Interview: Lee Shapiro' by Bill Ramey, *Batman-on-Film.com*, 28 July 2005

'*It's* somewhat *based on Frank Miller's novel* ...' Darren Aronofsky, quoted in 'Aronofsky Talks *Batman: Year One* ... Again' by Brian Linder, *IGN.com*, 6 December 2000

## BATMAN BEGINS (2005)

'*The studio had decided that they wanted to* ...' Charles Roven, *Batman Begins* LA Press Junket, 8 June 2005

'*The creative mandate was really to do* ...' Christopher Nolan, *Batman Begins* LA Press Junket, 8 June 2005

'*Frankly, as much as I love Batman* ...' David S. Goyer, San Diego Comic-Con International, 23 July 2004

'*We wanted to create a character in Bruce Wayne* ...' Charles Roven, *Batman Begins* LA Press Junket, 8 June 2005

'*DC and Warner Bros were great* ...' David S. Goyer, San Diego Comic-Con International, 23 July 2004

'*What I see in Christian is the ultimate* ...' Christopher Nolan, quoted in '*Batman Begins* Press Release', Warner Bros, 11 September 2003

'*In this movie we're making it much more* ...' Christian Bale, WonderCon, 19 February 2005

'*Just to get to work with Chris even* ...' Cillian Murphy, San Diego Comic-Con International, 23 July 2004

'*I felt very strongly that we should* ...' David S. Goyer, San Diego Comic-Con International, 23 July 2004

'*The way that we approached Gotham* ...' Christopher Nolan, quoted in 'Interview: Christopher Nolan', *IGN.com*, 6 June 2005

'*My main task was to make you* ...' Nathan Crowley, quoted in '*Batman Begins* Set Visit', by Paul J. Wares, *Batman-on-Film.com*, 5 January 2005

'There are certain things that you …' Nathan Crowley, quoted in 'Batman Begins Set Visit', by Paul J. Wares, *Batman-on-Film.com*, 5 January 2005

'Strong but unimpressive by today's …' Brandon Gray, quoted in 'Batman Begins in the Shadows', *BoxOfficeMojo.com*, 20 June 2005

'Deliver the full noir with a side order …' Kim Newman, quoted in 'Batman Begins', *Empire* magazine, 2005

'You've got to put credit where …' Michael Uslan, quoted in 'An Interview with Michael Uslan' by Bill Ramey, *Batman-on-Film.com*, 8 November 2005

### THE DARK KNIGHT (2008)

'Chris [Nolan] originally said that he would …' David S. Goyer, San Diego Comic-Con International, 23 July 2004

'Chris and I both felt that Bruce…' Christian Bale, WonderCon, 19 February 2005

'The next one would have Batman enlisting …' David S. Goyer, quoted in *Premiere*, June 2005

'We're waiting for Chris Nolan to declare himself …' Charles Roven, *Sci Fi Wire*, August 2005

'It felt like a very easy job …' Jonathan Nolan, quoted in 'Interview: Jonathan Nolan and David Goyer' by Bill Ramey, *Batman-on-Film.com*, 2 July 2008

'Our challenge in casting the Joker …' Christopher Nolan, quoted in 'The Dark Knight Press Release', Warner Bros, 31 July 2006

'Unlike Batman, who I wanted very much …' Christopher Nolan, quoted in 'A Chat with Chris Nolan' by Bill Ramey, *Batman-on-Film.com*, 30 June 2008

'The idea with the Joker is that …' Jonathan Nolan, quoted in 'Interview: Jonathan Nolan and David Goyer' by Bill Ramey, *Batman-on-Film.com*, 2 July 2008

'It became apparent as we were talking …' David Goyer, quoted in 'Interview: Jonathan Nolan and David Goyer' by Bill Ramey, *Batman-on-Film.com*, 2 July 2008

'The cameras are enormous and much heavier …' Wally Pfister, quoted in 'The Dark Knight: Post in 3mm and IMAX' by Oliver Peters, *Videography.com*, 18 July 2008

'The Chinese government was a nightmare …' Wally Pfister, quoted in 'Dark Knight Director Shuns Digital Effects for the Real Thing' by Scott Brown, *Wired.com*, 24 June 2008

'Watching him come up with the characterization …' Christopher Nolan, quoted in 'Writer/Director Christopher Nolan Talks About *The Dark Knight*' by Rebecca Murray, *About.com*, undated

'It was very important to me that his performance …' Christopher Nolan, quoted in '*The Dark Knight* Cast and Director Remember Heath Ledger' by Scott Huver, *ComingSoon.net*, 14 July 2008

'An ambitious, full-bodied crime epic …' Justin Chang, quoted in '*The Dark Knight*', *Variety*, 6 July 2008

'Spectacular, visionary blockbuster entertainment …' Mark Dinning, quoted in '*The Dark Knight*', *Empire* magazine, 2008

'Looking back, I think it's sometimes easy …' Emma Thomas, quoted in 'A Chat with Emma Thomas' by Bill Ramey, *Batman-on-Film.com*, 1 July 2008

'The wonderful thing about The Dark Knight …' Michael Uslan, quoted in 'Michael Uslan at New York Comic Con 2009' by Bill Ramey, *Batman-on-Film.com*, 8 February 2009

## CATWOMAN (2004)

'The most ridiculously awful lame-ass attempt …' Harry Knowles, *AintItCool.com*, 29 September 2003

'To the dimmest recesses of popcorn inanity …' David Rooney, quoted in 'Catwoman', *Variety*, 22 July 2004

'This is only worth seeing if you can …' Roberto Sadovski, quoted in 'Catwoman', *Empire* magazine, August 2004

'A stodgy, yowly, no fun to play with …' Harry Knowles, quoted in 'Catwoman review' *AintItCool.com*, 22 July 2004

## THE DARK KNIGHT IN THE DC ANIMATED UNIVERSE

'I never thought that [Warner Bros] would …' Eric Radomski, quoted in 'No Boundaries An Interview with Eric Radomski' by Amid Amidi, *Animation World Magazine*, November 2000

'We came up with a fairly successful formula …' Bruce Timm, quoted in 'Interview: Bruce Timm and Glen Murakami' by Emru Townsend, *The Critical Eye*, 17 September 1999

'We didn't want it to be just action/adventure …' Eric Radomski, quoted in 'Knight Vision' by Bob Miller, *Comics Scene*, June 1994

'[Batman] was groundbreaking in a lot of ways …' Dick Sebast, quoted in 'Interview: Dick Sebast' by Stu Hamilton, *WorldsFinestOnline.com*, 17 January 2006

'I was writing this show called "Joker's Favor" …' Paul Dini, quoted in 'Interview: Paul Dini' by Emru Townsend, *The Critical Eye*, 17 May 1999

'I have to say that Fox were actually pretty good …' Bruce Timm, quoted in 'Interview: Bruce Timm and Glen Murakami' by Emru Townsend, *The Critical Eye*, 17 September 1999

'The upper hierarchy of Fox Television was expecting …' Alan Burnett, quoted in '*BTAS* 15th Anniversary Special: Alan Burnett' by Stu Hamilton, *WorldsFinestOnline.com*

'I knew immediately what to do with Batman…' Bruce Timm, 2004

'I wanted the story to be about Bruce Wayne …' Alan Burnett, quoted in 'BTAS 15th Anniversary Special: Alan Burnett' by Stu Hamilton, *WorldsFinestOnline.com*

'Up until the day we shipped out the storyboards …' Alan Burnett, quoted in '*Mask of the Phantasm* 15th Anniversary Interview: Alan Burnett', *WorldsFinestOnline.com*

'Better-plotted than Tim Burton's live action movies …' quoted in '*Empire*'s Batman: Mask of the Phantasm Movie Review', *Empire* magazine

'When they came back at us and said that …' Bruce Timm, quoted in 'Interview: Bruce Timm and Glen Murakami' by Emru Townsend, *The Critical Eye*, 17 September 1999

'Warner Bros Animation decided to do one last …' Michael Reaves, quoted in 'Interview: Michael Reaves' by James Harvey, *WorldsFinestOnline.com*, 20 June 2008

'I doubt that we'll be formally, "officially" …' Bruce Timm, quoted on 'DC Animation Forum', *ToonZone.net*, 19 September 2009

## THE FURTHER ANIMATED ADVENTURES OF THE CAPED CRUSADER

'*Unlike* Batman: The Animated Series, we had …' Duane Capizzi, quoted in 'Interview: Duane Capizzi', *WorldsFinestOnline.com*, 2005

'If you group all of the animated Batman movies …' Bill Ramey, quoted in 'DVD Review: *The Batman vs Dracula*', *Batman-on-Film.com*, 28 December 2005

'If Sam [Register] had presented it to me as just …' James Tucker, quoted in 'James Tucker Interview' by Matt MacNabb, *LegionsofGotham.org*, October 2008

'I think whenever you work with Batman …' Michael Jelenic, quoted in 'Michael Jelenic Interview' by Matt MacNabb, *LegionsofGotham.org*, October 2008

'My temptation with Batman was always to go …' Andrea Romano, quoted in 'Andrea Romano Interview' by Matt MacNabb, *Legionsof Gotham.org*, October 2008

## DC UNIVERSE ANIMATED ORIGINAL MOVIES

'When we decided to make this film …' Gregory Noveck, *WorldsFinestOnline.com*, May 2008

'I think the film works as a standalone …' Bruce Timm, quoted in 'Bruce Timm Interview: *Batman: Gotham Knight*' by Simon Brew, *DenofGeek.com*, 16 July 2008

'Something new and entirely fresh …' quoted in '*Batman: Gotham Knight* Review', *Worlds FinestOnline.com*

'A must-see for all Caped Crusader completists …' Glen Ferris, quoted in '*Empire*'s *Batman: Gotham Knight* Movie Review', *Empire* magazine

'Superb voice cast, excellent character designs …' Zack Demeter, quoted in '*Superman/Batman: Public Enemies* Review', *WorldsFinestOnline.com*

'This is Superman's film first and foremost …' Bill Ramey, quoted in '*Superman/Batman: Public Enemies* Review', *Batman-on-Film.com*, 23 September 2009

'The most mature DC Universe Animated Original Movie …' James Harvey, quoted in '*Batman: Under the Red Hood* Review', *WorldsFinest Online.com*

'Better than both SubZero and Batman Beyond …' Bill Ramey, quoted in '*Batman: Under the Red Hood* Review', *Batman-on-Film.com*, 12 July 2010

'Batman: Year One *could benefit from some …*' Tommy Cook, quoted in 'Comic-Con 2011 – *Batman: Year One* Review', *Collider.com*, 23 July 2011

# INDEX